Care, Climate, and Debt

Benjamin C. Wilson
Editor

Care, Climate, and Debt

Transdisciplinary Problems and Possibilities

palgrave
macmillan

Editor
Benjamin C. Wilson
State University of New York College
at Cortland
Cortland, NY, USA

ISBN 978-3-030-96354-5 ISBN 978-3-030-96355-2 (eBook)
https://doi.org/10.1007/978-3-030-96355-2

This Palgrave Macmillan imprint is published by the registered company Springer Nature Switzerland AG
The registered company address is: Gewerbestrasse 11, 6330 Cham, Switzerland

To Sara, Ned, and Spencer with love and joy!

Contents

List of Contributors

Badurek Christopher A. Department of Geography, State University of New York College at Cortland, Cortland, NY, USA

Feinig Jakob Department of Human Development, Binghamton University, Binghamton, NY, USA

Ferguson Scott University of South Florida, Tampa, FL, USA

Jimenez Jeremy Foundations and Social Advocacy Department, School of Education, State University of New York College at Cortland, Cortland, NY, USA

Kadas Szilvia Art and Art History Department, State University of New York College at Cortland, Cortland, NY, USA

Kaltefleiter Caroline K. State University of New York College at Cortland, Cortland, NY, USA

Kelton Stephanie Stony Brook University, Stony Brook, NY, USA

kioni-sadiki déqui Brooklyn, NY, USA

Leclaire Joëlle College at Buffalo, State University of New York, Buffalo, NY, USA

Lee Hedwig Washington University, St. Louis, MO, USA

Ponirakis Julian S. State University of New York College at Geneseo, Geneseo, NY, USA

Robinson Jacob T. State University of New York College at Cortland, Cortland, NY, USA

Saas William O. Global Institute for Sustainable Prosperity, Granville, OH, USA;
Tulane University, New Orleans, LA, USA

Seijo Maxximilian Global Institute for Sustainable Prosperity, Granville, OH, USA;
University of California, Santa Barbara, CA, USA

Wessell Kelly J. Tompkins Cortland Community College, Dryden, NY, USA

Wildeman Christopher Duke University, Durham, NC, USA;
ROCKWOOL Foundation Research Unit, Copenhagen, Denmark

Wilson Benjamin C. State University of New York College at Cortland, Cortland, NY, USA

List of Figures

Can Household Debt Cause a Financial Crisis?

How Are You Going to Pay for It? The Macroeconomic Benefits of Student Debt Cancellation

"Solidarity Is a Force Stronger Than Gravity": Money, Aesthetics, and the Abstractness of Care

Introduction

Benjamin C. Wilson

Introduction

Each year, the State University of New York, College at Cortland's Cultural and Intellectual Climate Committee (CICC) chooses a theme and a common read that frame a series of lectures, discussions, film screenings, and art exhibitions. The committee selects these themes to promote cultural and intellectual life on campus and cultivate campus and Cortland community engagement with current and relevant issues in the world. For the 2019–2020 academic year, the CICC selected *Care, Climate & Debt: Transdisciplinary Problems and Possibilities* as its theme, and with additional support from the State University of New York (SUNY) "Conversations in the Disciplines" grant program, CICC developed and hosted a wide-ranging series of events. This volume is a collection of these transdisciplinary investigations, critiques, and new imaginings.

B. C. Wilson (✉)
State University of New York College at Cortland, Cortland, NY, USA
e-mail: bcw@cortland.edu

B. C. Wilson, *Care, Climate, and Debt*,
https://doi.org/10.1007/978-3-030-96355-2_1

Margaret Atwood's 2008 Massey Lecture *Payback: Debt and the Shadow Side of Wealth*[1] opened our conversation, as the year's common read. In this text, Atwood describes debt from its ancient origins to its contemporary form as a structural force in human societies. Her examination of debt set us free to move well beyond the narrow constraints of finance and money management. Atwood's central claim helped to thematize our conversations and the chapters in this book:

> Like all our financial arrangements, and like all our rules of moral conduct—in fact, like language itself—notions about debt form part of the elaborate imaginative construct that is human society. What is true of each part of mental construct is also true of debt, in all its many variations: because it is a mental construct, how we think about it changes how it works. (Atwood 2008, 203)

To change how we think about the workings of debt, and to imagine new possibilities, this transdisciplinary text spans history, sociology, law, economics, graphic design, religion, environmental science, politics, and more. Written for an undergraduate audience with upper level electives and masters coursework in mind, it is ideal for provoking classroom discussions that not only point out the gravity of the social and environmental crises we face in the twenty-first century, but also strives to open spaces for students to create innovative solutions.

Because we tend to think about debt in the narrow sense as belonging to the realm of money and finance, Atwood urges us to embrace a broader perspective: When she proposed "debt" as her topic to the Massey Lecture Series, the committee was at first skeptical.

> They thought I was going to write about economics. They were much relieved when I explained that, no, my subject was simply the way human beings have thought about what is owed, who owes it, and how it should be repaid—balancing the scales, in religion, literature, the criminal world, the revenge tragedy, and in Nature, an area in which we have, alas, vastly overdrawn our account. (Atwood 2008, xii)

The Massey Lecture Committee's reaction reveals how much debt's imaginary is constrained by its near-exclusive existence in the domain of

[1] Margaret Atwood. (2008). *Payback: Debt and the Shadow Side of Wealth*. Toronto, ON, Canada. House of Anansi Press Inc.

business and economics. By looking at debt from a literary perspective, Atwood demonstrates the power of narrative in shaping the public's understanding of debt. Beginning with how we use language and specifically metaphors, such as, "going into debt" as though we are going somewhere (like into prison) informs and inhibits our monetary imagination (Atwood 2008, 81). With her analysis, Atwood encourages us to move beyond, not only, metaphorical confines but also "debt as plot" themes[2] and to reject our auto-pilot-like retreat to confined conceptions of debt as a devil's bargain or a place that we must escape.

The authors in this volume examine climate change, the carceral state, housing, health care, education, and social justice by expanding upon Atwood's literary analysis of debt. Who and what do we owe? Where are the offsetting credits? Can we imagine novel approaches to balance sheets, measures of value, and justice? Why does such a persistent deficit of care permeate so much of our lives? Similar inquiries also abound about the role of debt in the climate crisis. Are we exploiting free environmental services? What do we owe the planet for rich soil, carbon sequestration, and photosynthesis? Can we continue to take advantage of these environmental services paying nothing back? The planet does not have a bank account, so what would payback look like? Challenging the inclination that debt is a constraint on our ability to meet the pressing issues of our time, this volume offers contributions that allow us to reimagine it as a social construct capable of empowering people to organize sustainable prosperity for all.

This is not a simple task, as even though Atwood succeeds in expanding readers' thinking about debt, she too remains mired in a conventional understanding of debt and money. In the finale of her text, for instance, she imagines a twenty-first century edition of the Charles Dickens' tale, *A Christmas Carol* that only updates, rather than reimagines, debt from the ground up. In Atwood's greening of this classic, we find a generous billionaire version of Scrooge lavishing his money on green organizations and supporting micro-lending programs, all while wearing a stylish hemp suit. Atwood's transformation of Scrooge from miser to green philanthropist billionaire as the solution to our climate debt fails to break with the conventional thinking about money and debt that exists today.

[2] Chapter 3 of Atwood's text is titled "Debt as Plot".

One group of rogue economists have created concepts that allow us to break with conventional thinking about money. As such a brief introduction of the work done by Modern Monetary Theory (MMT) economists will help readers understand the more expansive arguments about money as debit and credit found in this volume. For MMT, money is a score-keeping practice that allows people and institutions to keep track of what they owe each other. From this perspective, money has to be credit and debit at the same time because someone's debt is always someone else's credit. One does not go into debt without a corresponding party extending credit. This simple observation is often overlooked because mainstream economics does not view money as a social relation but as a commodity. This money mythology contributes to the repressed imagination we as a society have for money.

When we challenge conventional perceptions of debt, we need to begin by asking what money is. From MMT's perspective, money is an IOU, a debtor's promise to pay a creditor. While the technical balance sheet language of credit/debit or asset/liability sounds sophisticated, our lives are filled with simple examples. A neighbor lending a cup of sugar in exchange for the future delivery of cupcakes, or the picking up of a dinner tab with the implicit or explicit promise of a future dinner from your friend, are examples of IOUs or balance sheet operations. What MMT brings into view is how such promises change as the relationships that structure these promises become more complex and formalized. The criminal justice system (Chapters 2 and 3), municipalities (Chapter 11), financial institutions (Chapter 12), and the federal government (Chapter 10) all make and receive promises. Once we become aware of the myriad IOUs we experience on a day-to-day basis and how they are structured, cultural and institutional differences between these promises and why we accept them introduce new possibilities for defining what we want to promise and for whom.

When we ask what we can promise to deliver for one another, rather than what we owe, very different stories about our future become possible. We must think bigger than finite and redistributive Robin Hood stories or Faustian promises to collect our souls. Money is not scarce as a social construct and does not grow on rich people. This volume encourages the construction and development of fresh stories, stories where "credit as plot" drives themes of abundance or forgiveness, rather than finite redistribution and extraction. We need stories that unleash our capacity to wield money as a boundless public utility and celebrate our collective dependence.[3] This volume unfolds by exploring our common villains, racism, inequality, and the climate crisis, then reveals emergent heroes as activists, educators, and producers that remind us of our power to organize and bring novel strategies to make and deliver promises and their corresponding aesthetics. Through these tales, we hope to push money and debt beyond its current confines and invite the writing of new stories informed by collective and democratic dialogue and debate in your classrooms, homes, and wherever else a good story can be told.

The Structure of the Book

The book is divided into four sections. The first section investigates debt from the perspective of race. The second section discusses our environmental debts and how we can use education, technology, and media to achieve sustainable outcomes. Section three explores the causes and consequences of personal debt and the potential of public forgiveness. To conclude, the last section explores monetary experimentation and the future of credit from questions of monetary design and the aesthetics novel monetary systems create.

Criminal Justice: Race and Resistance

This section explores how race and our legal systems construct debt relations at the societal level and how those institutions impact everyday life.

We begin with an examination of our criminal justice system. In Chapter 2, Christopher Wildeman and Hedwig Lee explore the common trope that people must "pay their debt to society" when individuals are convicted of crimes. What is generally meant by that is that an individual should suffer prison or jail incarceration, state supervision after release in the form of parole or probation, and directly "giving back" whether in the form of community service or the payment of legal fines and fees. In this chapter, they develop the concept of being indebted by proxy, focusing on how adult women connected to men who experience prison and jail incarceration end up also paying a debt to society. They do so in three stages. In the first, they show how common family member incarceration

[3] Ferguson, Scott. Declarations of Dependence. Lincoln, NE. University of Nebraska Press. (2018).

is for women. In the second, they discuss how family member incarceration is, more often than not, disruptive to their lives. In the third, they highlight the negative consequences women suffer as a result of family member incarceration.

Chapter 3 continues our discussion of debts to society and the criminal justice system's inequities by honoring resistance. Black August is a thirty-one-day commemoration of people and events that center around Black/New Afrikan lives, voices, perspectives, and acts of resistance. Margaret Atwood argues that without memory there can be no debt, and dequi kioni-sadiki provides us with memories from the experiences of those who the United States has attempted to eliminate, assimilate, and enslave. In this chapter, she describes the history of resistance in the Black/New Afrikan tradition giving voice to political prisoners and prisoners of war, paying homage to the historical and contemporary acts of resistance, and raising fundamental questions about the relationship between a civilized society and its prison system.

Ecological Debt, Education, and the Art of Communication

In this section, our examination of debt turns to its application as a tool for environmental extraction and the role of education in transforming these relationships to better value and engage with the natural world.

Chapter 4 opens this discussion with Kelly Wessell describing the ways in which ecology and economy are inextricably linked. Everything from the glass that makes up our phone screens to the materials used to build our houses originates in the environment before making it into our economy. He reminds us that in addition to these goods, a healthy, functioning ecosystem also provides us with services like soil regeneration and water filtration, all of which have value. Depleting natural resources or degrading ecosystem services puts us in a sort of ecological debt that eventually must be paid because ecosystems have real value. The debt we incur by degrading natural systems manifests itself in tangible ways as we struggle to replace ecological goods like soil nutrients to maintain food production or to treat drinking water polluted by industrial activity. However, the values of diverse, functioning natural systems are hard to quantify. We cannot necessarily put a price tag on the enjoyment of a walk in the woods, but we experience a sort of spiritual deficit when we see local forests turned into housing developments. To avoid the ecological debt that results from unsustainable development, Wessell provides examples of how we might expand the ways in which we value nature beyond the goods it provides and learn to live within our ecological means.

Building on Wessell's pedagogical lessons outlined at the end of his chapter, Christopher Badurek and Jeremy Jimenez argue, in Chapter 5, that students from an array of disciplinary perspectives are increasingly interested in course work and educational experiences that address the climate crisis. Although academic departments often prepare students through education on the scientific foundations of climate change from the perspectives of such fields as conservation biology, environmental geoscience, or environmental geology, their college aims to provide a broader perspective on the climate change issue. Student enrollment at SUNY Cortland has a high percentage of education majors, their teaching experiences indicate a need for an interdisciplinary perspective that includes science, social science, humanities, and applied course work that appeals to future educators. To do so, they describe how they engage students in a more targeted manner, based on their disciplinary and program focus. For some students, this involves the application of geotechnology and modeling applications so they are more informed on the technology necessary for monitoring greenhouse gases and their related impacts. For others, they focus more on promoting dialogue on the educational and societal implications of climate change by integrating perspectives from environmental economics, entrepreneurship, art, and social foundations of education through serviced applied learning. In this chapter, they present an interdisciplinary perspective on sustainability rooted in the concept of climate debt.

Continuing our pedagogical intervention into climate change, Szilvia Kadas, in Chapter 6, argues that higher education has an obligation not only to teach discipline-specific skills but also to provide a safe place for students to practice expressing their voices and develop critical thinking skills. In describing a class project, Kadas demonstrates the power of graphic design as a vessel for shaping public perception around climate, public health, and inequality. In most cases, graphic design is mass-produced and targets general audiences; therefore it is vital to establish strong ethical conduct regarding its public responsibility. It is well known that graphic design has close ties with commerce, however, its primary focus is to promote ideas in a visual manner and influence ideologies on a larger scale. It is fair to say that the graphic design profession not only has a direct link with consumer culture and the economy, but also shapes social norms, beliefs, and behaviors; therefore, it is essential that designers initiate new narratives, by standing up for social values and by creating a sustainability mindset.

Micro and Macro Consequences of Debt and the Possibility of Forgiveness

This section examines the dynamic relationships between debt held by the individual and society. Together, these chapters reflexively demonstrate the harm debt causes the individual, beyond the balance sheet, and for society at large, while also expressing the power of the collective to forgive or cancel debt and expand our capacity for care.

This section begins with the household. In Chapter 7, Joëlle Leclaire investigates the relationship between levels of household debt and financial crisis. In this inquiry, she finds that household debt can cause a financial crisis via five channels. It influences the consumption levels of households, the leverage of financial institutions, rate of return on mortgage and other debt held by banks and other financial institutions, the rate of return on the production of goods and services, and the overall well-being of households in our economy. Her inquiry is framed by the father of the financial instability hypothesis, Hyman Minsky, and makes a significant contribution to our understanding of Post-Keynesian economics and the integration between micro- and macroeconomic dynamics.

Complementing Leclaire's examination of household budget stress is the work of Caroline K. Kalteflieter, Julian S. Ponirakis, and Jacob T. Robinson. In Chapter 8, they examine the problematic elements of the student debt crisis and the corresponding reality that an entire generation might be written off or disposed of. Several candidates in the Presidential Election of 2020 addressed the student loan crisis in their platforms. However, research and stories focusing on debt numbers fail to address the physical, and psychological burdens of debt, seared into one's everyday cognitive existence. To overcome this shortcoming in our understanding of student debt, they provide analysis grounded in critical race theory and construct an intersectional narrative and textual analysis of those struggling not only financially with debt, but also psychologically. Drawing upon the work of Eric Fromm and Michel Foucault, they explore notions of self-care, creativity, and collective action as forms of resistance and discuss anarchist concepts of mutual aid and cooperation. Finally, they highlight community outreach projects of debt resistance and elimination and call for student actions within the university.

Continuing the examination of student debt, Stephanie Kelton describes an alternative form of collective action. Starting at the very top, Chapter 9 describes the political consequences of what Kelton defines as *The Deficit Myth*. Drawing on her experience as chief economist to the Democrats on the U.S. Senate Budget Committee (2015/16), she describes how this myth places undue limits on our collective capacity to both extend credit and forgive debt. Informing her description is an economic modeling exercise that compares the macroeconomic implications of two prominent approaches to economic stimulus: tax cuts and student loan cancellation, she dispels the deficit myth's core narratives and encourages an alternative set of stories from which healthier and more productive political discourse can be achieved.

The Aesthetics and Potential of Alternative Monetary Design

The final section begins the process of challenging the design and aesthetic of money. In Chapter 10, Scott Ferguson labors to transcend apparent oppositions between money and aesthetics for a Green New Deal care economy. To do so, he turns a critical eye toward a seemingly unrelated aesthetic tradition: modern Western visual culture and its largely unquestioned preoccupation with finite material experience. Mobilizing the alternative conception of money articulated by Modern Monetary Theory (MMT), Ferguson contends that the monetary medium, rather than representing a private, finite, and alienating technology that behaves like a physical system, is a fundamentally inexhaustible government abstraction that harbors still unrealized powers for sensuous cultivation across economic and aesthetic spheres. To fully overcome today's exhausted dialectical oppositions between money and aesthetics, however, Ferguson critiques what he calls modernity's "gravitropic visuality" from Renaissance perspectival painting to the Hollywood blockbuster. On his analysis, this gravity-based visuality variously represses abstraction's wide-scale potentials with assuring sensations of material finitude. Rather than ground a Green New Deal in an austere physics, then, Ferguson affirms the essential abstractness of care as expressed powerfully by contemporary union leader Sara Nelson's dictum: "Solidarity is a force stronger than gravity."

Gently pulling us down from the lofty clouds of Ferguson's abstractness of care, Jakob Feinig takes us to eighteenth-century New York City. In Chapter 11, he challenges Georg Simmel's observation that money, "the means of means," (Simmel) always has to become an end in itself. Instead, he shows that forgetting money's character as a means for organizing society, mobilizing resources, and coordinating activities depend on historically changing conditions. Faced with a lack of drinking water, eighteenth-century New York City policymakers issued waterworks currency to pay for a high-tech steam pump and a system of wooden pipes. This currency was a public good, and money users understood it as such. During the war, British soldiers destroyed the steam pump. Decades later, the New York State Assembly chartered a corporation that was charged with improving access to water. But most lawmakers did not realize that they had chartered a bank that saw water provisioning as a side business. Money was no longer a transparent public good that mobilized resources for water provisioning. Instead, water had become a pretext for corporate money creation. Through this historical example, Feinig contributes a vision for public money that enables large public projects like a Federal Job Guarantee and the Green New Deal. Understanding money as a public good enables democratic societies to mobilize people and resources to address the many challenges we face today.

The final chapter harnesses Feinig's vision and describes a novel policy mechanism for revitalizing U.S. higher education in the age of COVID-19. In place of the current tuition-as-revenue model, William Saas, Benjamin Wilson, Scott Ferguson, and Maxximillian Seijo propose the "Uni" model, whereby public colleges and universities tap their latent fiscal authority to issue and circulate complementary currencies. Like their U.S. dollar counterparts, Uni currencies will obtain value because they will be accepted by colleges and universities in payment for tuition, fees, meal plans, and rents. Unis may also be disbursed by their issuers in payment of local property taxes, creating new liquidity for their host communities. In order to satisfy its dual mandate, and in line with its current monetary experimentation with the Municipal Liquidity Facility, the Federal Reserve Bank of the United States is capable of accommodating the Uni system. When implemented, the Uni system will enable colleges and universities to abandon the austere business as usual approach to crises, and instead return to and reimagine how best to execute their missions as critical public institutions.

Acknowledgements In my first experience contributing a chapter for an edited volume, its editor Julia M. Puashunder would close her correspondences with the "honored authors" using the valediction, "With the highest appreciation for your noble gift of care." These words always struck me as not only very kind but also especially appropriate for the work that goes into the development of scholarship. So I thank Dr. Puashunder for her words, and I too would like to express my gratitude and appreciation for all those who helped bring this edited volume to life, with the highest appreciation for your noble gift of care.

Specifically, I am very grateful to Palgrave Macmillan for launching this endeavor and granting the contributors the opportunity to share their creative scholarship. I'd also like to thank SUNY Conversations in the Disciplines, SUNY Cortland President Erik Bitterbaum, Provost Mark Prus, Dean Bruce Mattingly, the Campus Artists and Lecture Series, my colleagues in the Economics Department, as well as, Mavis Lefever, Sandra Wohlleber, Tom Frank, and Liz Speziale for supporting this project financially, professionally, and logistically. Special thanks go out to my colleagues and the contributors who have made this volume possible. I am humbled and privileged by the opportunity to learn from each of you both during the development of this project and beyond. Thank you to Nikolay Karkov, Jeremy Jimenez, and Evan Faulkenbury for their support in developing this project's grant proposal and call for chapter proposals, and thank you to Brian Barrett, Scott Moranda, Howard Lindh, and Jena Curtis for teaching me the ropes of the CICC and giving me the confidence to take on the role of chair.

I'd also like to thank my colleagues at the Global Institute for Sustainability, President Fadhel Kaboub, Research Director Mathew Forstater, and Micheal J. Murray for supporting this project and providing helpful feedback from the very beginning. In addition, I need to express my gratitude and appreciation to the crew at the Modern Money Network and Money on the Left Editorial Collective for their inspiring efforts to bring the worlds of money and the humanities together. As part of that inspirational force, special thanks to Jakob Feinig for his sharp editorial eye and uncanny ability to help me write what it is I am trying to say.

And finally, thank you to my wife and partner Sara and my boys Ned and Spencer for the endless care and love they have and continue to give to this, admittedly at times, grumpy political economist. I am so very grateful to have so many supportive and brilliant people in my life!

Criminal Justice: Race and Resistance

Indebted by Proxy: How Women Are Faring Under the Carceral State

Christopher Wildeman and Hedwig Lee

Introduction

At one point or another, virtually all of us will have heard someone else—a politician, judge, family member, or friend—say or said ourselves that someone who has been convicted of crime needs to "pay their debt to society" for what they have done (or, rather, been convicted of doing). What is generally meant by "paying their debt to society" is that an individual should suffer prison or jail incarceration, supervision after release, usually in the form of parole, and directly "giving back" whether in the form of community service or the payment of legal fines and fees.

In this article, we build upon much of our previous work on the prevalence and consequences of having a family member incarcerated (Enns et al. 2019; Lee and Wildeman 2013, forthcoming; Wildeman and Lee

C. Wildeman (✉)
Duke University, Durham, NC, USA
e-mail: christopher.wildeman@duke.edu

ROCKWOOL Foundation Research Unit, Copenhagen, Denmark

H. Lee
Washington University, St. Louis, MO, USA

B. C. Wilson, *Care, Climate, and Debt*,
https://doi.org/10.1007/978-3-030-96355-2_2

2021) to develop the concept of being indebted by proxy. Put most directly, we will argue that women who are tied to men who experience incarceration through blood, marriage, children, love, or some combination thereof are also forced to "pay a debt to society" on the basis of their family member's incarceration and that paying this debt does them deep harm, with potential implications for racial/ethnic and class differentials in women's well-being.

We develop this argument in three stages. In the first, we show how common family member incarceration is for American women (e.g., Enns et al. 2019). Although in this stage we focus only on immediate family members, it is important to remember that even the incarceration of extended family members and broader members of kin can have important consequences for women (e.g., Stack 1974). In the second, we discuss how family member incarceration is, more often than not, disruptive to their lives. Here we tread close to our recent review articles on this topic (Lee and Wildeman, forthcoming; Wildeman and Lee 2021), although we also draw out textured qualitative research that lets women who have experienced the incarceration of a family member speak for themselves. In the third, we highlight the negative consequences women suffer as a result of family member incarceration. Here again we stick closest to what we know in the form of recent reviews (Lee and Wildeman, forthcoming; Wildeman and Lee 2021) while simultaneously trying to provide some real, concrete examples of how this process unfolds.

Although our core goal of this chapter is to show how women must "pay their debt to society" just as often as men do despite experiencing prison and jail incarceration directly at much lower rates, we hope that this chapter can also be used to show how debt pervades entire families and can be influenced by broader social policies in ways that may not always be readily apparent.

How Common Is Being Indebted by Proxy?

For most of human history—and, indeed, most of American history—incarceration in a prison or jail was an either wholly unknown event or something that happened only very, very rarely. As recently as the early 1970s, only about 100 per 100,000—0.1% of the population—of Americans were imprisoned on any given day (Blumstein and Cohen 1973). Although a full description of the nature, causes, and consequences of what has come to be called "mass incarceration" (Garland 2001; Western

2006) is beyond the score of this chapter, three key features of this phenomenon bear mentioning. First, as we mentioned above, imprisoned started to take place on a historically novel scale. While 1 in 1000 individuals were in prison on any given day in the early 1970s, that number had quintupled by the early 2000s. Second, this level of imprisonment was not only historically novel within the United States; it was also totally out of step with the imprisonment rates of every other developed democracy in the world. Put directly, no country that we would usually compare ourselves to imprisons at nearly the same rate. Finally, the combination of very high and very unequally distributed rates of imprisonment has made prison incarceration a "normal" event in the life-course of marginalized men. Between one in three and one in four African American men will be sent to prison at some point (Bonczar and Beck 1997; Bonczar 2003; Pettit and Western 2004); more than three in five African American men who did not complete high school will experience this event at some point (Pettit and Western 2004).

Imprisonment is thus common, especially for African American men who did not finish high school. If these men were totally detached from family life or simply did not have families—though virtually all Americans have contact with at least some immediate family members—then these high rates of imprisonment would be important for men but less so for women. Yet research that closely documents the experiences of women with an immediate family member—often a romantic partner—who has been to prison or jail highlights how embedded in family life many of these men were before being locked up (e.g., Braman 2004; Comfort 2008, 2016). To be sure, many of these men did have their struggles prior to entering prisons or jails—as do many of us, we would argue. Sociologist Megan Comfort's (2008, 2016) work is especially relevant in this regard, as she shows that many men who experienced incarceration were loving men who cared for their families and partners, while also struggling with mental health problems, drug and alcohol addiction, infrequent employment, and housing instability and even homelessness.

Because these men were valued family members even prior to experiencing incarceration, their departure likely leaves women with more to manage in their absence, an issue we return to in the next section. Before doing so, however, it is worth noting just how common family member incarceration is and how unequally distributed that event is. To do this, we rely on a figure that we made for a previous article (Wildeman and Lee

2021: 547) and data that we helped collect—the Family History of Incarceration Survey (FamHIS), the first dataset designed primarily with the goal of documenting common an experience family member incarceration is for Americans.

As we have noted elsewhere (Enns et al. 2019; Wildeman and Lee 2021), Fig. 1 provides support for several conclusions. The first one we imagine will be the most shocking, and so we want to challenge you before looking at the figure (or the next sentence) to write down your answer to the following question: What percentage of women do you think has ever had an immediate family member—a serious partner, parent, sibling, or child—sent to prison or jail? Thinking back to when we designed the FamHIS, I can tell you that most of us thought the answer would be between 20 and 30% based on everything we knew at that point. But we were so very wrong—and this project included some of the most central experts in the field. If you said something around 50%, you got it right, meaning that our best guess for what percentage of women would have experienced, this event was about half as high as it should have been.

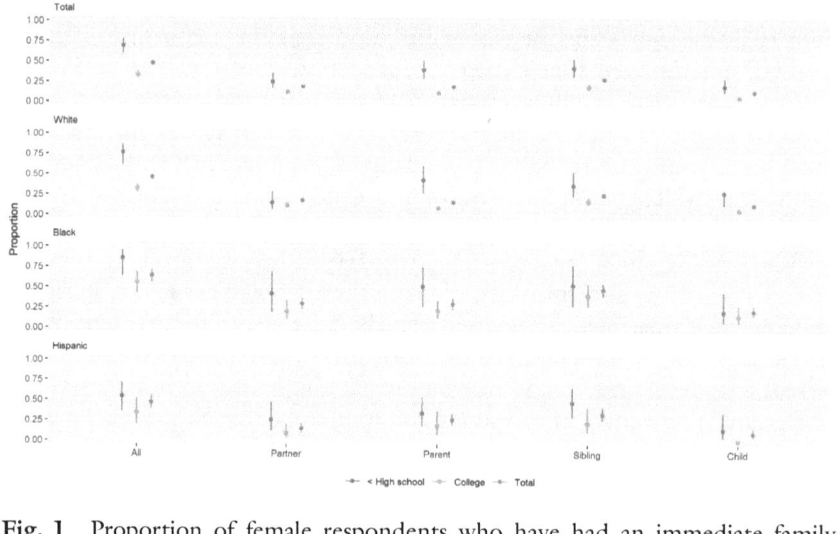

Fig. 1 Proportion of female respondents who have had an immediate family member incarcerated, by race and education

A second set of core findings revolves around racial/ethnic—for the purposes of this study, African Americans, Hispanics, and Whites—and class—for the purposes of this study, women who did not finish high school and who had completed some college—inequality in the risk of experiencing this event. African American women who did not complete high school had the highest risks at about 75%, although highly educated African American women also had high risks. And White women who did not complete high school had far, far higher risks than other White women. Yet at each stage, African American women had higher risks than White women. As a result, the FamHIS date indicate that there are large racial/ethnic and social class differences in the chance of having an immediately family member incarcerated at some point.

A third finding revolves around the relationship women have with the incarcerated family member. Because many of the respondents in the FamHIS data did not have children over the age of 18, risks of child incarceration tend to be fairly low in that sample. Yet the risks for other family members, especially siblings, are quite high across racial/ethnic and class groups. This suggests that when we think about the consequences of family member incarceration, we should think about what women might "owe society" if their romantic partner or father of their child, their own father or mother, or their own brother or sister had ever been incarcerated before.

Taken together, the bottom line from this section is this: Family member incarceration happens to about half of women, is unequally distributed by race/ethnicity and class, and is not limited to just one type of family member. Many types of family members experience incarceration.

(How) Does Family Member Incarceration Disrupt Family Life?

As we have argued elsewhere (Lee and Wildeman, forthcoming; Wildeman and Lee 2021), there are many ways in which having a family member incarcerated could be disruptive to family life, both during the incarceration period and after release. Although it is easy to focus on how the actual incarceration period disrupts family life—the period when the family member is actually gone and can contribute very little to family life and funds must be diverted to their commissary account and money must be spent visiting them—we focus of how family member incarceration could disrupt family life even after the individual has been released from a correctional facility. There are many different ways in which this process could play out—indeed, there are a virtually infinite number of ways in which having a family member sent to such a brutalizing institution could change everything for families—but we focus here on three that may seem mundane but are actually vitally important: (1) the labor market chances of formerly incarcerated men; (2) the mental and physical health of formerly incarcerated men; and (3) shifts in the structure and texture of family life that take place as individuals shift back into daily life after incarceration.

Men who go on to experience incarceration were, on average, not doing well in the labor market even prior to incarceration (e.g., Apel and Sweeten 2010; Western 2006). Yet there is strong and consistent evidence that having been incarcerated does serious harm to labor market prospects, even above and beyond the factors that would have led men to struggle in the labor market even absent incarceration. There are two potential ways in which having ever been incarcerated could lower employment: through (1) the stigma attached to having ever been incarcerated; and (2) the reductions in what economists call human capital—skills, education, and motivation, to name just three pieces—as a result of being confined. Although providing evidence for reductions in human capital as a result of incarceration is challenging, research provides a strong, consistent evidence that prospective employers respond very negatively to the "negative credential" of having ever been incarcerated in experimental studies (Pager 2003, 2007). As a result, most studies indicate that individuals who have been incarcerated earn somewhere between 10 and 30% less than they would as a result of incarceration, a substantial decrease (Western 2006).

Diminishing men's economic contribution both during incarceration and after release is but one way in which family member incarceration strains women's family lives. Decreased physical and mental health of formerly incarcerated men is another mechanism. Although, paradoxically, men's health may, in some circumstances, improve during the incarceration period, evidence strongly and consistently shows that men who have been incarcerated tend to be in poor physical and mental health after release and that the incarceration experience partially causes this poor health (e.g., Massoglia 2008; Schnittker et al. 2012; Schnittker and John

2007). As many women with formerly incarcerated family members indicate (e.g., Braman 2004; Comfort 2008, 2016), female family members are often the ones who manage the heavy burden of a family member's poor physical and mental health, coordinating care, providing emotional support, and increasing their own labor market activity to offset losses due to disability. As a result, these effects on physical and mental health are very real as a source of family stress.

Although these indirect effects on family life are important, the consequences of having a family member incarcerated for both the structure and texture of family life are maybe more vital—and are certainly more direct. Family structure is important in no small part because men, on average, commit more resources to children and families they are living with. As a result, the large effects having been incarcerated have on the probability of a relationship, whether a marital one or a cohabiting one, ending (Lopoo and Western 2005), when combined with the decreased earnings of formerly incarcerated men (Western 2006) lead to dramatic declines in men's financial contributions to families (Geller et al. 2011). This decrease in funds available to the family can lead to increases in serious material deprivation (Schwartz-Soicher et al. 2011) and even homelessness (Wildeman 2014). And this is to say nothing of how women—and large-scale quantitative analyses—indicate that family member incarceration, on average, harms the interactions within the family (Braman 2004; Comfort 2008, 2016; Turney and Wildeman 2013).

Although all of this research seems to suggest that family member incarceration *on average* is disruptive to family life, there are likely certain situations in which the incarceration of a family member would either have no effect on the family or might even benefit the family. On the most basic level, the incarceration of a family member who has no contact with their families is unlikely to have significant effects on family life. And when the incarcerated family member is actively detrimental to family life—through domestic violence or spiraling addiction and mental health problems, for instance—there may even be some short-term benefits of family member incarceration for the individuals left behind. Nonetheless, research tends to indicate that family member incarceration is, more often than not, something that disrupts family life significantly.

(How) Does Family Member Incarceration Harm Women?

In the last two sections, we showed that family member incarceration is common and unequally distributed and that this event seems to place a strain on families. In this section, we demonstrate the costs of this heavy burden that women bear by showing how family member incarceration is tied to women's health. Although there is a great deal of research on how parental incarceration affects the physical and mental health of children (see Lee and Wildeman, forthcoming; see also Wildeman et al. 2018), we focus on how the incarceration of a romantic partner or former romantic partner or a son affects the health of adult women tied to that individual.

Thinking first in terms of romantic partners and former romantic partners, there is quite strong evidence that family member incarceration increases the risk of major depressive disorder—what we colloquially call "depression" much of the time—in the months and years after incarceration (Wildeman et al. 2012). Thinking back to the prior section, this makes good sense, as family member incarceration disrupts the households women manage in vital ways—and this is to say nothing of the sadness and sense of loss that come with knowing that a loved one is sitting in a prison or jail cell with no family and friends to support them. Beyond these effects on mental health, there are also indications that family member incarceration is tied to increase risk factors for cardiovascular disease and that these effects fall especially heavily on adult women relative to adult men. Indeed, research in this area indicates that women who have ever had a family member incarcerated have higher risks of being obese, having diabetes, or having had a heart attack or stroke (Lee et al. 2014), all core indicators of poor health.

The incarceration of a son also seems to take a toll on women's health. Although research in this area first appeared over 15 years ago (Green et al. 2006), this area of research lay mostly dormant until just a couple years. Recent research on how a son's incarceration shapes maternal health findings large negative effects on this event on maternal health at around age 50—or even before, in some instances. The health outcomes considered in the very best research on this topic might sound strange to those of us more interested in debt than health—self-rated health, functional impairments, and functional limitations—but the evidence of harm is strong and quite consistent (Goldman 2019; Sirois 2020). The short version here, again, is that having had a son incarcerated takes a serious toll on women's health, leading them to report that they are in worse health than otherwise similar women who had not experienced this event and to report that they are able to do less things that they need to do to take care of themselves. Given what we discussed earlier, this seems like a logical conclusion in light of what we know about how family member incarceration disrupts family life. Yet thinking also just of our own experiences either as a parent or a child, it is also just patently obvious that seeing a child be locked up and knowing that you were unable to help them during that time would be absolutely devastating to all of us.

Compelling though this area of research is, the reality is that it is quite new, and we simply need more data on how family member incarceration affects women's health. Despite the relative novelty of the evidence in this area, it is clear that family member incarceration generally does harm to women's health and that this harm extends to myriad different health outcomes.

Conclusion

We introduced this chapter with the phrase "indebted by proxy," explaining that what we meant by that is that women—many or even all of whom had committed no crime and may not have even known about any criminal activity their incarcerated family member had engaged in—were forced to pay the "debt to society" that their family members had incurred. This is a nice rhetorical flourish, and we find it satisfying that such a flourish extends our understanding of debt—and especially the role that systems of social control have in meting out debt in ways that we might not have even thought about before. Yet rhetorical flourishes aside, it is important to close with what this specific flourish means. It means, as we have shown in the core of this chapter, that poor, disproportionately minority women experience family member incarceration at very high rates in the contemporary United States. Because this event is highly disruptive to household functioning and women's health as a result, it also means that this new form of debt has the effect of exacerbating racial/ethnic and class disparities in women's health and well-being.

References

Apel, R., & Sweeten, G. (2010). The Impact of Incarceration on Employment during the Transition to Adulthood. *Social Problems*, *57*(3), 448–479. https://doi.org/10.1525/sp.2010.57.3.448

Blumstein, A., & Cohen, J. (1973). Theory of the Stability of Punishment, A. Symposium: Perspectives on Innovation and Reform in Criminal Justice. *Journal of Criminal Law and Criminology*, *64*(2), 198–207. https://heinonline.org/HOL/P?h=hein.journals/jclc64&i=204

Bonczar, T. P. (2003). *Prevalence of Imprisonment in the U.S. Population, 1974–2001* (Statistics No. 197976; BJS Special Reports). Bureau of Justice Statistics. https://www.ncjrs.gov/App/abstractdb/AbstractDBDetails.aspx?id=197976

Bonczar, T. P., & Beck, A. J. (1997). *Lifetime Likelihood of Going to State or Federal Prison*. U.S. Department of Justice, Office of Justice Programs, Bureau of Justice Statistics.

Braman, D. (2004). *Doing Time on the Outside: Incarceration and Family Life in Urban America*. University of Michigan Press. https://doi.org/10.3998/mpub.17629

Comfort, M. (2008). *Doing Time Together: Love and Family in the Shadow of the Prison* (6.1.2008 edition). University of Chicago Press.

Comfort, M. (2016). "A Twenty-Hour-a-Day Job": The Impact of Frequent Low-Level Criminal Justice Involvement on Family Life. *The Annals of the American Academy of Political and Social Science*, *665*(1), 63–79. https://doi.org/10.1177/0002716215625038

Enns, et al. (2019). https://journals.sagepub.com/doi/full/10.1177/2378023119829332

Garland, D. (Ed.). (2001). *Mass Imprisonment: Social Causes and Consequences* (First Edition). Sage Publications Ltd.

Geller, A., Garfinkel, I., & Western, B. (2011). Paternal Incarceration and Support for Children in Fragile Families. *Demography*, *48*(1), 25–47. https://doi.org/10.1007/s13524-010-0009-9

Goldman, A. W. (2019). Linked Lives in Double Jeopardy: Child Incarceration and Maternal Health at Midlife. *Journal of Health and Social Behavior*, *60*(4), 398–415. https://doi.org/10.1177/0022146519882328

Green, K. M., Ensminger, M. E., Robertson, J. A., & Juon, H.-S. (2006). Impact of Adult Sons' Incarceration on African American Mothers' Psychological Distress. *Journal of Marriage and Family*, *68*(2), 430–441. https://doi.org/10.1111/j.1741-3737.2006.00262.x

Lee, H., & Wildeman, C. (2013). Things Fall Apart: Health Consequences of Mass Imprisonment for African American Women. *The Review of Black Political Economy*, *40*(1), 39–52. https://doi.org/10.1007/s12114-011-9112-4

Lee, H., & Wildeman, C. (Forthcoming). Assessing Mass Incarceration's Effects on Families. *Science*. https://www.science.org/doi/abs/10.1126/science.abj7777

Lee, H., Wildeman, C., Wang, E. A., Matusko, N., & Jackson, J. S. (2014). A Heavy Burden: The Cardiovascular Health Consequences of Having a Family Member Incarcerated. *American Journal of Public Health, 104*(3), 421–427. https://doi.org/10.2105/AJPH.2013.301504

Lopoo, L. M., & Western, B. (2005). Incarceration and the Formation and Stability of Marital Unions. *Journal of Marriage and Family, 67*(3), 721–734. https://doi.org/10.1111/j.1741-3737.2005.00165.x

Massoglia, M. (2008). Incarceration as Exposure: The Prison, Infectious Disease, and Other Stress-Related Illnesses. *Journal of Health and Social Behavior, 49*(1), 56–71. https://doi.org/10.1177/002214650804900105

Pager, D. (2003). The Mark of a Criminal Record. *American Journal of Sociology, 108*(5), 937–975. https://doi.org/10.1086/374403

Pager, D. (2007). The Use of Field Experiments for Studies of Employment Discrimination: Contributions, Critiques, and Directions for the Future. *The ANNALS of the American Academy of Political and Social Science, 609*(1), 104–133. https://doi.org/10.1177/0002716206294796

Pettit & Western (2004). https://journals.sagepub.com/doi/abs/10.1177/000312240406900201?casa_token=v4W_hOdCWUUAAAAA:beKfTTiVfkmQZzAGFBCf7DSRgFoF1e29l2rQrVNZQ5jxe9ttp8FbCz0TZs67tGTsxNPf-5qGqtB-w

Schnittker, J., & John, A. (2007). Enduring Stigma: The Long-Term Effects of Incarceration on Health. *Journal of Health and Social Behavior, 48*(2), 115–130. https://doi.org/10.1177/002214650704800202

Schnittker, J., Massoglia, M., & Uggen, C. (2012). Out and Down: Incarceration and Psychiatric Disorders. *Journal of Health and Social Behavior, 53*(4), 448–464. https://doi.org/10.1177/0022146512453928

Schwartz-Soicher, O., Geller, A., & Garfinkel, I. (2011). The Effect of Paternal Incarceration on Material Hardship. *Social Service Review, 85*(3), 447–473. https://doi.org/10.1086/661925

Sirois, C. (2020). The Strain of Sons' Incarceration on Mothers' Health. *Social Science & Medicine, 264*, 113264. https://doi.org/10.1016/j.socscimed.2020.113264

Stack, C. (1974). *All Our Kin: Strategies for Survival in a Black Community*. Harper & Row.

Turney, K., & Wildeman, C. (2013). Redefining Relationships: Explaining the Countervailing Consequences of Paternal Incarceration for Parenting. *American Sociological Review, 78*(6), 949–979. https://doi.org/10.1177/0003122413505589

Western, B. (2006). *Punishment and inequality in America*. Russell Sage.

Wildeman, C. (2014). Parental Incarceration, Child Homelessness, and the Invisible Consequences of Mass Imprisonment. *The ANNALS of the American Academy of Political and Social Science*, *651*(1), 74–96. https://doi.org/10.1177/0002716213502921

Wildeman, C., Fitzpatrick, M. D., & Goldman, A. W. (2018). Conditions of Confinement in American Prisons and Jails. *Annual Review of Law and Social Science*, *14*(1), 29–47. https://doi.org/10.1146/annurev-lawsocsci-101317-031025

Wildeman, C., & Lee, H. (2021). Women's Health in the Era of Mass Incarceration. *Annual Review of Sociology*, *47*(1), 543–565. https://doi.org/10.1146/annurev-soc-081320-113303

Wildeman, C., Schnittker, J., & Turney, K. (2012). Despair by Association? The Mental Health of Mothers with Children by Recently Incarcerated Fathers. *American Sociological Review*, *77*(2), 216–243. https://doi.org/10.1177/003122411436

Black August: A Black Radical Tradition

déqui kioni-sadiki

> To understand the United States you have to see it not just from the story it tells about itself, but from the perspectives of the people it has tried to eliminate, assimilate, and enslave.[1]

These words speak-truth-to-power about the centering of Black/New Afrikan[2] lives, voices, perspectives, and resistance across the thirty-one days in summer known as Black August.

Black August is not a celebration.

[1] Nick Estes is a citizen of the Lower Brule Sioux Tribe, cofounder of Red Nation, an Indigenous resistance organization, professor and author of Our History is the Future: Standing Rock Versus the Dakota Access Pipeline and the Long Tradition of Indigenous resistance.

[2] "Black" is the political term used by Kwame Ture as the clarion call of the 1960s Black Power Movement. "New Afrikan" reflects a Pan African identity, purpose, direction, and refers to the descendants of enslaved Afrikans born in the United States and across the Afrikan diaspora. https://freethelandmxgm.org/why-we-say-new-afrikan/.

d. kioni-sadiki (✉)
Brooklyn, NY, USA
e-mail: kioni.sadiki@verizon.net

B. C. Wilson, *Care, Climate, and Debt*,
https://doi.org/10.1007/978-3-030-96355-2_3

Black August is a month-long commemoration of the lives of eight imprisoned Black/New Afrikan men murdered by California law enforcement and prison guards during the 1970s, the Black Radical Tradition of resistance and Black/New Afrikan U.S. held Political Prisoners and Prisoners of War (PPOWs).[3]

Black August was borne inside the dungeons of San Quentin, a men's state prison built on land once inhabited and cared for by the Chochenyo and Ramaytush Ohlone people in the city and state today known as San Francisco, California. Conceived in LOVE. LOVE as the Argentine revolutionary, Ernesto Ché Guerva, said all revolutionaries are guided by. LOVE for four-hundred years of Black/New Afrikan resistance to state-sanctioned violence, white settler-colonialism, mercantile imperialism, predatory capitalism, white supremacy, institutionalized racism, patriarchy, xenophobia, and sexism.

Black August came into being in the aftermath of the revolutionary struggles of the 1960s and 1970s, a period when Afrikan, Caribbean, South and Central American countries were winning their independence from European colonialism and imperialism. Here on Turtle Island,[4] the pre-colonial name for the united states, hundreds of thousands, if not millions of youth, across multi-racial, multi-ethnic identities, and backgrounds were taking to the streets, organizing and building solidarity with oppressed people all over the world in the fight against capitalism and the status-quo. Kwame Ture was challenging youth to "organize, organize, organize" and demanding "Black Power."[5] The Black Panther Party for Self-Defense (BPP) had declared "What We Want. What We Believe" with a 10-Point Platform and Program[6] that served the basic material needs of

[3] A Political Prisoner is a person held in confinement because of their support of, or identity with, a people struggling for freedom from an oppressive government or against its oppressive policies. A Political Prisoner of War is a national combatant of an oppressed nation held in confinement by the oppressor nation because of their support of, or identity with, the oppressed nation's war for self-determination, independence, or national liberation from the oppressor nation.

[4] Turtle Island is the name given this land by millions of Indigenous people thousands of years before it was invaded, colonized and renamed the united states of America by European settlers.

[5] Pan-Africanist revolutionary formerly known as Stokely Carmichael and leader of Student Non-Violent Coordinating Committee (SNCC) coined the term Black Power.

[6] National Alumni Association of the Black Panther Party—https://naabpp.org/what-we-want/.

cash-poor and working-class Black/New Afrikan communities. The air was thick with the culture of Black pride and Afrikan-centered consciousness that made clear Black was indeed beautiful and so was wearing natural hair, dashikis and changing a slave name into an Afrikan name. And the streets were filled with Black folk dancing and signifying to the rhythms of Black music that proclaimed "Say It Loud, I'm Black and I'm Proud," "To Be Young, Gifted & Black," and "Keep on Pushin."[7] Yes, the 1960s and 1970s were a decade when people truly believed change was gonna come and the revolution would happen in their lifetime.

Sadly, the revolution didn't happen. It was put down by U.S. law enforcement and the FBI's Cointelpro—counterintelligence program[8]—war on radicals, revolutionaries, and movements of that era, and in particular, the Black Liberation Movement (BLM) and BPP.

Change, however, did come. And it came with Black August.

In its early manifestations, Black August existed primarily behind the prison walls and prison towers of San Quentin. It made space and time for the Black/New Afrikan population to honor the lives, sacrifices, and martyrdom of Jonathan Jackson, William Christmas, James McClain, W.L. Nolan, Cleveland Edwards, Alvin "Jug" Miller, George L. Jackson and Khatari Gaulden. The majority of whom were murdered by California law enforcement and prison guards during the month of August.

W.L. Nolan was a leader in the New Afrikan Revolutionary Prison Movement, when he and two others, ***Cleveland Edwards*** and ***Alvin "Jug" Miller*** were shot and killed by a white prison guard as they defended themselves against a racist attack orchestrated by prison guards.

W.L. Nolan, Cleveland Edwards, and Alvin "Jug" Miller

Murdered on January 13, 1970

Jonathan Jackson was the eighteen-year-old younger brother of George L. Jackson, when he led an armed action to liberate his brother from a northern California courtroom.

[7] Songs by James Brown, Nina Simone, Curtis Mayfield, and the Impressions.

[8] COINTELPRO—the FBI's Counter Intelligence Program, a covert operation used to "disrupt, discredit and otherwise neutralize" surveil, infiltrate, progressive, radical and revolutionary organizations, and movements.

In the annals of Black/New Afrikan resistance history, this action is proudly known as the Marin County Courthouse Rebellion. Despite George's absence in court that morning, a young Jonathan was not. Continuing with intended mission, he led the presiding judge, court reporter, deputy district attorney, and three Black/New Afrikan men—William Christmas, James McClain, and Ruchell "Cinque" Magee—out of the courthouse, onto the streets of San Rafael and into a white getaway van.

When it looked like the van might get away, California law enforcement and prison guards unleashed a fusillade of gunfire into their moving vehicle. When the shooting stopped, everyone lay dead, except Magee and the deputy district attorney, who were both seriously wounded.

Magee, as the sole Black/New Afrikan male survivor and co-defendant of Angela Davis in another trial, was charged, convicted, and sentenced to life in prison. Fifty-eight years later, he remains imprisoned in the state of California, having served decades in the isolation, torture, and deprivation in the state's notoriously punitive and inhumane Solitary Housing Units (SHU).

Jonathan Jackson, William Christmas, and James McClain

Murdered on August 7, 1970

George L. Jackson was himself an eighteen-year-old when he was arrested and railroaded into a one-year-to-life prison term. Although he'd entered into a plea deal on a $70 robbery charge, once convicted instead of receiving a lesser sentence or one more commiserate with the charge against him, he was given an indeterminate prison sentence.

On the surface one might think this is an anomaly. It is not. Rather, it is more the rule than the exception when it comes to the sons and daughters of cash-poor and working-class Black/New Afrikan mothers and fathers entangled in the crosshairs of amerikkka's criminally unjust court system. These are the folk that the late-great comedian, Paul Mooney, often said "lack the complexion for the protection." And it is their lack of white skin privilege coupled with their lack of financial means to hire private legal counsel that makes for their lack of access to "equal" protection of the law, appropriate application of sentencing, offers of probation, community service, or even charges dropped as is generally the case for the sons and daughters of white middle-upper-middle class mothers and fathers. This tracking of Black/New Afrikan youth into the prison system didn't have a name sixty years ago. Today, it is aptly called the "school-to-prison-pipeline." Both are demonstrative of the systematic practice and underlying message that (a) "the Negro has no rights the white man is bound to respect"[9] and (b) the lives of Black/New Afrikan youth are irredeemable, disposable, expendable, not worthy of the equitable distribution of justice or opportunity in the courtrooms of amerikkka.

After being in prison for several years, as is often the case, George became politicized. A journey in self-actualization, heightened socio-political awakening, and consciousness that transformed him from social prisoner with a criminal mentality into one with a radical/revolutionary mentality and politic. Expressing that "freedom means warmth and protection against harsh exposure to the elements. It means food, not garbage. It means truth, harmony, and the social relations that spring from these. It means the best medical attention whenever it's needed. It means employment that is reasonable, that coincides with the individual necessities and feelings." George attributed his new-found knowledge, understanding, interrogation, analysis of capitalism, and its manipulation of the criminal injustice apparatus to target, demonize, criminalize and ultimately, warehouse cash-poor and working-class Black youth into prison to his readings of Marx, Lenin, Fanon, Trotsky, Engels, and Mao who "redeemed me." He joined a prison chapter of the BPP was appointed Field Marshall by its co-founder, Huey P. Newton,[10] evolving into an effective prison activist, advocate, leader, and spokesperson not only within San Quentin, but for a then growing national Prison Movement. He'd grown into a brilliant theoretician and writer who developed a well-publicized personal-political relationship with scholar-activist Angela Davis had his much-celebrated, *Soledad Brother: The Prison Letters of*

[9] Dred Scott was an enslaved Afrikan who sued to maintain his Freedom after traveling with a slave owner to a non-slaving hold state. The U.S. Supreme Court ruled that living in a free state and territory did not entitle an enslaved person to his freedom. In essence, the decision argued that, as someone's property, Scott was not a citizen and could not sue in a federal court. The majority opinion by Chief Justice Roger B. Taney also stated ...that African Americans could never become U.S. citizens. This is known as the Dred Scott Decision rendered March 6, 1857.

[10] Huey P. Newton and Bobby Seale co-founded the Black Panther Party for Self-Defense in Oakland, California in October 1966.

George Jackson[11] published as he stood trial for the murder of a prison guard. All of which on one hand, earned him tremendous respect, admiration, and notoriety within, across, and beyond the California prison system. But on the other, made him a threat and target of the prison administration. This sentiment was shared by Davis, a leader of the Soledad Brothers Defense Committee, in an article she wrote and published in *The Black Scholar* which said, "under the surface of the murder indictment lurked the real charges: revolutionary insubordination, failure to conform to the established order of things, inciting dissent, planting the seeds of liberation in the minds of their comrades in captivity."[12]

And so it happened one August morning, a little more than three weeks after the one-year anniversary of the Marin County Courthouse Rebellion, that George L. Jackson was shot and killed by guards on the San Quentin prison yard.[13]

As justification for his murder, the administration claimed George was attempting an escape, had hidden a 0.32 caliber gun in his hair and was planning to use on prison guards. Then and now, this claim is so outrageous as to never be believed other than by the state or prison administration. An idea affirmed when prominent scholar-writer-activist James Baldwin wrote "no black person will ever believe that George Jackson died the way they tell us he did."

[11] George Jackson, Fleeta Drumgo, and John Clutchette became the Soledad Brothers when they charged with the murder of a prison guard at the Soledad prison where they were held. They were facing the death penalty if convicted.

[12] Davis, Angela. April–May 1971. "THE BLACK PRISONER." The Black Scholar. Vol. 2 No. 8/9. pp. 2–7. https://www.jstor.org/stable/41202900.

[13] Following the murder of George Jackson, three prison guards were killed. Six Black/Brown men—Fleeta Drumgo, David Johnson, Hugo "Yogi" Pinell, John Larry Spain, Luis Talamantez, and Willie Tate—were charged. They were known as the "San Quentin Six" and were subjected to horrific torture, violence, brutality, and punitive segregation by the prison administration before being acquitted of all charges. In retaliation, the Aryan Brotherhood murdered Yogi on the prison yard days after his release into general population following decades of solitary confinement.

George L. Jackson

Murdered on August 21, 1971

Khatari Gaulden was a founder and leader of Black August. Also imprisoned at San Quentin, he had escaped on a previous occasion, but was recaptured and returned to San Quentin. It was on that prison yard that he suffered an injury which led to his death, and as he lay bleeding, the prison administration denied him much-needed medical treatment. Their blatant disregard for his life caused Khatari to bleed to death.

Khatari Gaulden

Murdered on August 1, 1978

To honor of these eight lives, during the month of August, brothers behind the wall wore black arm bands, participated in the collective ritual of morning and nighttime prayers, fasted from sun-up to sun-down, boycotted the prison commissary, exercised daily, attended mandatory political education classes, discussion sessions, cultural, social consciousness-building events, and activities. They read and studied revolutionary books and writings, turned off the radio and television, refrained from drugs and alcohol, or engaging in arrogant or loud behavior. The month of August was dedicated to sacrifice, developing and fostering self-restraint, self-reliance, self-discipline, unity, community solidarity and strengthening their physical, mental, emotional, financial, and spiritual health.

It was coined Black August both as an identity and political nod to the Black/New Afrikan nation, the 1960s Black Power Movement, and homage to the many historical and contemporary acts of Black resistance that occurred during the month of August.

These include but are not limited to:

August 1st

- 1979: Veronza Bowers attempts escape from UPS Lompoc, CA;

August 2nd

- 1850: Underground Railroad network forms;

August 3rd

- 2010: Marilyn Buck, a white anti-imperialist, Black Liberation Army ally, and former PPOW succumbs to cancer;

August 8th

- 1950: Birthday of Dr. Mutulu Shakur, acupuncture healer and PPOW;
- 1977: Rebellion at Napanoch-upstate NY prison against Klu Klux Klan guards;
- 1978: MOVE compound in Philadelphia, PA home is bombed by Mayor Wilson Goode;

August 10th

- 1970: Rebellion at lower Manhattan Tombs-New York City jail;
- 2014: Rebellions in Ferguson, Missouri following the police murder of unarmed 18-year-old Black male, Mike Brown;

August 11th

- 1965: Rebellion in Watts, Los Angeles in protest of continuing unpunished police violence and murder of unarmed Black men, womyn, and children;

August 12th

- 2015: Hugo "Yogi" Pinell, one of the San Quentin Six, is murdered by a member of the Aryan Brotherhood following his release into general population after decades of solitary confinement;

August 17th

- 1887: Birthday of Marcus Mosiah Garvey, Jamaican Pan-Africanist activist/founder United Negro Improvement Association;

August 18th

- 1971: the Provisional Government of the Republic of New Afrika (PGRNA) defends Black/New Afrikan citizens against violent FBI assault in Jackson, Mississippi;

August 20th

- 1619: arrival of first enslaved Afrikans in Jamestown, Virginia;
- 1985: Ohio prisoners take over supermax unit;

August 21st

- 1791: start of the Haitian Revolution;
- 1831: Rebellion led by Nat "the Prophet" Turner in Southampton County, Virginia;

August 22nd

- 1843: Henry Highland Garnett calls upon enslaved Afrikans to go on a general strike;
- 1964: Fannie Lou Hamer, founder of Mississippi Freedom Democratic Party, testifies about Black voter disenfranchisement at the Democratic National Convention;
- 1989: Huey P. Newtown, co-founder Black Panther Party for Self-Defense, is killed

August 23rd

- 1943: Birthday of Russell 'Maroon' Shoatz, PPOW;

August 24th

- 2003: Safiya Bukhari, veteran BPP, former PPOW, and co-founder of The Jericho Movement for Amnesty & Recognition of U.S. held Political Prisoners & Prisoners of War dies;

August 27th

- 1963: W.E.B. DuBois, New Afrikan scholar and theoretician dies in Ghana;

August 28th

- 1955: Emmitt Till, fourteen-year-old Black teen from Chicago, IL is murdered by three white men in Money, Mississippi;
- 1963: "Poor People's March" to demand Jobs & Freedom is held in Washington, DC;
- 2005: Hurricane Katrina destroys communities and displaces thousands of Black/New Afrikans in New Orleans, LA;
- 2016: Colin Kaepernick, activist/NFL player holds a press conference explaining his refusal to stand for the National Anthem in defense of unarmed Black men, women, and children being murdered by police;

August 30th

- 1800: Rebellion led by enslaved Gabriel Prosser in Henrico County, Virginia;
- 1938: Birthday of Fred Hampton, Chairman of the Chicago, IL chapter of the Black Panther Party.

Black August transcended the prison walls and towers in the 1980s, when a coalition of activists and organizations from the New Afrikan Independence Movement (NAIM), Malcolm X Grassroots Movement (MXGM), and New Afrikan People's Organization (NAPO) joined forces to form the Black August Organizing Committee (BAOC). Their goal was bridging the gap between the inside world of prisons and the outside. To accomplish this, the BAOC set out to (1) introduce Black August to Black/New Afrikan communities' nationwide; (2) educate the outside world about the horrific and inhumane prison conditions endured by those on the inside; (3) build awareness and support for Black/New Afrikan U.S. held PPOWs.

The support of PPOWs includes the understanding that PPOWs do not exist in a vacuum. That PPOWs exist because where there is oppression, there is resistance. And where there is resistance, there is systematic repression. The U.S. government and capitalist propaganda doggedly denies and/or ignores the existence of PPOWs, but Freedom-loving people all over the world recognize that they do exist. In the words of the late Yuri Kochiyama, a warrior for Black Liberation and survivor of Japanese internment camps, "of course there are Political Prisoners in the u.s. They are the heartbeat of the struggle,..., reminders of what struggle is really about." And they are! PPOWs do remind us that the struggles of the 1960s and 1970s existed. The proof government the extreme lengths the U.S. government went to criminalize, demonize, surveil, frame, outright assassinate, punish, and perpetually imprison those who dared to struggle against them.

That it's long been said "if you want to know how civilized a society is all you have to do is take a look inside its prisons," we need look no further than the Movements of the 1960s and 1970s when prison population hovered in the low hundreds of thousands. In the decades since, the numbers have exploded closer to 2.5 million, with millions more on parole and/or probation. The U.S. makes up just 5% of the world's population yet imprisons an astonishing 25% of the world's prison population. The Attica Rebellion and Massacre[14] exposed rampant rodent-bug infestations, lack of nutritional food, healthcare, educational opportunities, personal hygiene products, forced unpaid prison labor.[15] The violence and brutality of prison guards, overt racism, white supremacy, and other inhumanities that made prison life intolerable shocked the nation; but for some it was very familiar reality. Fifty years later, those same conditions persist, sparking rebellions, hunger strikes, and work stoppages in federal, state, local prison, and detention camps across this stolen land. That said, we must ask ourselves, what can be said about a "civilized" society that imprisons more of its citizenry than any other country in the world, and what can be said about a society that sanctions, condones,

[14] Attica is a men's prison in upstate New York where from September 9 to 13, 1971 it was taken over by the prison population who held prison guards hostage in order to negotiate for their list of demands for better living conditions. Then NYS governor Nelson Rockefeller's response was a bloody police siege that ended with state-sanctioned shooting deaths of ten (10) prison guards, forty-three (43) Attica Brothers, and the vicious torture and beating of hundreds more.

[15] McDonald's, Starbucks, Wendy's, Walmart, Sprint, Verizon, Victoria Secret, JC Penney, American Airlines, Avis Rent-a-Car, Kmart are just some of the corporations who exploit prison labor to reduce operating costs. Per hour wages are anywhere between \$.10 and \$.50 cents per hour, in states like Georgia prison labor is unpaid.

supports the torture of solitary confinement, death by prison medical neglect, and administrative indifference.

Black August raises these questions and more with its month-long hosting of social, political, cultural, and educational events and activities to bring the inside out and reminds us of the importance of reaching back into those prison death camps to stay connected to those we Love inside, including PPOWs.

The names below are of those Black/New Afrikan PPOWs currently held in federal and state prison death camps, along with the year their imprisonment began:

- Imprisoned since 1963 ~ Ruchell "Cinque" Magee (*politicized in prison*)
- Imprisoned since 1970 ~ Ed Poindexter
- Imprisoned since 1971 ~ Joseph "Joe-Joe" Bowen
- Imprisoned since 1973 ~ Sundiata Acoli (Clarke Squire, 84 years old)[16]
- Imprisoned since 1973 ~ Veronza Bowers Jr.
- Imprisoned since 1977 ~ Russell "Maroon" Shoatz (recently released to Hospice care)
- Imprisoned since 1977 ~ Kenny "Zulu" Whitmore
- Imprisoned since 1981 ~ David Gilbert (*white anti-imperialist*) recently granted parole
- Imprisoned since 1982 ~ Mumia Abu-Jamal
- Imprisoned since 1986 ~ Dr. Mutulu Shakur
- Imprisoned since 2000 ~ Imam Jamil Al-Amin (formerly H. Rap Brown)
- Imprisoned since 2002 ~ Kamau Sadiki (Freddie Hilton)

Like George Jackson, they wanted "to leave a world that is liberated from trash, pollution, racism, nation-states, nation-state wars and armies, from pomp, bigotry, parochialism, a thousand different brands of untruth, and licentious, usurious economics."[17] They are also veterans of the

[16] Sundiata is the co-defendant of Assata Shakur, and was in the car on the NJ Turnpike during the May 2, 1972 police involved shooting that resulted both of them being wounded and the death of their comrade, Zayd Shakur.

[17] George L. Jackson quote.

BPP that J. Edgar Hoover, the FBI's decades-long Director, called "the greatest threat to the internal security of the united states" as he waged a vicious, unrelenting, and then illegal Cointelpro campaign to destroy the organization and its membership. Although the BPP was a primary Cointelpro target, the Black Liberation Army (BLA), Republic of New Afrika (RNA), Nation of Islam (NOI), and other progressive revolutionary organizations were targeted as well. The impact of which was not just the crushing of the 1960s and 1970s movements, but the inertia within the movement—or lack thereof—that exists today.

This includes the fact that these PPOWs have now aged into their 60s, 70s, and 80s having served decades more time in prison than individuals convicted of similar so-called crimes that are not of a political nature. Despite their advanced age, poor health, and exemplary accomplishments, PPOWs are routinely singled out for disparate treatment, harassment, isolation, and punishment. Nearly all are battling multiple serious and life-threatening illnesses—COVID, bone cancer, liver cancer, blindness, and more—while the capitalist power structure, courts, prison administrations, and parole boards continue to label them a threat to the outside world. Just as George was labeled a threat prior to being murdered, and with decades and dozens of denials for parole, compassionate release, clemency, and commutation of sentence, each is effectively sentenced to death in prison without a judge actually having sentenced them to death.

Most disturbing is how PPOWs have been largely forgotten, ignored, marginalized, and erased out of our current struggles. As the New Year approaches, we who work with and advocate on their behalf, believe it is well past time they be allowed to come home to be with their families. They do not deserve to die alone shackled to a prison cot. They need us, the beneficiaries of their hard-fought sacrifices and organizing on the streets, to make a determined and persistent demand of pressuring elected officials to release them. We ask you to visit The Jericho Movement for Amnesty and Recognition of U.S. held Political Prisoners and Prisoners of War website to consider ways you can help bring these elders home where they belong.[18]

We have already lost too many PPOWs to state-sanctioned medical neglect, misdiagnosis, mistreatment and murder behind the wall:

[18] The Jericho Movement for Amnesty & Recognition of u.s. held Political Prisoners & Prisoners of War supports, advocates and fights for the release of Black/Brown, Indigenous, Asian, Puerto Rican, white (anti-imperialist) PPOWS. For more info and facility listings, visit: www.TheJerichoMovement.com.

- Imprisoned in 1969 ~ Romaine "Chip" Fitzgerald, RIP 2021
- Imprisoned in 1970 ~ Mondo we Langa, RIP 2016
- Imprisoned in 1971 ~ Albert "Nuh" Washington,** RIP 2000
- Imprisoned in 1973 ~ Teddy "Jah" Health, RIP 2001
- Imprisoned in 1981 ~ Kuwasi Balagoon, RIP 1986
- Imprisoned in 1982 ~ Bashir Hameed, RIP 2008
- Imprisoned in 1982 ~ Abdullah Majid, RIP 2016
- Imprisoned in 1984 ~ Warren Wells, RIP 2001
- Imprisoned in 1985 ~ Tom Manning (*white anti-imperialist*), RIP 2019
- Imprisoned in 1985 ~ Richard Williams (*white anti-imperialist*), RIP 2005

Black August also aided in the victories that have brought some of our PPOWs home:

- Released 1990: Imprisoned since 1971 ~ Dhoruba bin-Wahad
- Released 1997: Imprisoned since 1972 ~ Geronimo JiJaga Pratt, *RIP 2011*
- Released 2001: Imprisoned since 1972 ~ Albert King* (*politicized in prison*)[19]
- Released 2013: Imprisoned since 1972 ~ Herman Wallace* (*politicized in prison*), *RIP* 3 days later
- Released 2014: Imprisoned since 1975 ~ Sekou Kambui, RIP 2017
- Released 2014: Imprisoned since 1981 ~ Sekou Odinga
- Released 2016: Imprisoned since 1972 ~ Albert Woodfox* (*politicized in prison*)
- Released 2016: Imprisoned since 1979 ~ Maliki Latine Shakur
- Released 2017: Imprisoned since 1981 ~ Zolo Azania
- Released 2018: Imprisoned since 1973 ~ Herman Bell**
- Released 2018: Imprisoned since 1973 ~ Robert Seth Hayes, *RIP 2019*
- Released 2020: Imprisoned since 1971 ~ Jalil Muntaqim**

[19] *Albert Woodfox, Robert King and Herman Wallace were known as the Angola 3, who spent 30 + years in solitary confinement as punishment for membership in a prison chapter of the BPP.

Black August is rooted in Black/New Afrikan peoples' human right to struggle for self-determination, justice and Liberation "by any means necessary"—armed and otherwise. It neither holds nor accepts the white supremacist narrative and systematic erasure, exclusion, sanitizing, mythologizing and demonizing of the Black Freedom Struggle, especially our PPOWs, however, that resistance is manifested.

That said, Black August honors

- the resistance waged by kidnapped Afrikans onboard Christian-named slave ships like "Jesus," "Faith," "John the Baptist," "Hope," even "Independence" being forcibly transported across the Transatlantic Slave Trade/Middle Passage into the horrific two-hundred-and-forty-two-year "peculiar institution"[20] of buying, trading, selling, and enslaving Black bodies on auction blocks and plantations north, south, east and west of this stolen land;
- the resistance waged by enslaved Afrikans and their descendants on those plantations who sometimes killed slave masters, poisoned food, over-harvested crops, ran away, refused to wed, bear children, pick cotton, tobacco, or chop sugar cane from "can see in the morning till can't see at night," and most dangerously, acquire the skill of reading and writing;
- the resistance waged by armed self-defense patrols such as the Afrikan Blood Brotherhood, Deacons of Defense, Jamaica Rifle Association, BPP, BLA, Revolutionary Action Movement (RAM), RNA, and others, that organized to protect and defend Black/New Afrikan families, communities and property from roving mobs of violent white men—uniformed and not—intent to tarring, feathering, lynching, burning, bombing, massacring, shooting, discarding, and dumping Black bodies in rivers, mass graves, in cities and towns from that Red Summer,[21] to Tulsa, OK, Elaine, AR, Wilmington, NC, Rosewood FL, to dozens of other cities and towns across this stolen land.

[20] Euphemist term white southerners used for the enslavement of Afrikan people. Also a book by the same name: Peculiar Institution: Slavery in the Ante-Bellum South by Kenneth M. Stampp. Vintage Publisher. December 1989.

[21] From April to November 1919, white supremacists terrorized and engaged in mob violence, murder, and racist attacks of Black communities in more than three dozen cities across the U.S., including a three-day-long massacre in Elaine, Arkansas.

While the dominate narrative presents these patrols as violent "hate whitey" groups, the truth is the purpose they have always served has been in self-defense against the terror of white on Black violence—state or private.

- the resistance waged across the Long Hot Summer,[22] Watts, Ferguson,[23] and other urban cities that saw Black/New Afrikan communities burn down capitalist enterprises that exploit their everyday needs, help themselves to over-priced poor-quality goods, break windows, smash and overturn cars. Toss and lock themselves into prison cells that hold them hostage, refuse mess hall, organize hunger strikes and work stoppages.

Because Black resistance has always been viewed through a liberal white gaze, terms like violent, destructive, unjustified, angry mobs "rioting and looting" are applied to these spontaneous, generally unorganized and unsustainable, powder keg rebellions. These rebellions are part and parcel spoken in the "language of the unheard" by a people who are simply "sick and tired of being sick and tired" of the business-as-usual practice of violence and human rights violations that is sanctioned, perpetuated, condoned, supported by laws and policies that deny Black/New Afrikan people their right to live, breathe, travel, work, and be free every second of every day.

The gift that Black August offers the descendants of kidnapped and enslaved Afrikans is its connecting of the past with the present and with an eye toward the future. Throughout the month of August, we speak the names Jonathan Jackson, George L. Jackson W.L. Nolan, William Christmas, James McClain, Cleveland Edwards, Alvin "Jug" Miller, Khatari Gaulden. We hold the beating hearts of the Black Freedom Struggle, our PPOWs, in our hearts and minds. We pass on the radical revolutionary histories/herstories of David Walker, Rosa Parks, Robert and Mabel Williams, Ida B. Wells, Malcolm X, Fannie Lou Hamer, and a myriad of other Black/New Afrikan Freedom Fighters who sacrificed in

[22] The summer of 1967 was marked by over 150 Black rebellions that erupted in cities across the u.s.—Atlanta, Boston, Cincinnati, Buffalo, Tampa, Detroit, Toledo, Watts, and elsewhere in protest of the oppression, injustice, inequities in cash-poor and working-class Black/New Afrikan communities.

[23] Weeks and months of rebellions and protests after the murder of Michael Brown, an unarmed Black teenager by white police officer, Darren Wilson, who the grand jury refused to indict.

our long walk, run, and fight toward Black self-determination, justice and liberation.

Through Black August we

a. ensure that we never forget the words of Shirley Graham-DuBois who told us, "we must always remember that this land was founded on the genocide of one nation and the enslavement of another;"[24]
b. center the centuries-old question raised by Frederick Douglass, "*What to the Slave Does Your 4th of July Mean*" and the hypocrisy of a nation celebrating its own independence from British colonial subjugation while denying it to millions of enslaved Afrikans and their descendants;
c. challenge the misnomer that ameriikkka is a "safe" harbor for people escaping violence, oppression, and persecution rather than "the greatest purveyor of violence in the world" as Dr. King said;
d. make clear that white on Black violence in all its forms—physically, socially, culturally, economically, spiritually, and mentally—is "as American as cherry pie."[25]

We do this through Black August to position violence in ameriikkka in its proper historical context. Not just in the enslavement of Afrikan people, genocide of Indigenous people, hundreds of broken treaties and policies, the litany of blood-soaked invasions and bombs dropped in Japan, Korea, Grenada, and Panama, but in the present. As in missile and drone strikes in Iraq, Afghanistan, Libya, Syria, the funding of Israel and its killing of Palestinian men, women, and children. The unrestrained and unpunished police terror and murder of unarmed Black/Brown, Asian, and Indigenous men, women, and children, political and mass imprisonment, poverty, homelessness, lack of access to quality education, housing, and healthcare that is imposed on cash-poor and working-class Black/Brown, Asian, Indigenous, and white people.

Black August does heavy lifting when it comes to sharing the history/herstory of Black resistance. It is why in the 1990s, two veterans

[24] Shirley Graham DuBois (November 11, 1896-March 27, 1977), author, playwright, human rights/political activist and wife of W.E.B. DuBois.

[25] Quote from Imam Jamil Al-Amin, formerly known as H. Rap Brown, and Student Non-Violent Coordinating Committee (SNCC) Chair and current Political Prisoner. Quote by Shirley Graham-DuBois, Pan-African scholar, activist, comrade and wife of W.E.B. DuBois.

of the Black Freedom Struggle exiled in Cuba , Assata Shakur,[26] and the late Nehanda Abiodun,[27] encouraged MXGM organizers to create a vehicle that would introduce Black August and Black/New Afrikan PPOWs to an audience of Afrikan-descended people worldwide. Their idea was brought into fruition with MXGM's Black August Hip-Hop Project and organizing of the Black August Annual Hip-Hop Benefit Concerts. These concerts brought activists-artists such as *dead prez, Yasiin Bey (formerly known as Mos Def), Talib Kweli, Erykah Badu, The Roots, Dave Chappelle, Common, David Banner, Fat Joe,* and a host of others together on performance stages in New York City, Oakland, Los Angeles, Philadelphia, Washington DC, Atlanta, Houston, Dallas and Austin, Texas, New Orleans, and internationally in Cuba, Venezuela, Haiti, Tanzania, South Africa and Brazil. Each artist donating their time, activism, talent, and voice to raising funds and awareness of PPOWs and introducing Black August to hip-hop music lovers, new generations of activists-artists and Freedom-loving people world-wide.

When the COVID-19 pandemic was raging across the globe putting much of the world on lockdown, MXGM took these benefit concerts onto the virtual stage. In collaboration with the Movement 4 Black Lives, Black August 2020 was held on the YouTube[28] social media platform with past artists, Yasiin Bey and M1 of dead prez, sharing the virtual stage with a younger group of activists-artists—*Rhapsody, Big Krit, Audio Push, Oswin Benjamin , Sampa The Great, and poet jessica Care moore.*[29] Once again, to introduce and edu-tain concert-goers about Black August and the existence of U.S. held Black/New Afrikan PPOWs.

The Black August Hip-Hop Project is important because it helps to remind and teach the legacy of Black resistance. Black August reminds that before there was a Jonathan Jackson, a George Jackson and the

[26] Assata Shakur is a NY-based Panther who was liberated from a NJ prison on November 2, 1979. In 2002, she was placed on the FBI's Most Wanted List with a $1 million bounty offered for her capture. It has since increased to $2 million with a mislabeling as a "Domestic Terrorist" added. She is the Mother of one adult and has several Grandchildren.

[27] Nehanda Abiodun was a NY-based Panther when she escaped capture in the October 1981 Nyack, NY-Brinks expropriation. She remained in exile until her Transition on January 30, 2019. She leaves behind two children.

[28] Black August Virtual Benefit Concert—https://www.youtube.com/watch?v=eykdlRfvUQc&t=1s.

[29] Jessica Care Moore is a five-time Apollo winner, an internationally renowned poet, playwright, performance artist, producer, author, and publisher. Her latest book of poetry, *We Want Our Bodies Back* is available on her website: https://mooreblackpress.com/.

brothers who form the bedrock of its legacy, there was a Harriet Tubman, Nat Turner, Gabriel Prosser, Denmark Vesey, and a host of Black/New Afrikan heroes/ sheroes—known and unknown—who also refused to acquiesce their Freedom-dreams and instead planned and executed armed rebellions and insurrections.

And while some might question the logic or futility of a lone Jonathan Jackson executing a plan to liberate his brother from the bowels of prison life, it must be remembered that it was a lone Harriet Tubman who also carried out similar actions to liberate hundreds of her brothers and sisters from the bowels of plantation life. Yes, the Marin County Courthouse Rebellion was put down, but the courage, tenacity, and determination demonstrated by this young man reminds us of the potential young Black/New Afrikan folk have to develop radical/revolutionary politics and leadership if and when they are guided more by the principles of self-determination, justice, and liberation versus the perverse nihilistic glorification of capitalism and violence they have been indoctrinated to value. Unfortunately, the latter has become a normalized consequence and legacy of the Cointelpro war on Black Liberation in general and the BPP in particular.

There is no doubt that George L. Jackson was a prophetic man. He spoke of wanting to live in a world free from the "technology of killing" and the "consumption practices" that capitalism and imperialism are imposing on our bodies, health, environment, climate, air, lakes, rivers, and oceans. His 1970s vision resonates with as great an urgency and relevancy as the global demands made in 2021 for environmental justice, end to climate change, global warming, fossil fuel dependence, fracking, perpetual war, occupation, and militarism. George L. Jackson was a visionary way ahead his and our time.

For this writer, the George Jackson and Black August legacy bring to mind the words of Fred Hampton, head of the Chicago chapter of the BPP, who said, you can jail or kill a revolutionary, but you can't jail or kill the revolution. In the fifty-plus years since the assassination of George (and Jonathan), their names stretch far and wide into the hearts, minds, and spirits of Freedom-dreaming, Freedom-Loving Black/New Afrikan people inside and out the prison system. That simply being in the possession of George's name or image anywhere in the California prison system, will send the owner into indefinite placement in the SHU or hole is the proof. George's second book, *Blood in My Eye*, published after his death continues to be widely read and circulated outside the California prison system, among intellectuals, prison rights activists, college students, progressives, and developing radical and revolutionaries.

With that in mind, if we are to make a better world for the next seven generations of children to live, we must heed his call to "*settle your quarrels, come together, understand the reality of our situation, understand that fascism is already here, that people are dying who could be saved, that generations more will live poor butchered half-lives if you fail to act. Do what must be done, discover your humanity and your love in revolution.*"[30]

May the spirit and legacy of Black August continue to carry the Black/New Afrikan nation forward!.

Dare to Struggle! Dare to Win!!!!

[30] George L. Jackson quote.

Ecological Debt, Education, and the Art of Communication

Ecological Debt and the Holistic Value of Nature

Kelly J. Wessell

Environment as Driver of Economy

All life on Earth depends on the natural processes that support and sustain it. Nutrients cycle through biotic and abiotic compartments, enriching soil and providing the basic building blocks for life. Plants use sunlight to excite electrons harvested from water to build sugars out of carbon dioxide, exhaling oxygen in the process. Most organisms can then use this oxygen in a complex suite of reactions to harvest energy and nutrients from their food to live and grow. Over time, ecological communities—through the process of natural selection—have evolved a fine-tuned efficiency with no appreciable waste that builds soil by recycling and transforming nutrients in a balanced and truly sustainable way. The Gaia Hypothesis, proposed by James Lovelock and Lynn Margulis (1974), posits that organisms interact with the physical environment to form a synergistic, self-regulated system that helps to maintain and perpetuate the conditions for life. Although this hypothesis has been widely criticized as being teleological and, therefore, non-Darwinian, the general

K. J. Wessell (✉)
Tompkins Cortland Community College, Dryden, NY, USA
e-mail: WesselK@tompkinscortland.edu

B. C. Wilson, *Care, Climate, and Debt*,
https://doi.org/10.1007/978-3-030-96355-2_4

idea of Earth as a superorganism is hard to completely abandon. A visitor to Leticia, Colombia, is greeted with signs declaring the Amazon region the "Lungs of the Earth." Similarly, rivers deliver nutrients to floodplains and drain waste from their watersheds much like our own circulatory system. Wetlands filter water and sequester toxins just like our kidneys and liver do. Just as each of our individual organs depend on the function of the whole body through a network of feedback loops and synergies, the balance of Earth's biosphere depends on ecological linkages that connect all living things through the cycling of nutrients through food webs and the maintenance of services such as soil regeneration and water filtration.

Ecosystems, then, are natural economies. The words "ecology" and "economy" share the same root, "*oikos*," which is derived from the Greek word for "house." The fields of ecology and economics both are aimed at understanding things like supply of various resources, how that supply impacts demand for those resources, and the processing of wasted production. Similar to how an economist might look at the effect of a new product or process on job growth, the ecologist might strive to make predictions of how an increase in a resource base will impact niche space in an ecological community. Similarly, both ecologists and economists often try to better understand the impacts of resource scarcity in ecosystems and economies, respectively.

The connections between ecosystems and economies go well beyond etymology. Economies are inextricably linked to both local and global ecosystem goods and services. From the first economies, based primarily on agricultural production, to the globalized economy we live in today, humans have always relied on available ecosystem goods such as timber, water, and soil as well as ecosystem services such as air and water filtration, nutrient cycling, and climate moderation. For example, early periods of economic development were facilitated by the discovery or exploitation of natural resources. The Atlantic Cod fishery fueled the industrial revolution in Europe and North America, and the cod fishery itself was made possible by building ships with North American timber.

Despite the obvious importance of natural resources in making both ecosystems and economies resilient, these resources often don't show up in ledgers. For example, even though global pollination services are worth up to US$387 billion annually (Porto et al. 2020), the pollinators themselves are not factored into the true value of the food we eat. More importantly, many of us do not consider how much our food would cost if pollination services were not provided to us for free by bees and other insects. Of course, nature should be valued beyond the tangible and monetary. Those of us lucky enough to live in areas of the world where fresh air, clean water, and natural beauty abound live longer and are generally happier and healthier than those of us who do not (WHO 2006), and this alone makes environmental issues uniquely intersectional with other social justice issues. What follows is a discussion of the different ways we value nature, the ways in which human activities degrade ecosystem services, suggestions for ways we might engage in a more holistic valuation of ecosystems and the services they provide, and the role education can play in facilitating the cultural shift needed to help us learn to live within our ecological means.

How Do We Value Nature?

In order to appreciate the value of ecological goods and services, it is helpful to explore the various ways in which nature has been ascribed value. Like many indigenous groups, the Haudenosaunee of Central New York value nature for the bounty it provides them. They necessarily extract resources for food, shelter, and textiles, but their overarching philosophy is one of sharing space with other organisms, honoring the gifts of nature, and ensuring those gifts are "tended and preserved unto the Seventh Generation" (Oneida Nation, n.d.). They value natural services and practice stewardship of natural resources to sustain these services. This Native American belief system is so deep-rooted that it sometimes shows up in their language. Robin Wall Kimmerer writes in *Braiding Sweetgrass* that, while English is a noun-based language, appropriate to a culture obsessed with things, the Potawatomi language has more verbs than nouns. For example, the verb "*wiikwegamaa*" (to be a bay) "releases the water from bondage and lets it live...and holds the wonder that, for this moment, the living water has decided to shelter itself between these shores...[The water] could do otherwise–become a stream or a waterfall, and there are verbs for that, too" (Kimmerer 2013).

In contrast with traditional indigenous belief systems, early European colonists saw the bounty of the New World in terms of goods. They looked at the forests of North America as commodities: Wood to build with and burn for fuel, pelts to support the burgeoning European felt hat market, and land for the production of commodity crops for export. This focus on short-term, immediate economic development rather than long-term, sustainable support resulted in cleared forests, declining population densities of nearly all non-cultivated native organisms, and local extinctions. In some cases—for example, certain wild fisheries—this unsustainable exploitation of resources in the interest of maximizing short-term profit has resulted in the collapse of entire economies (Grafton et al. 2007).

There are some important exceptions to this simplistic, one-dimensional view of the value of nature in the Western world, and these views have helped develop a more holistic valuation of nature and the goods and services it provides. Alexander von Humboldt (1769–1859), the German explorer and polymath, is widely considered the first real ecologist. While many European colonists sought riches in their exploration of the New World, Humboldt emphasized the connectedness of natural systems (undoubtedly influenced by his native guides) and viewed nature as a complex and interconnected force not for the use of humankind alone (Wulf 2015). Humboldt's ideas helped spark the modern conservation and preservation movements by reframing the value of nature. Furthermore, his friendships and collaborations with poets and artists helped propel his ideas beyond the scientific community and into the imaginations of the wider population.

Although Charles Darwin (1809–1882) is not normally thought of as a conservationist, his work has helped counter the Western oversimplification of how we should value nature. Taken together, descent with modification and natural selection connect all living things on Earth to each other and to the physical world and implies that the balance of natural systems is the result of long-term coevolutionary relationships that have resulted in a sort of dynamic equilibrium of matter cycling and energy flow through interconnected ecosystems. At the end of Chapter 4: Natural Selection from his *Origin of Species*, Darwin writes:

> As buds give rise by growth to fresh buds, and these, if vigorous, branch out and overtop on all sides many a feebler branch, so by generation I believe it has been with the great Tree of Life, which fills with its dead and broken branches the crust of the earth, and covers the surface with its ever branching and beautiful ramifications. (Darwin 1859)

Like Humboldt, Darwin saw beauty in nature and wrote with reverence for natural processes and deep-rooted connections. His work helped us see value in nature for all that it is, not only what it can give us.

In addition, the early conservation movement in the U.S. was, in a sense, a response to the rapid decline of natural resources as a result of western expansion and the laissez-faire private land ethic. Conservationists, led by Gifford Pinchot and others, advocated for a long-term plan to maximize the economic benefits of natural resources. Preservationists like John Muir, founder of the Sierra Club, had a different view. He believed that natural areas should be preserved for their inherent value, and opposed the conservationists' focus on economic uses of natural areas. Muir, who was raised in a Christian home and liked to frame forays into the wilderness as spiritual experiences, described his duty to immerse in "mountain baptism" to everyone he could. He saw nature as a great teacher "revealing the mind of God" (Williams 2002), which stood in stark contrast to the prevailing culture of expansion and extraction of the times. Rachel Carson, helped connect all the different ways we value nature to the ways in which we disrupt natural systems. In her book, *Silent Spring*, Carson described the ways that chemicals like DDT can lead to an almost dystopian chain of events where the very ways we see (and hear!) the world change. By doing this, Carson ignited a movement that pitted nature against industry and helped the public more clearly see the true costs of pollution and all that we have to lose by not considering all the different ways nature contributes to our well-being.

More recently, there have been efforts to quantify the value of ecosystem services. By necessity, global estimates of the value of ecosystem services employ simplistic models and important assumptions. One approach is to use local case studies to estimate the unit value (in US dollars per hectare per year; \$/ha/y) of, for example, a coral reef, and then simply scaling this value based on the total area of global coral reef habitat. Using this approach, Costanza et al. (1997) estimated the total value of global ecosystem services to be \$45.9 trillion per year (2007 values). Since the publication of this important work, methods have been refined, and our understanding of specific ecological services has increased, resulting in a trend of increasing unit value estimates in virtually every terrestrial and marine biome. For example, the value of coral reefs have increased from about 8000 to 352,000 \$/ha/y due to additional studies of storm protection, erosion protection, and recreation (Costanza et al. 2014a). In a review of different valuation methods (Costanza et al. 2014a), the authors compare the results of using a more sophisticated method which takes into account spatial differences in unit values for ecosystem services (instead of simply scaling one value based on the total area of a particular biome) (de Groot et al. 2012) to that initial 1997 study by Costanza and colleagues. They also consider the changes in area of each biome in calculating these new values. For example, based on a clearer understanding of the overall value of tropical forests, the unit value increased from 2769 to 5382 $/ha/y, but the overall land area of tropical forests decreased. Taking these things into consideration for 16 different biomes, they estimate the total value of global ecosystem services to be approximately $124.8 trillion per year (Costanza et al. 2014a). For reference, global GDP is estimated to be approximately $84.7 trillion per year (World Bank 2021).

While estimating the value of ecological services in monetary units is useful to show their importance, it could encourage the oversimplification of their value in schemes like carbon markets. A better way of thinking about these services are as public goods, as much of their value is difficult to quantify. For example, while a functioning wetland can help defray the costs of municipal water treatment or buffer storm surge from hurricanes, they also increase human well-being in less tangible ways (e.g., their esthetic value). Despite the fact that global GDP is estimated to be US$84 trillion per year (World Bank 2020), ecosystem services contribute more than twice as much to human well-being (Costanza et al. 2014a). In other words, the monetary value of these services is only part of their value.

Human Impacts and Ecological Deficits

Although many of us see the holistic value in ecosystems and the services they provide, and there are cultures and communities that strive for sustainable development and use of natural resources, the last several centuries have nonetheless resulted in important ecological deficits. Forests are home to most of the world's terrestrial biodiversity, and they provide important ecological services, support livelihoods, mitigate climate change, and are critical to the production of food. Despite the fact that deforestation has decreased over the last 30 years, it is estimated that 420 million hectares of forest have been lost through conversion to other land uses. As of December 2020, a total of 20,334 tree species (approximately, one-third of all described tree species) are listed as threatened, and more than 1400 tree species are assessed as critically endangered and in urgent need of conservation (FAO 2020). Most often, this conversion of forest land is driven by increasingly intensive agricultural production.

The cattle industry in Brazil, for example, is responsible for about 80% of the deforestation in the Brazilian Amazon, where more than 19% of the total forest area has disappeared (Amigo 2020).

Freshwater ecosystems have been similarly degraded. Damming alone has impacted approximately 60% of the world's large river basins, affecting downstream water availability, thermal regimes, and in some cases, complete desiccation of entire aquatic ecosystems. Overharvesting and invasive species have changed entire ecological communities and affected aquatic ecosystem productivity and other physical and chemical parameters such as light availability and nutrient cycling (Carpenter et al. 2001). Industrial pollutants such as mercury, nonpoint source nutrient run-off from farms, and soil erosion from clearing of riparian zone habitat have disrupted natural nutrient cycling and accelerated the process of eutrophication, leading to periods of hypoxia (low dissolved oxygen) and anoxia (no dissolved oxygen). Taken together, these impacts result in degradation of water quality, and the availability of water for human uses.

Degradation of terrestrial and freshwater resources also impacts marine systems. Nutrient run-off in the Mississippi River Watershed contributes to a hypoxic zone in the Gulf of Mexico averaging over 13,000 km^2 in size over the last five years (EPA 2021a). This results in massive fish die-offs, disruptions to food webs, and depletions in valuable fisheries. In addition to creating dead zones, nutrient pollution along with warming and ocean acidification is causing coral bleaching, already impacting corals around the world. The most recent global coral bleaching event exposed 75% of coral reefs to bleaching-level heat stress, and approximately 30% of reefs experienced mortality-level stress (Eakin et al. 2018). Bleaching is expected to occur on every reef in the world by the year 2050 (Manzello 2015). Since corals provide structure, buffer storm surge, and support coastal fisheries, the decline in coral reef habitat will have widespread economic and social costs. In the U.S. alone, the total annual economic value of coral reef services is estimated at US$3.4 billion. Worldwide, over 500 million people depend on reefs for food, income, and coastal protection (NOAA 2021).

Degradation of forests, freshwater systems, and marine environments both cause and are exacerbated by climate change, and the evidence for the ways in which human activity contributes to global climate change is unequivocal (IPCC 2021). At the same time humans are increasing greenhouse gas (GHG) concentrations in the atmosphere by burning fossil fuels, we are reducing Earth's natural ability to sequester carbon by degrading carbon sinks through activities such as deforestation and other activities which reduce ecosystem productivity. Between 1990 and 2015, global carbon dioxide (CO_2) emissions increased by 51%. The U.S. is the second largest GHG contributor, though national emissions have declined slightly since 2007 (EPA 2021b). The impacts of climate change are numerous and include increasing unpredictability of weather, increasing incidence of extreme weather events (e.g., droughts, floods, etc.), and loss of biodiversity. The monetary costs of climate change are dependent on a host of variables including the timing of action and the actual increase in global temperature. According to one study, its toll on agriculture, disease, and physical infrastructure could cause the global economy to lose $23 trillion—10% of its value—by 2050 (Swiss Re Institute 2021). In 2020, there were 22 separate billion-dollar weather and climate disasters in the U.S., costing the nation $95 billion in damages (NOAA 2021). Since unchecked climate change is predicted to increase the frequency and severity of such disasters, these costs will increase if significant action is not taken to mitigate further change and adapt to the change to which we're already committed. The human costs are nearly impossible to quantify.

Taken together, these impacts are resulting in a decline of natural capital and ecosystem services. Using only the unit values calculated by Costanza et al. (1997), which considers the impact of decreasing habitat area but not the functionality of each biome, the total net decrease in the value of ecosystem services is about $4.3 trillion per year. This is largely driven by the decrease in high value biomes like tropical forests, wetlands, and coral reefs (Costanza et al. 2014a). Using updated unit values (de Groot et al. 2012), the decrease in the value of ecosystem services between 1997 and 2011 has been $20.2 trillion annually (Costanza et al. 2014a). For context, in 2020, the GDP was estimated to be just over $20 trillion for the U.S., $14.7 trillion for China, and $15.2 for the European Union (World Bank 2021). In other words, due to habitat loss and degradation of ecosystem function in critical biomes, humans have contributed to the decline in ecosystem services valued at or above the world's largest economies. The problem with this, of course, is that the world's economy is based on a history of these services being provided by nature free of charge.

Another way of looking at this is to consider our individual and collective ecological footprints, which measure human demand on natural capital. Ecological footprint is calculated by contrasting the resources it takes to support an individual or population with the productive area that can regenerate—the biocapacity—what people demand from nature. If a population exceeds a region's biocapacity, that region runs an ecological deficit. If a region's biocapacity exceeds its ecological footprint, it has an ecological reserve (Global Footprint Network 2021). Footprint calculators are widely available (see https://www.footprintnetwork.org/our-work/ecological-footprint/ for an example) for individual footprint assessment, and footprint data exist for countries, municipalities, and regions. Ecological-footprint quizzes are often used by individuals to assess their personal impacts to the environment: The typical footprint calculator asks users about how much meat they eat, what proportion of their food is grown locally, how far they drive in a typical week, how often they fly, how energy efficient their house is, and how much waste they generate. This gives users an indication of how much land (in global hectares, gha) is required to support their lifestyle and provides a comparison of how much land is available to individual humans, given the total biocapacity of the Earth and the current human population size. Most people reading this will find that the demands of their lifestyles exceed the biocapacity of the Earth, which means their lifestyle is unsustainable. Individual footprint results can be useful to help us evaluate our own lifestyles and target aspects of them for change. They may, for example, help us see that there are some things we could actually do to reduce our footprints such as moving toward a more plant-based diet (for the typical American, diet is the single largest component of their impact) or investing in their home's energy efficiency. Individual results also may help people understand that consumption patterns have an ethical element: What allows some of us to live beyond the Earth's biocapacity is the fact that others live considerably below it.

While it may be useful for an individual to evaluate his or her footprint, it is essential that nations do this in order to evaluate their resource sovereignty and national security. When we look, for example, at the U.S., we see worrying trends. The biocapacity of the U.S. is approximately 3.4 gha per person. This means that if resources were divided equitably among all Americans, we would each be allocated 3.4 gha. One way of looking at this is to consider it our ecological income. However, the amount of land required by the average American—our ecological expenditures—is 8.1 gha (2017 data; Global Footprint Network 2021). This means that we are running an ecological deficit of 4.6 gha and must compensate for this by borrowing biocapacity from other parts of the world through trade and/or the reliance on ecosystem services outside of our borders. Other countries that are currently running ecological deficits include Mexico, China, India, along with the European Union and the entire Middle East.

Mexico provides an example of some important drivers of ecological deficits. Right around 1975, Mexico went from running an ecological surplus to running a deficit. This occurred at a point in time when both per capita biocapacity was falling and ecological footprint was increasing. The reasons for this are not adequately captured in the data, but undoubtedly due at least in part to two factors: Population growth in Mexico meant that available resources needed to be shared with more people, and economic development was causing an increase in the per capita consumption of those limited resources.

Increased consumption is often the result of economic development. In 1970, the population of China was approximately 843 million, and the country was living within its biocapacity with a per capita footprint equal to about 1.0 gha. At this time, the GDP of China was $202. By the year 2017, the population of China was 1.4 billion, the per capita footprint was 3.7 gha, the GDP was $7347, and the ecological deficit was 2.8 gha. During this time, the biocapacity remained relatively stable (Global Footprint Network 2021). What this means is that even though the population of China doubled, the typical Chinese citizen's footprint almost quadrupled due to individual consumption rates increasing as a result of economic development. More people were able to buy more stuff, and this taxed their resource base.

Not all countries run an ecological deficit. For example, Brazil continues to live within its ecological means. As of 2017, the biocapacity per person in Brazil was 8.6 gha whereas the footprint per person was only 2.8 gha. It should be noted, however, that in 1961, the biocapacity of this extremely productive nation was 22.9 gha per person. The reduction in Brazil's overall per capita biocapacity is mostly driven by its increase in population: Between 1961 and 2017, its population size increased by about 2.8 times, whereas its per capita biocapacity decreased by about 2.6 times (Global Footprint Network 2021).

Toward a More Holistic Valuation of Nature

The Earth's life-support system clearly must continue to function if humans hope to prosper—indeed, if they hope to survive. The discussion so far has focused mostly on the monetary value of natural services.

The danger in this, as Costanza et al. (2014a) note, is the potential for commodification and privatization of natural resources. This oversimplification of the true value of functioning ecosystems could result in an area or biome becoming valued for a single good or service. For instance, a singular focus on the carbon sequestration potential of a tropical forest could result in a sort of "green capitalism" (Fairhead et al. 2012) that places the same value on a monocultural stand of oil palms as it would on a diverse tropical forest. In the case of cap and trade schemes, this might allow for a sort of double-dipping where carbon emitters might try to count such extractive activities toward carbon offsets. To avoid this, we need a more holistic way to assign value to natural resources that encompasses their many benefits.

Recreational value of ecosystems may serve as an example. While most estimations of the value of ecosystem goods and services consider recreational value, these values are typically tied to commercial activities like tourism. While these values should certainly be considered, we must acknowledge that many recreational activities have little or no direct monetary value. While a state park may increase economic activity in nearby communities by driving demand for hotels and restaurants, preserved natural spaces provide other values as well, and although these values may be more difficult to quantify, they are equally—if not more—important. In other words, these values accrue directly to humans without passing through the money economy at all (Costanza et al. 1997).

The challenge of assessing non-material benefits of nature stems from its interdisciplinarity. While many of us probably have an intuitive understanding that nature provides rich social and cultural benefits, to systematically examine these benefits requires the collaboration of disparate disciplines like anthropology, sociology, philosophy, art, medicine, and ecology. The structure of universities and discipline-specific literature often makes this sort of endeavor difficult. Truly holistic assessment of cultural values also is constrained by researchers' tendency to limit their exploration of the literature to a specific language. For example, review articles used in this chapter are all published in English, and so have a Western bias. Bearing in mind these challenges and biases, Russell et al. (2013) have used 10 constituents of human well-being to structure their synthesis of the literature on intangible connections between humans and nature: Physical health, mental health, spirituality, security, learning, inspiration/imagination, sense of place, identity/autonomy, connectedness/belonging, and subjective overall well-being. An in-depth discussion of each of these constituents is beyond the scope of this chapter, but some specific examples will help us understand some of the intangible, non-monetary values of nature to humans.

Anyone who has experienced the feel of mist from a waterfall or the majesty of a mountain view knows that nature can have a profound effect on well-being. It is good for the body and mind, and there is a wide body of literature to support this intuition. For example, proximity to green spaces has been shown to increase longevity in the elderly (Takano 2002). Similarly, residents in neighborhoods with significant greenspace have better health outcomes even after controlling for various demographic characteristics like race and poverty (Maas et al. 2006). Conversely, ecological degradation has been correlated with declines in physical health (e.g., mosquito-borne diseases) (Donovan et al. 2013; Jardine 2007) and the increased likelihood of emergent zoonotic diseases (Morand and Lajaunie 2021). Time spent in nature also has a positive effect on our mental health. For example, urban dwellers who spend time in green spaces like parks have been shown to exhibit better concentration, focus, and reduced fatigue (Herzog and Nebel 2003) and quicker recovery from crisis and traumatic loss (Ottosson and Grahn 2008).

While it is challenging to put a monetary value on the sorts of benefits described above, it would be difficult for most of us to discount them. The spiritual value and sense of place that intact natural systems provide us are, indeed, more valuable in the long term than many of the monetary values are. This is why tourists flock to places like the Grand Canyon and Yellowstone National Park on family vacations. This is why many of us would rather spend a Sunday afternoon walking our dogs at a local park than spend it at the mall. This is why some of us find our higher power sitting aside a giant sequoia tree. We need to work to preserve these resources and *all* the value they provide.

One sort of practical way to do this is to encourage a more holistic measure of progress is to move away from GDP as a primary indicator of growth. When GDP was adopted as the primary indicator of a nation's growth and well-being following WWII, it was a relevant indicator of progress. At that time, increased economic activity was credited with providing employment, income, and amenities that reduced social conflict. Today, the emphasis on GDP fuels social and environmental instability and distracts developing countries from the possibilities for truly sustainable development (Costanza et al. 2014b). The simplicity of using GDP as the sole economic indicator also often results in the assessment of the causes and consequences of unsustainable practices as net positive growth. For example, despite the destruction and loss of life caused by the Deepwater Horizon oil spill in 2010 and Hurricane Sandy in 2012, both events boosted U.S. GDP because of the ways in which they stimulated rebuilding. In this way the fossil fuel industry and the havoc our dependence on their products cause are—at least on paper—a net positive for economic growth.

In contrast, the Human Development Index (HDI) focuses more holistically on people and their capabilities, as opposed to economic growth alone. The HDI integrates three dimensions of human development: a long and healthy life, being knowledgeable, and achieving a decent standard of living. The health dimension is assessed by mean life expectancy at birth, the education dimension is measured by mean years of schooling in adults 25 years and older, along with expected years of schooling for children entering school. The standard of living dimension is measured by per capita gross national income (UN 2021a). The HDI has recently been expanded to include aspects of energy systems (e.g., carbon emissions and renewable energy consumption), material cycling (e.g., material consumption, use of N fertilizer, and electronic waste), equity indicators (e.g., gender equality, food insecurity), and stewardship measures (e.g., percent total terrestrial land area protected) (UN 2021a).

The United Nations Sustainable Development Goals (SDGs) set conservation targets directly aimed at protecting and restoring terrestrial and aquatic resources, encouraging responsible consumption, and acting on climate change. Because sustainable development also must address economics and equity, the UN sets targets related to poverty reduction, food security, and reducing inequalities, they also serve as a reminder that people are part of the equation, and that the overall goal of sustainable development is to create a global society that preserves ecosystems and the services they provide while allowing humans to thrive. The SDGs are meant to serve as a roadmap for policy makers, and they require us to consider ourselves as part of nature, rather than apart from it. In most cases, reaching the goals will require systemic change at all levels of society, and for countries like the U.S., this means garnering the political will to institute widespread changes in our policy priorities. This will require a cultural shift and a focus on conservation and preservation of natural resources and the people who depend on them.

Paying Our Ecological Debt and Living Within Our Means

As discussed above, our unsustainable development and oversimplification of the value of nature as a provider of goods have resulted in a sort of ecological debt that must be addressed. Relying on more holistic indicators of growth like the HDI or using the SDGs as a framework for growth and development might help us begin to focus our efforts as a nation and a global community on truly sustainable growth that incorporates growth in human well-being, increasing ecosystem integrity, along with the traditional purely economic indicators. However, if we are to avoid widespread collapse of the ecosystem services that support our economy and our well-being, we must pay our debts. New environmental regulation, enforcement of existing regulations, and carbon taxes, along with tax incentives to private landowners for conservation and/or direct payments for ecosystem services are some of the possibilities for incorporating the true cost of unsustainable practices into the price of products which contribute to degradation of natural ecosystem services. At the same time, we must restore degraded areas, consider more sustainable, non-extractive economic development options that allow us to maintain existing ecosystem services and biodiversity, and, over the long term, change our culture to one of appreciation and conservation of natural resources. The following are some examples of how we might do this.

Ecosystem restoration could begin to ensure natural services are not further degraded and even begin to rebound. The United Nations Decade on Ecosystem Restoration is an international movement to protect and revitalize natural ecosystems and the valuable services they provide (UN 2021b). In general, ecosystem restoration results in a net gain for biodiversity, ecosystem integrity, and human well-being, and it also can promote participatory governance and equity by involving multiple stakeholders including those most severely-impacted by the degradation itself. When done right, ecological restoration strives to incorporate all kinds of knowledge, including indigenous, traditional, local, and scientific ways of knowing. It is also a great investment in the future. Not only can restoration projects help reduce some of the tangible and intangible costs of unsustainable development, but as part of a federal jobs-guarantee program, could serve as a sort of social safety net that can help communities train workers with skills that not only make them more employable, but also add true value to communities through, for example, the creation of parks which would support local tourist economies.

The reforestation of 2000 hectares of surface mined lands in Appalachia serves as an example of how restoration can simultaneously restore important ecosystem services—in this case, carbon sequestration—while creating jobs and uniting communities around the importance of intact natural systems. Started in 2009, the project is aimed at mitigating the destruction caused by coal mining by reforesting portions of the Monongahela National Forest in West Virginia, U.S. The project is overseen by Green Forests Work, a non-profit organization based in Kentucky, U.S., which creates renewable and sustainable multi-use resources by enhancing the natural environment and providing economic opportunities. Coal mining has ravaged much of West Virginia's landscape by polluting air, water, and destroying entire watersheds, but it remains a vital part of the state's economy. However, since 2005 coal production in Appalachia has fallen by 65% due to declining costs of new renewables and natural gas, along with our dire need to reduce carbon emissions to head off the worst impacts of climate change. During the same period, employment fell by 54%, and these job losses were higher in counties with the greatest dependence on the coal industry (Bowen et al. 2021). Reforestation projects like this create jobs for seed collectors, equipment operators, and tree planters while they reestablish habitat for endemic species and involve local communities in establishing a sustainable multi-use resource base for the future. They also benefit local landowners by increasing land values and by establishing new potential sources of income (e.g., selling hunting leases and other entrepreneurial activities).

In addition to restoration, we need to move away from high carbon, extractive economies. The development of ecotourism can support local and national economies while facilitating conservation, restoration, and overall awareness of the many values of biodiversity and ecosystem services. Ecotourism is broadly defined as "environmentally responsible travel and visitation to relatively undisturbed natural areas, in order to enjoy and appreciate nature (and the accompanying cultural features–both past and present) that promotes conservation, has low visitor impact, and provides for beneficially active socio-economic involvement of local populations" (IUCN definition cited by Stem et al. 2005). Criticism of ecotourism as a means of sustainable development includes the ways in which ecotourism (and tourism in general) can negatively affect local land use rights and that it fails to deliver promises of community and conservation benefits. When ecotourism infrastructure is owned by multinational corporations, for example, it can actually result in the expatriation of revenues, exploitation of labor, the loss of traditional cultures and lifestyles, and what Fairhead et al. (2012) term a green grab. At its worst, ecotourism can backfire, resulting in environmental degradation and cultural commodification (Johnson 2000).

However, when conducted responsibly, benefits of ecotourism include building environmental awareness, generating direct financial benefits for conservation projects, local economic development, and increased cultural awareness. In a study of the economic, social, and environmental benefits of ecotourism in Costa Rica, Hunt et al. (2015) found that ecotourism jobs offer local residents higher incomes and ecotourism is viewed as the activity contributing most to residents' quality of life. They also found that it was linked to increased levels of financial and attitudinal support for conservation projects, which highlights ecotourism's potential to change worldviews and policy priorities. The study found that awareness of threats to local diversity was higher in tourism workers than non-tourism workers (Hunt et al. 2015). Not only did survey respondents working in the ecotourism industry in the study report higher monthly incomes than respondents who worked in non-tourism sectors (e.g., agricultural workers and small business owners), tourism workers were far more likely to have been born in the Osa region than non-tourism workers, suggesting that when ecotourism is controlled by local communities, it benefits local economies and results in increased awareness of conservation issues and increased allocation of funds for conservation projects. In this way, ecotourism helps shape the worldviews of both tourists and locals.

The Role of Education in Facilitating Connections

Education has long been recognized as a key contributor to economic growth. Many also view education—both formal and informal—as a way to address the rapid decline of the Earth's biocapacity and concurrent drive to transition to more sustainable forms of development. Education—especially formal education in a classroom full of diverse experiences and worldviews—can help us come together around these issues, bridge political divides, and create a sense of empathy for other people and other species. The following is a discussion of some of the ways in which teachers can help our students understand the value of natural services to our economy and, more broadly, to our continued growth.

There is reason to be optimistic that higher education may be addressing this issue. For example, Tompkins Cortland Community College (TC3) (Dryden, NY USA) faculty recently voted to include the following institutional learning outcome (ILO): Upon graduation, students will be able to "describe the ways in which social, economic, or environmental sustainability depends on their own and the collective contributions of a diversity of ideas and people." More recently, the State University of New York (SUNY) added a "Diversity, Equity, Inclusion, and Social Justice" category to its general education requirements. Both of these examples mean that at the institutional level, these goals will be assessed, which has spurred conversations among faculty and administrators on how to make this happen. At TC3 in particular, this has helped start interdisciplinary conversations about how to infuse concepts of sustainability across the curriculum at the degree program and institutional levels.

At the course level, there are many opportunities to foster a more ecocentric worldview in our students. In my own classes, I have a mix of students from all walks of life. Each student is a product of his or her history and community, and so each student has a slightly different worldview. Many of my urban students, for example, have concerns about municipal water quality, air quality, and green spaces in their neighborhoods. Rural students, on the other hand, are often concerned with energy policy, food security, and overall conservation of natural resources. Both groups rank environmental issues as important, but have very different ideas of the role of government (particularly state and federal government) regulations and other policy measures that could help address challenges like water security and climate change (Bonnie et al. 2020). On the first day of classes, the two groups might see each others' overall environmental interests as being completely different. By giving each group a voice, and by making sure each voice is valued in the class, students start to see common ground. Everyone wants clean air, clean water, and healthy food. Everyone needs ecosystems to continue to function as our life-support system. Discussing pressing issues like climate change and biodiversity loss, along with the economic and moral implications of those problems helps students see that we are in this together, and that we all stand to gain by addressing these problems now rather than later.

I've found that one of the most powerful points of connection is the food system. Everybody cares about food, and both consumers and producers of food rely on the sustainability of the food system. Unsustainable cultivation of food degrades soil, water, and air, and food production often competes with water supplies for urban areas. Climate change and biodiversity loss (e.g., pollinators and other beneficial insects) are causing food prices to rise, disportionately impacting poor and marginalized people. These things, in addition to inefficiencies in food distribution systems all result in food insecurity, which is not felt equally by all Americans. In 2020, approximately 10.5% of U.S. households experienced food insecurity. However, food insecurity was higher in households with children headed by single women (27.7%), single men (16.3%) as well as those with Black (21.7%), and Hispanic (17.2%) reference people (USDA 2021). In this way, the food system is an entry point to talking about sustainable development with and beyond the food system: Food is a race issue, a poverty issue, and a gender issue. It also is a way to get students to consider their own environmental impacts as well as how they depend on functioning ecosystems for their own survival.

Developing a sense of biophilia—or ecophilia—also can encourage a more holistic valuation of nature. Access to natural areas definitely helps facilitate this. As a child, I spent my summers in the woods observing the ebb and flow of seasonal streams, watching Pileated Woodpeckers mine for insects as they built their nest cavities, and marking the seasons with the sounds of Spring Peepers and the cracking of frozen trees as they blow in the winter winds. This led to an undergraduate major in zoology, graduate projects on ecosystem restoration and large river bioassessment, and a career teaching about the reasons we should value nature. A starting point to encouraging similar passion for nature is to incorporate more natural history across the science and non-science curriculum, including the arts, humanities, and the social sciences. Although the focus on inquiry-based labs has been effective in honing students' research skills and their overall understanding of how the scientific method is used to answer questions regarding how the natural world works, it has shifted focus away from pure natural history. While this shift may help build scientific literacy and analytical skills, it leaves little room for unstructured appreciation for how the world works. Science teachers at all educational levels could help address this by planning activities that get students outside to learn their local flora and fauna. Since we're more likely to value the things we can name, starting with a campus bioblitz or a backyard birding assignment can help foster a sense of place and an appreciation for biodiversity. Deep exploration of a particular place can have profound experiences for students, allowing them to appreciate the interconnectedness of organisms and ecosystems. Don Burgess, an ornithologist who facilitates a field experience focused on migratory birds in Maine, leads a field experience in which students are able to freely observe bird social behavior, foraging behavior, and predator–prey interactions. He reports that on one trip, they witnessed a Merlin capture, kill, and then drop a migrant Sanderling. After they examined the dead bird, they prepared it as a museum specimen. During this activity, Burgess taught them about migration, predation, foraging behavior, and a host of other ecological and evolutionary concepts. At the end of the weekend, the students no longer saw the shorebird as an isolated entity but rather as part of a community of interconnected species. By studying one species' migration, they made connections that unify continents (Burgess 2017).

Interdisciplinary experiences are effective at fostering a holistic valuation of nature, and this is particularly meaningful for students of learning communities. The TC3 faculty contract allows for the creation of learning communities, in which two professors work together to link two different classes. Students cannot take one class without taking the other, and the two classes typically meet back-to-back. I have participated in several learning communities linking environmental science and biology with math, sociology, anthropology, and literature. In all cases, the linkage of the two courses resulted in a reinforcement of both classes' material. The biology and anthropology learning community culminates in a trip to Colombia, where students explore the linkages between culture, history, and natural resources. We work with traditional basket weavers from the Central Andes to learn about how cloud forest conservation is necessary for their livelihoods and identities. We travel to the Amazon region to learn about how ecotourism has changed the land use priorities for indigenous groups in the region. Overall, students see for themselves the direct connections between natural resources, local economies, and culture. The interdisciplinary synergism reinforces the value of nature and the connections to our livelihoods and cultural identity.

Conclusion

This chapter went into some detail about the various ways humans are degrading natural capital and the services it provides to human economies and overall well-being. However, simply relying on our own observations and experiences, it makes intuitive sense that development in recent history has not been sustainable, and that we are incurring a sort of ecological debt. This debt must be addressed if we wish to avoid collapse, and this involves addressing the ways in which humans have already degraded natural ecosystem services along with a culture shift toward a more holistic valuation of intact ecosystems. To address historical degradation, we must put in place policies that encourage ecological restoration, conservation, and preservation, and that recognize the real human costs of our extractive past. We also must work to minimize externalization of costs of unsustainable growth with both environmental regulations that punish polluters and with economic incentives that encourage and reward responsible production, consumption, and land use. These types of policies will help address our ecological debt in the short term and ensure that we create a global society that lives within its ecological means over the longer term.

Education can play a role in encouraging a long-term cultural shift whereby people—citizens—see nature not only as a source of goods that flow through economies, but as a life-support system that allows us to prosper. By acknowledging the importance of truly sustainable development in institutional learning outcomes, schools create a culture that encourages real dialogue around these issues in faculty and students that necessarily addresses the intersectionality of issues like climate change, poverty, race, and gender. Such dialogue helps students see other worldviews, and that there are many entry points for action. A revival of natural history across the curriculum and the implementation of interdisciplinary learning communities encourage students to not only understand that we rely on natural services for our survival, but to see the beauty in the interconnectedness of humans, other species, and the ecosystems that connect us.

There is reason to be optimistic that this is already happening. Policy proposals like the Green New Deal are helping citizens see the immediate and long-term benefits of addressing climate change, poverty, and marginalized communities together. Other proposals to tax carbon and to encourage a shift to renewable energy will help us address the climate crisis. The rise of Sunrise Movement, and the importance they played in shaping policy priorities during the 2020 U.S. presidential election, demonstrated that activists are getting organized and politically savvy. Activism also has played a key role in the movement to divest from fossil fuels: Endowments, portfolios, and pension funds worth almost $40 trillion (an amount worth more than the GDP of the U.S. and China combined) have now committed to full or partial divestment from fossil fuel stocks (Global Fossil Fuel Commitments Database. n.d.). The Water Protectors of the Dakota Sioux helped many of us see the important connection between people and place. Modern Monetary Theory is helping us see that we don't have to choose between the cost and the value of action. Taken together, these things and more are important first steps in rethinking what we value and what we're willing to invest in helping our values become reality. We are beginning to pay our ecological debts and to figure out how to live within our ecological means.

References

Amigo, Ignacio. 2020. When will the Amazon hit a tipping point? Retrieved on October 29, 2021 from: https://www.nature.com/articles/d41586-020-00508-4

Bonnie, R., E. Pechar Diamond, E. Rowe. 2020. Understanding Rural Attitudes Toward the Environment and Conservation in America. NI R 20–03. Durham, NC: Duke University.

Bowen, Eric, Christiadi, Deskins, John, and Lego, Brian. 2021. "An Overview of Coal and the Economy in Appalachia: Fourth Quarter 2020 Update." Bureau of Business & Economic Research. 329. https://researchrepository.wvu.edu/bureau_be/329

Burgess, D. 2017. "Nurturing biophilia: Merlin and Sanderling." *Journal of Natural History Education and Experience* 11: 1–4.

Carpenter, S.R., E.H. Stanley, and M.J. Vander Zanden. 2001. "State of the World's Freshwater Ecosystems: Physical, Chemical, and Biological Changes." *Annual Review of Environment and Resources* 36: 75–99.

Carter A. Hunt, William H. Durham, Laura Driscoll & Martha Honey. 2015. Can Ecotourism Deliver Real Economic, Social, and Environmental Benefits? A Study of the Osa Peninsula, Costa Rica. *Journal of Sustainable Tourism*, 23:3, 339–357 https://doi.org/10.1080/09669582.2014.965176

Costanza, R., dArge, R., de Groot, R., Farber, S., Grasso, M., Hannon, B., Limburg, K., Naeem, S., Oneill, R.V., Paruelo, J., Raskin, R.G., Sutton, P., van den Belt, M., 1997. The value of the world's ecosystem services and natural capital. *Nature* 387: 253–260.

Costanza, R., R. de Groot, P. Sutton, S. van der Ploeg, S. Anderson, I. Kubiszewski, S. Farber, adn R. K. Turner. 2014a. "Changes in the Global Value of Ecosystem Services." *Global Environmental Change* 26: 152–158.

Costanza, R., Kubiszewski, I., Giovannini, E., Lovins, H., McGlade, J., Pickett, K.E., Ragnarsdottir, K.V., Roberts, D., De Vogli, R., Wilkinson, R., 2014b. "Time to Leave GDP Behind." *Nature* 505: 283–285.

Darwin, Charles. 1859. On the Origin of Species by Means of Natural Selection, or Preservation of Favoured Races in the Struggle for Life. London :John Murray.

de Groot, R., Brander, L., van der Ploeg, S., Costanza, R., Bernard, F., Braat, L., Christie, M., Crossman, N., Ghermandi, A., Hein, L., Hussain, S., Kumar, P., McVittie, A., Portela, R., Rodriguez, L.C., ten Brink, P., van Beukering, P. 2012. Global Estimates of the Value of Ecosystems and Their Services in Monetary Units. *Ecosystem Services* 1: 50–61.

Donovan, G.H., Butry, D.T., Michael, Y.L., Prestemon, J.P., Liebhold, A.M., et al. 2013. "The Relationship Between Trees and Human Health: Evidence from the Spread of the Emerald Ash Borer." *American Journal of Preventive Medicine* 44: 139–145.

Eakin, C.M., Liu, G., Gomez, A.M., De La Cour, J.L., Heron, S.F., Skirving, W.J., Geiger, E.F., Marsh, B.L., Tirak, K.V., Strong, A.E. 2018. "Unprecedented Three Years of global coral bleaching 2014-17 in 'State of the Climate in 2017'." *Bulletin of the American Meteorological Society* 99: S74–S75.

Environmental Protection Agency (EPA). 2021a. Retrieved October 31, 2021, from https://www.epa.gov/ms-htf/northern-gulf-mexico-hypoxic-zone.

EPA. 2021b. Inventory of U.S. Greenhouse Gas Emissions and Sinks. https://www.epa.gov/sites/default/files/2021-04/documents/us-ghg-inventory-2021-main-text.pdf?VersionId=wEy8wQuGrWS8Ef_hSLXHy1kYwKs4.ZaU

FAO and UNEP. 2020. The State of the World's Forests 2020. Forests, Biodiversity and People. Rome. https://doi.org/10.4060/ca8642en

Fairhead, James, Melissa Leach & Ian Scoones. 2012. "Green Grabbing: A New Appropriation of Nature?" *Journal of Peasant Studies* 39 (2): 237–261. https://doi.org/10.1080/03066150.2012.671770

Global Footprint Network. 2021. "Ecological Footprint: Overview." footprintnetwork.org. Retrieved 16 July 2021.

Global Fossil Fuel Commitments Database. (n.d.). Database of Fossil Fuel Divestment Commitments Made by Institutions Worldwide. Retrieved October 30, 2021, from https://divestmentdatabase.org/.

Grafton, R.Q., Kompas, T., Hilborn, R.W. 2007. "Economics of Overexploitation Revisited." Science (New York, N.Y.) 318 (5856): 1601. doi:https://doi.org/10.1126/science.1146017.

Herzog, T.R., Colleen, P.M., Nebel, M.B. 2003. "Assessing the Restorative Components of Environments." *Journal of Environmental Psychology* 23: 159–170.

Hunt, Carter A., W.H. Durham, L. Driscoll, M. Honey. 2015. "Can Ecotourism Deliver Real Economic, Social, and Environmental Benefits? A Study of the Osa Peninsul, Costa Rica." *Journal of Sustainable Tourism* 23 (3): 339–357.

IPCC, 2021. Climate Change 2021: The Physical Science Basis. Contribution of Working Group I to the Sixth Assessment Report of the Intergovernmental Panel on Climate Change [Masson-Delmotte, V., P. Zhai, A. Pirani, S. L. Connors, C. Péan, S. Berger, N. Caud, Y. Chen, L. Goldfarb, M. I. Gomis, M. Huang, K. Leitzell, E. Lonnoy, J. B. R. Matthews, T. K. Maycock, T. Waterfield, O. Yelekçi, R. Yu and B. Zhou (eds.)]. Cambridge University Press. In Press.

Jardine A, Speldewinde P, Carver S, Weinstein P. 2007. "Dryland Salinity and Ecosystem Distress Syndrome: Human Health Implications. EcoHealth 4:10–17.

Johnson, Alison. 2000. "Indigenous Peoples and Ecotourism: Bringing Indigenous Knowledge and Rights into the Sustainability Equation." Tourism Recreation Research 25(2): 89–96.

Kimmerer, R. W. (2015). Braiding Sweetgrass. Milkweed Editions.

Lovelock, J.E., and Margulis, L. 1974. "Atmospheric Homeostasis by and for the Biosphere: The Gaia Hypothesis. *Tellus*. Series A. Stockholm: International Meteorological Institute 26 (1–2): 2–10.

Manzello, D. 2015. "Rapid Recent Warming of Coral Reefs in the Florida Keys." Scientific Reports, 5(16762).

Maas, J., Verheij, R.A., Groenewegen, P.P., de Vries, S., Spreeuwenberg, P. 2006. "Green Space, Urbanity, and Health: How Strong Is the Relation?" *Journal of Epidemiology and Community Health* 60: 587–592.

Morand S and Lajaunie C. 2021. "Outbreaks of Vector-Borne and Zoonotic Diseases Are Associated With Changes in Forest Cover and Oil Palm Expansion at Global Scale." Frontiers in Veterinary Science 8: 661063. https://doi.org/10.3389/fvets.2021.661063

NOAA. 2021. 2020 U.S. Billion-Dollar Weather and Climate Disasters in Historical Context | NOAA Climate.gov. Retrieved October 30, 2021, from https://www.climate.gov/news-features/blogs/beyond-data/2020-us-billion-dollar-weather-and-climate-disasters-historical.

Oneida Indian Nation. nd. Retrieved from (https://www.oneidaindiannation.com/conservation-a-haudenosaunee-view/) on September 7, 2021.

Ottosson, J., and Grahn, P. 2008. "The Role of Natural Settings in Crisis Rehabilitation: How Does the Level of Crisis Influence the Response to Experiences of Nature with Regard to Measures of Rehabilitation? Landscape Res 33: 51–70

Porto, R.G., de Almeida, R.F., Cruz-Neto, O. et al. 2020. "Pollination Ecosystem Services: A Comprehensive Review of Economic Values, Research Funding and Policy Actions." Food Security 12, 1425–1442. https://doi.org/10.1007/s12571-020-01043-w; https://livingplanetindex.org/home/index

Russell, Roly, Guerry, Anne D., Balvanera, Patricia, Gould, Rachelle, K., Basurto, Xavier, Chan, Kai M.A., Klain, Sarah, Levine, Jordan, and Tam, Jordan. 2013. "Humans and Nature: How Knowing and Experiencing Nature Affect Well-Being." *Annual Review of Environment and Resources* 38 (1):473–502

Swiss Re Institute. 2021. The Economics of Climate Change. Swiss Re. Retrieved October 30, 2021, from https://www.swissre.com/institute/research/topics-and-risk-dialogues/climate-and-natural-catastrophe-risk/expertise-publication-economics-of-climate-change.html.

Takano, T., Nakamura, K., Watanabe, M. 2002. "Urban Residential Environments and Senior Citizens' longevity in Megacity Areas: The Importance of Walkable Green Spaces." *Journal of Epidemiology and Community Health* 56: 913–918

United Nations (UN). 2021a. Human Development Reports. Interactive Dashboard: Human Development and the Anthropocene | Human Development Reports. (n.d.). Retrieved October 28, 2021a, from http://hdr.undp.org/en/dashboard-human-development-anthropocene.

United Nations (UN). 2021b. Un Decade on Restoration. Retrieved October 16, 2021b, from https://www.decadeonrestoration.org/

USDA ERS—Key Statistics & Graphics. 2021. Retrieved October 26, 2021, from https://www.ers.usda.gov/topics/food-nutrition-assistance/food-security-in-the-us/key-statistics-graphics.aspx#householdtype.

WHO. 2006. Preventing Disease through Healthy Environments. Prüss-Üstün, A.; Corvalán, C. (Eds.). WHO, Geneva.

Williams, Denis C. 2002. God's Wilds: John Muir's Vision of Nature. College Station: Texas A&M Univ. Press. ISBN 978-1585441433.

World Bank. 2020. GDP (current U.S.). https://data.worldbank.org/indicator/NY.GDP.MKTP.CD. Accessed June 2, 2022.

World Bank. 2021. https://data.worldbank.org/indicator/NY.GDP.MKTP.CD

Wulf, A. 2015. The Invention of Nature: Alexander von Humboldt's New World.

Our Carbon Debt: A Curriculum for Interdisciplinary Education on Climate Change

Christopher A. Badurek and Jeremy Jimenez

Introduction

Despite the impacts of the pandemic, climate change remains as one of the most pressing issues to college students. Students from an array of disciplinary perspectives are increasingly interested in course work and educational experiences that address the climate crisis. Although academic departments often prepare students through education on the scientific foundations of climate change from the perspectives of such fields as conservation biology, environmental geoscience, or environmental geology, our college aims to provide a broader perspective on the climate change issue. Student enrollment at SUNY Cortland has a high percentage of education majors, our teaching experiences indicate

C. A. Badurek (✉)
Department of Geography, State University of New York College at Cortland, Cortland, NY, USA
e-mail: christopher.badurek@cortland.edu

J. Jimenez
Foundations and Social Advocacy Department, School of Education, State University of New York College at Cortland, Cortland, NY, USA

B. C. Wilson, *Care, Climate, and Debt*,
https://doi.org/10.1007/978-3-030-96355-2_5

a need for an interdisciplinary perspective that includes science, social science, humanities, and applied course work that appeals to future educators. To do so, we engage students in a more targeted manner, based on their disciplinary and program focus. For some students, this involves application of geotechnology and modeling applications so they are more informed on the technology necessary for monitoring greenhouse gases and their related impacts. For others, we focus more on promoting dialogue on the educational and societal implications of climate change by integrating perspectives from environmental economics, entrepreneurship, art, and social foundations of education through active learning activities. In this chapter, we present an interdisciplinary perspective on sustainability rooted in the concept of climate debt.

Interdisciplinary Perspectives

The authors, Badurek and Jimenez, first collaborated on organizing a well-attended panel in the Fall of 2020 that was open to the public though primarily attended by students. This panel was targeted to the theme of debt, with a panel entitled "Our Climate Debt: Examining Environmental Legacies and Burdens for Future Generations (a Climate Keywords Panel Discussion)." Here a panel of SUNY Cortland faculty members shared their perspectives on the issue of climate change, including its impacts on the human and natural world, ranging from measuring carbon sources, impacts of increased carbon in the ocean and atmosphere, and ecosystem changes to plant life locally and abroad. In addition to Badurek and Jimenez, ecologist Andrea Davalos (Assistant Professor of Biology), and geoscientist Li Jin (Professor of Geology) joined the panel presentation.[1]

In part, Jimenez's motivation to organize the panel was to bridge the gap between the "hard" and social sciences, given his increasingly shared viewpoint that scholars can no longer afford to address the multi-faceted problem of our climate crisis by examining it from higher education's proclivity to study issues in limited, disciplinary lenses. Increasingly, many scientists working in the fields of climate change mitigation and/or

[1] Cornell University Associate Professor of Earth and Atmospheric Sciences Toby Ault had intended on participating but was unable to make it; however, he virtually responded to some questions contributions about global dimming and other carbon lagging indicators.

adaptation are discussing the importance of finding ways to work collaboratively with social scientists. For example, in his discussion about working with nature based approaches to flood management, Dr. Todd Bridges (2021), U.S. Army Corps of Engineers Senior Research Scientist for Environmental Science, said on the podcast "America Adapts":

> "there's a social science component to this that's every bit as significant as the natural or physical science component ... in my experience, the social science component of these problems has received less attention than the physical science, and for us to be able to make more progress and to implement better solutions for the future, we're going to have to find a way to address the social science considerations more effectively." [2]

Atmospheric scientist and former NASA engineer Dr. Kalmus is even more blunt about the need for social scientists to step up to the plate to deal with our climate crisis, stating in the New York Times, "I feel like the climate scientists have kind of done our job…We've laid it out pretty clearly, but nobody's doing anything. So now it's kind of up to the social scientists" (Branch and Plumer 2020). In this spirit, Jimenez has also organized and moderated an earlier climate change panel featuring professors of economics, education and history in March 2019 entitled "***Is it too late to avert apocalyptic climate change?,***" where SUNY Cortland faculty members shared their perspectives regarding our likelihood of preventing and/or delaying the many catastrophic climate change impacts looming on our horizon. During these conversations, the need to better understand carbon accounting (e.g., quantifying our carbon debt) by both students and other members of the academic community became apparent. Badurek has suggested SUNY Cortland students would benefit from increased understanding of methods for carbon quantification by country and sectors of human activity.

Interdisciplinary Geotechnology and Sustainability

How is each country's carbon debt counted and verified? Sources of greenhouse data are often quantified using spatial data and verified using

[2] https://www.americaadapts.org/episodes/2019/1/13/flood-management-nature-based-approaches-andinternational-collaborations.

remotely sensed imagery. Yet, most citizens and students are unaware of these carbon accounting measures despite their interest in the climate change crisis. The discipline of geography and geographic information technology tools can be effectively harnessed to inform students on the challenges in acquiring US and international greenhouse gas GIS and remotely sensed data. Access to these data are helpful for better understanding the root causes of the increasing carbon debt held by most developed nations. Students can examine carbon dioxide emissions and aggregation approaches through "hands-on" mapping exercises using these data sources with geographic information technology such as geographic information systems (GIS) and satellite image processing.

Anthropogenic contributions to carbon dioxide emissions are the single largest driver of climate change. The main sources of anthropogenic carbon dioxide emissions are cement manufacture, human respiration, domesticate-animal respiration, and the consumption of coal, petroleum, natural gas, and biofuel. Since 1750, it is estimated that two thirds of atmospheric carbon dioxide come from fossil fuel burning, and 80% of the increase in atmospheric carbon dioxide since the pre-industrial era is as a result of fossil fuel combustion (IPCC 2007). It is therefore necessary to monitor anthropogenic contributions to carbon dioxide for a variety of uses ranging from models of the global carbon budget to identifying the regional distribution of carbon dioxide sources (Gurney et al. 2009, 2012). The spatial distribution of fossil fuel carbon dioxide is most commonly estimated at coarse resolutions of national and annual scales from fossil fuel consumption statistics.

International agreements to limit or trade carbon dioxide emissions also make it necessary to monitor and confirm carbon dioxide emissions at finer scales (Andres et al. 2011). By improving the spatial and temporal resolution of bottom-up emissions inventories, it may be possible to corroborate atmospheric composition with remotely sensed data, making confirmation of international emissions possible. The primary approach to improve these resolutions is through GIS methods.

Methods used to create fine resolution emissions inventories include both top-down and bottom-up approaches. Top down approaches disaggregate data from coarse resolutions at the regional or country level and annual time scale through the use of population or nightlights data sources. Bottom-up approaches compile data at fine scales at the road and building level using point data and then aggregate these measures to a sum of total carbon dioxide emissions. Point sources are stationary, large, identifiable discrete points of pollution emissions that release carbon dioxide into the atmosphere. Point sources include power plants, cement manufacturing facilities and other industrial facilities (US EPA, 2001). Top down approaches generally rely on data from non-point source emissions inventories and rarely use point data when disaggregating fossil fuel carbon dioxide emissions.

The primary data used in the development of fossil fuel carbon dioxide emission inventories are fossil fuel consumption statistics at annual and national scales. All of these emissions inventories are global or national in spatial scale, and annual in temporal scale. However, the time periods over which each emissions inventory spans varies from source to source and datasets at national and annual scales often contain inconsistencies between state- and national-level totals. These inconsistencies in data sources lead to inevitable amount of uncertainty in resulting CO_2 estimates (Andres et al. 2011; Gregg and Andres, 2008).

Bottom-up approaches, in which fossil fuel carbon dioxide emissions for individual sources are summed up to estimate emissions at the county, state, or national levels, generally involve data collection on fuel consumption or CO_2 emissions at the building scale (US EPA 2001). Two point source emissions inventories currently exist, the Emissions and Generation Resource Integrated Database (eGRID 2021), produced by the US EPA and available for the United States only, and Carbon Monitoring for Action (CarMA 2012), available globally from the Center for Global Development up until 2012. Students in GIS courses are able to map these carbon dioxide sources as part of laboratory exercises in 300-level courses such as *Geographic Information Systems* and *Environmental Remote Sensing*.

A second topic used to inform students on climate debt is direct examination of greenhouse gas data using remotely sensed imagery. Acquisition and use of NASA data sources for mapping atmospheric concentrations of greenhouse gases and the extent of their data curation and discovery systems can be taught in geographic information technology courses. The parameters of scale, resolution, atmospheric column type, lack of cartographic knowledge, and selection of covarying atmospheric variables are found to be areas for potential bottlenecks for novice and moderately experienced GIS users. These issues represent a significant challenge in guiding student projects using greenhouse gas data sets in a variety of courses ranging from introductory to advanced remote sensing course work. However, these can be mitigated by effective data information literacy trainings and support materials that complement climate change education.

The COVID-19 pandemic has provided an opportunity to explore changes to greenhouse gas emissions due to it being an example of a "natural experiment" or the experimentation on a population due to conditions created by nature. They usually arise from tragedy but provide a rare opportunity to understand trends in a large scale settings. In particular, the pandemic has allowed for the analysis of the relationship between anthropogenic activities and emissions from fossil fuels.

Preliminary studies from NASA satellite monitoring show a decline in commuting for work and reduced electrical consumption are related to a decline in air pollution as evidenced by atmospheric measures of sulfur dioxide (SO_2) and nitrogen dioxide (NO_2). In April 2020, NASA released reports displaying the effect of the decrease in transportation on pollution levels. Within about a month there was a thirty percent drop in air pollution, including the pollutant NO_2, in the northeast United States (NASA 2021). This relationship can be explored by comparing rates of SO_2 and NO_2 using data from NASA's Ozone Monitoring Instrument (OMI) and second Modern-Era Retrospective Analysis for Research and Applications (MERRA-2) Model, gathered from NASA's GIOVANNI web GIS application.

NASA's web geographic information system (or GIS) application GIOVANNI, or the Goddard Earth Sciences Data and Information Services Center (or GES DISC) Interactive Online Visualization and Analysis Infrastructure (Acker and Leptoukh 2007) can be used to access data to explore these relationships. Web GIS tools enable direct mapping using an online interface and are often easier for students and the general public to use than desktop GIS software. GIOVANNI enables users to visualize NASA's satellite data directly, without conducting traditional analysis beforehand (NASA 2008). It is also efficient for data processing of an array of large data sets as it stores and processes hundreds of rows of data over the cloud and sends the resulting map back a user's web browser.

When providing instruction on use of the GIOVANNI web GIS tool, the following attributes should be defined and their relevance explained to students: date ranges, kinds of data set selected, and the pixel resolution of each image. For example, in exploring the relationship of the pandemic to greenhouse gas emissions, the data sets "SO_2 Column Mass Density (ENSEMBLE), time average (M2TMNXAER v5.12.4)" and "NO_2 Total

Column (30% Cloud Screened) (OMNO2d v003)" can be used. An important point for students and the general public to consider is how atmospheric concentration of greenhouse gas emissions are measured by sensors aboard each satellite. For example, the total column data of each gas preferred as an average of the reflectance of pollutant levels from the top of the atmosphere down to the Earth's surface, which better suits studies related to anthropogenic activity.

In addition, satellite data of greenhouse gas emissions can also vary in scale, temporal, and spatial resolution. For example, the MERRA-2 Model collects SO_2 data in units of kilograms per meter squared, at the large spatial resolution (e.g., pixel cell size) of 0.5 by 0.625 degrees, and at an hourly temporal resolution. OMI collects NO_2 measures in units of one per centimeter squared, at a spatial resolution of 0.25 by 0.25 degrees, and at a daily temporal resolution. After selecting the relevant search facets, these greenhouse gas data sets can be viewed directly in the GIOVANNI data visualization interface or downloaded as geostationary earth orbit tagged image files, or GeoTIFF files, and mapped with desktop GIS tools such as ESRI's ArcMap. These differences in spatial and temporal resolution are relevant in not only explaining differences in how the maps appear, but also in the interpretation of the data. For example, students and the general public should be careful to interpret direct relationships between ground based features such as interstate highways with concentrations of greenhouse gases co-located inside each pixel cell. Again, a certain degree of uncertainty needs to be explained in the interpretation of the maps and their potential relationships.

Using geographic information technology to educate students about our carbon debt has several benefits. Firstly, this approach is interdisciplinary in the sense that it integrates geography, geographic information technology, environmental science, and atmospheric sciences. Secondly, these data are also approachable as they are readily available through federal or non-profit based websites and are curated for data quality. The GIOVANNI website could be used effectively in an array of courses as it is a web GIS technology specifically developed by NASA to enable public use. The process of selecting the relevant search parameters in instructive in itself, particularly for explaining the relevance of spatial and temporal resolution of satellite imagery and in understanding of measuring greenhouse gas emissions in the atmosphere. Thirdly, the process of understanding fossil fuel emissions data and measures in the atmosphere would ideally lead to discussion of what global policy and individual actions that could be taken to reduce our overall carbon debt. Course work that explores environmental awareness and sustainability at the more local level would be an ideal follow-up to the exploration of how carbon dioxide emissions are measured.

Interdisciplinary Environmental Advocacy

Further to this spirit of interdisciplinary ways of engaging students with sustainability issues, Jimenez sought to collaborate with Graphic Design Professor Szilvia Kadas to develop a joint student project focused on the theme of environmental advocacy and regeneration. They applied for a Cortland Applied Learning Practitioner (CALP) Grant from the SUNY Cortland Institute for Civic Engagement in Spring 2020 with the aim to help raise "environmental awareness" through a collaboratively created children's literature book. CALP grants are internal funding to support collaboration between faculty members and community partners to engage students in course work that embraces civic engagement and applied learning.

After some discussion, Jimenez and Kadas decided on a multidisciplinary themed book about composting. Upon being awarded the CALP grant, they then reached out to a community partner Adam Michaelides to provide the expertise and guidance on composting. Thus, they aimed to develop a children's composting book that relies on the expertise of three distinct fields. Jimenez and the teacher candidates in his Foundations of Education course would construct the narrative, dialogue, and outline of images that would prioritize his programs' mission of being inclusive of a wide variety of students of different racial, gender, and ability backgrounds and that was appropriate for young primary school students. Kadas and her students would focus on creating the images, adding their expertise on engaging visuals in line with the principles of graphic design. Lastly, the community partner would ensure that the information and visuals about composting was accurate, by participating in multiple feedback sessions commenting on draft versions of the book that our students put together.

Of course, to some extent the COVID-19 disruption impacted our ability to carry out the project as originally attended. What was particularly problematic was that the Education students were attending an in-person class whereas the Graphic Design students were in an online course, which required considerable schedule adjustments because social distancing protocols limited seating capacity, meaning the class could only meet half as often. What was initially planned as in-person discussions and collaboration instead had to take place over Microsoft Teams meetings, which enabled the collaboration to take place but sometimes created frustrating internet connectivity issues for some students. COVID restrictions meant none of our students were able to visit the Cornell composting site to get a live demonstration on composting, given how research has often found such direct interactions with local, natural settings are pivotal to engendering pro-environmental attitudes and motivation (Jimenez and Moorhead 2021). Despite these obstacles, the project was completed on time, and post-surveys indicated that a significant majority of the students enjoyed the collaboration and found it meaningful.

Layers of a Stackable Worm Bin
Add your food scraps to the top layer. Cover your food scraps with shredded, moist newspaper to keep away fruit flies.
The middle layer used to be the top layer. This is where food scraps and newspaper are actively eaten by the worms. After they are done, you have vermicompost, which you can give to your plants!
The liquid from food scraps eventually drips through the layers into the bottom. Collect this "worm tea" because it is packed with nutrients which makes the plants happy and healthy!

Learn with Squirm
Composting
for
Beginners

Interestingly, Jimenez taught the same Education course that semester to students not participating in the composting collaborative project, which inadvertently served as a control group for the project intervention; students did not sign up for either section with any awareness that one section would entail this collaborative project. There were some modest indicators that the students in the collaborative group had a stronger connection to environmental issues. First of all, whereas only two students in both classes combined chose to write a final course paper with an environmental education theme, both of those students were in the collaborative section despite the fact that the control group was assigned their choice of an alternative activity to learn about composting and regenerative agriculture (i.e., a writing reflection to some related reading, lecture, or documentary).

There was also additional evidence, admittedly anecdotal, that the CALP classmates were more invested in the class overall and more bonded with each other than the non-CALP section. First of all, more students in the CALP section opted to partake in extra credit assignments related to the topic. Secondly, when class was occasionally conducted via

Webex or GroupMe chats, the overall student participation rates after the project was higher in the CALP section. Lastly, at semester's end when Jimenez invited both classes to his backyard to demonstrate four types of composting[3] (along with a primer on edible weeds and the advantages of planting perennials), only half the students in the non-CALP section accepted the offer to visit, whereas all but one (e.g., 27 out of 28) students in the CALP section came to observe Dr. Jimenez's ecological garden. Of course, class dynamics can vary considerably even without any experimental interventions, due to any combination of the personality mix, course day or time, room conditions, etc.; nonetheless, it was noteworthy that the CALP students tended to demonstrate in these informal ways greater empowerment in environmental advocacy, investment in learning, and a sense of commitment to their community.

Lessons Learned

What lessons learned have been learned by taking a perspective of teaching about our climate and carbon debt? Clearly, the need for interdisciplinary perspectives is needed as we move toward climate solutions. At the time of this writing, participants in COP26 are advocating for reducing carbon emissions by half before 2030 (McGrath 2021). This is only possible by significant changes to economic and government policies. Therefore, providing college graduates an interdisciplinary education on climate change will help to increase support for the rapid and significant reorientation of social-economic systems required to meet these carbon emission targets. Students can greatly benefit from learning about how carbon emissions are measured, monitored, and ultimately used in climate policy negotiation. Understanding how carbon debt is accruing is also not just for students in STEM disciplines, "hands-on" exploration of carbon emissions data can benefit students from all disciplines by increasing foundational knowledge through primary data sources.

At the conclusion of the "Our Climate Debt" Panel, the faculty participants engaged in dialogue on what next steps to take to expand this interdisciplinary collaboration on climate education. As a direct result of the panel, Badurek has initiated a new one credit course, *Climate Change and Urban Sustainability,* for students from any major. The

[3] Bird's nest compost bin, tumbler bin, bokashi buckets, and a tiered vermicomposting system.

course focuses on the science of climate change and also how carbon emissions are calculated and compared with content from academic, government, and media sources. Students without geographic technology experience are engaged by multimedia visualization of carbon monitoring with satellites and the promise it holds for improving climate negotiations as evidenced by recent media coverage related to COP26 (Fountain 2021). The class has been overenrolled each year and its popularity speaks to the high interest among students across campus. In addition, Badurek has begun a collaborative project with undergraduate research assistants to calculate carbon storage from vegetation on SUNY Cortland properties with GIS tools to aid the Campus Energy Manager in reporting net carbon emissions more accurately. Jimenez has constituted a Sustainability Curriculum Committee (of which he serves as Chair) and he has also begun adding more content on the relationships between race, social justice, and agricultural practices to his education courses.

An ideal learning outcome for students learning about our carbon debt at SUNY Cortland would be better preparation as consumers of climate change information as it enters the government and media ecosystem. As noted by Lejano and Nero (2020), climate inaction can be traced back to artificial debates on climate science in the mainstream media or to disinformation spread via social media channels. Clearly, there is a need for citizens with more advanced information literacy when consuming media content on climate science and policy. In addition, graduates with direct experience of exploring carbon data, collaborating with others on a sustainability project, or visiting demonstration compositing can also provide more content knowledge to be more informed on what actions are possible for addressing the climate crisis.

References

Acker, J.G., and Leptoukh, G. 2007. Online Analysis Enhances Use of NASA Earth Science Data. Eos, Trans. *AGU*, 88 (2): 14–17.

Andres, R.J, Gregg, J.S., Losey, L., Marland, G., and Boden, T.A.. 2011. Monthly, Global Emissions of Carbon Dioxide from Fossil Fuel Consumption. *Tellus*: 309–327.

Branch, J., and Plumer, B. 2020. Climate Change is Now Locked In. The Next Moves Will Be Crucial. *New York Times*, September 22, 2020.

Bridges, T. 2021. Engineering with Nature. US Army Corps of Engineers. https://ewn.erdc.dren.mil/. Last accessed 11 July 2021.

Carbon Monitoring for Action (CARMA). 2012. Carbon Monitoring for Action (CARMA). https://www.cgdev.org/topics/carbon-monitoring-action. Last accessed 11 July 2021.
Emissions & Generation Resource Integrated Database (eGRID). 2021. http://www.epa.gov/egrid. Last accessed 11 July 7 2021.
Fountain, H. 2021. Satellites Could Help Track if Nations Keep Their Carbon Pledges. *New York Times*, November 3, 2021.
Gregg, J.S., and R.J. Andres. 2008. A Method for Estimating the Temporal and Spatial Patterns of Carbon Dioxide Emissions from National Fossil-Fuel Consumption. *Tellus*: 60B, 1–10.
Gurney, K.F., I. Razlivanov, Y. Song, Y. Zhou, B. Benes, and M. Abdul-Massih. 2012. Quantification of fossil fuel CO_2 emissions on the building/street scale for a large U.S. city. *Environmental Science and Technology* 46: 12194–12202.
Gurney, K.R., D.L. Zhour, Y. Mendoza, C. Miller, S. Geethakumar, and S. de La Rue du can. 2009. High resolution fossil fuel combustion CO_2 emission fluxes for the United States. *Environmental Science and Technology* 43: 5535–5541.
IPCC. 2007. Contribution of Working Group I to the Fourth Assessment Report of the Intergovernmental Panel on Climate Change. Cambridge: Cambridge University Press.
Jeremy, Jimenez Laura, Moorhead. 2021. Don't Say It's Going to Be Okay: How International Educators Embrace Transformative Education to Support Their Students Navigating Our Global Climate Emergency. *Education Sciences* 11 (10): 593. https://doi.org/10.3390/educsci11100593.
Lejano, R.P. and Nero, S.J. 2020. The Power of Narrative: Climate Skepticism and the Deconstruction of Science. New York, NY: Oxford University Press.
Liu, Z., et al. 2020. Near-Real-Time Monitoring of Global CO_2 Emissions Reveals the Effects of the COVID-19 Pandemic. *Nature Communications*, 11 (1): 5172.
McGrath, M. 2021. COP26: Draft Deal Calls for Stronger Carbon Cutting Targets by End of 2022. BBC News, November 10, 2021.
NASA. 2008. Giovanni: An Easier Way to Visualize Earth Science Data. https://www.nasa.gov/audience/foreducators/9-12/features/giovanni-an-easier-way.html. Last accessed 11 July 2021.
NASA. 2021. EarthData COVID-19 Dashboard. https://earthdata.nasa.gov/covid19. Last accessed 11 July 2021.
US EPA. 2001. EIIP Volume II: Introduction to Stationary Point Source Emissions Inventory Development. United States Environmental Protection Agency.

An Effort to Integrate Social and Environmental Awareness into Graphic Design Education

Szilvia Kadas

The higher education arena not only teaches discipline-specific skills, but also provides a safe place for students to develop critical thinking and practice to express their authentic voices. This chapter is a brief overview of sustainable graphic design, followed by a review on some of the key graphic designers, who advocate for a more socially and environmentally aware design profession and sustainable design education. In this chapter, I will also present a socially and environmentally aware student designer project along with showcasing some of the final student's posters, and discusses the significance of training graphic designers with a sustainability mindset.

Graphic design can be a vessel to deliver multiple perspectives and shape the public perception. In most cases, it is mass-produced and targeting mass audiences, therefore it is vital to establish strong ethical conduct regarding its public responsibility. It is well known that graphic design has close ties with commerce; however, its primary focus is to

S. Kadas (✉)
Art and Art History Department, State University of New York College at Cortland, Cortland, NY, USA
e-mail: szilvia.kadas@cortland.edu

B. C. Wilson, *Care, Climate, and Debt*,
https://doi.org/10.1007/978-3-030-96355-2_6

promote ideas in a visual manner and influence ideologies on a larger scale. It is fair to say that the graphic design profession not only has a direct link with consumer culture and the economy, but also may shape social norms, beliefs, and behaviors; therefore, it is essential that designers initiate new narratives, by standing up for social and environmental values.

Today, many companies and trades are making efforts to reduce their negative impact on the environment and society, taking initiatives to rethink the way they design and integrate sustainable development into their business models (Verghese et al., 2012). Their goals may include commitments to tackle poverty, end inequalities, and mitigate climate change. A recent study showed that in 2016 corporate sustainability became mainstream, as many corporate executives reported that sustainability was on their company's agenda (Kiron et al., 2017). This means that these companies need manufacturers and service providers who can support these sustainability efforts. Graphic design is one of the service sectors within the market that connects production and consumption by providing visual communication for businesses (Davis, 2012). Therefore, mainstream graphic designers have a key function in the production chain; they are one of the connecting links "between client and producer, and raw materials and the manufacturer" (Sherin, 2013, p. 10).

There are growing interests and initiatives in sustainable graphic design (Benson & Perullo, 2017; Carroll 2012; Dritz 2014; Gavos, 2012; Jedlička 2009; Perkins, 2006; Sherin, 2013), but the graphic design profession has not yet come to a consensus on a clear definition or set of criteria to assure consistent standards for sustainable design (Dritz, 2014). Dritz cautioned the design profession that "this has created misunderstanding and potentially missed opportunities for graphic designers and the business they serve" (2014, p. 46). Furthermore, Anne Chick (2012) stated "contemporary design professionals have been struggling with the challenges posed by addressing the core concept of sustainability development in earnest for over thirty years" (p. 52). Alastair Fuad-Luke (2009) pointed out that "sustainability has many flexible definitions, depending on its context and the field of study" (p. 23). Dresner (2002) commented that the problem with the concept of sustainability is not that it is meaningless, but that it is an adverb or qualifier that has different meanings to different people, therefore "it is a contestable concept like liberty and justice" (p. 2).

Graphic design is a collective term to refer to the diverse field of creative expression that uses visual problem-solving techniques to integrate text and images conveying ideas and messages to a targeted audience. Graphic design emerged from the graphic arts and become a distinct discipline by the mid-1900s (Cramsie, 2010). Patrick Cramsie (2010) noted that there were several aspects that differentiated graphic design from fine arts. For instance, the fact that graphic design was functional, "it was either selling or informing, or sometimes doing it both" (p. 9) and its aspect of "reproduction is what distinguishes graphic design from most forms of art" (p. 11). Cramsie defined graphic designers as a "service provider" (2010, p. 9), which also differentiated them from the autonomy of the artists. In addition, graphic design has a direct link to consumer culture, and Davis (2012) brought to attention that "design and mass media are essential to capitalist economic system that assign social value to the consumption of material goods" (p. 98).

Cramsie (2010) further explained that graphic designers became worthy of study and being included in art history only in the last three decades. This lack of attention was due to "graphic design's role as a service provider [as it] masked whatever artistic merit it might have possessed" (p. 9). Graphic design occupies a creative realm that lays in between the two poles of the high arts and the applied arts. It contains both aspects at the same time, which made it difficult for art historians to classify graphic design. Graphic design cannot be completely utilitarian nor can it be completely symbolic. If it is the former, then it becomes solely pragmatic, and if it is the latter, then it becomes autonomous art. Furthermore, this little attention was also due to the "lack of clarity about the status of graphic design [which] has been compounded by its ephemeral nature" (2010, p. 9). Graphic design includes different creative activities such as typography, identity design, magazine and book illustration, art-direction, packaging design, branding, interactive design, game design, and advertisement. The various forms of media application may also create challenges to view graphic design as a unified field. Graphic designers may use many different media for conveying messages, such as print and digital, screen-based media. A single graphic designer regularly engages in various types of projects, which requires most graphic designers to be familiar with a multitude of work areas across media and different applications (Jedlička, 2009).

Still, it is fair to say that the collective focus of graphic design is neither the media nor the tools used in its production. Rather, it is on the creative methods that treat words and images on a two—three—or even four-dimensional surface and use reproduction (and often mass production) to communicate ideas to society. Graphic designers' work exists in a social context and often has material consequences. This means that they bear a social and environmental responsibility for the material on which their designs are printed or the messages their designs convey to the public. The outcome of the design has an impact on society and the environment whether disseminated in print or digital media. Designers working in the digital media are increasingly concerned with their ethical responsibility. In September 2017 at a technological design conference called *Techfest*, designers declared and signed the *The Copenhagen Letter*, in which they manifested:

> It is time to take responsibility for the world we are creating. Time to put humans before business. Time to replace the empty rhetoric of building a better world with a commitment to real action. It is time to organize, and to hold each other accountable. (n.p.)

This letter is the manifesto for a transparent society, a call for action to bring clarity and structure to the inherent chaos of the postmodern world in which ultimately business is put first.

Graphic design has a significant influence on society, the environment, and the economy. Research showed that currently brand identities and logos are more recognizable by the public than common animal species (Assadourian, 2010). Graphic designers create these brand identities and, thus, influence consumer ideologies. Design is a powerful tool for shaping the world and how we live in "marketing and advertising shapes consumer culture, including the self-image and personal values of buyers" (Perkins, 2006, n.p.). Davis (2012) stated that advertising "define[s] who we are and what we believe…" (p. 99). In this way, design may negatively influence consumer behaviors and practices, or not take advantage of the potential to positively influence consumers. For instance, The U.S. Environmental Protection Agency (EPA) urged American households and businesses to implement sustainable materials management (SMM) and embrace a system approach of the concept of Reduce, Reuse, and Recycle (EPA, 2016).

Today the main emphasis in packaging is placed on developing the sustainable supply chain by refining efficiency of the used materials to reduce the materials' environmental impacts (Dominic et al., 2015). However, the visual communication on the packaging or elsewhere that would inspire, motivate, and inform consumers to recycle has not yet been realized effectively (Nordin & Selke, 2010). Still more than 50 percent of municipal solid waste (MSW) in the United States ends up in landfills (EPA, 2016). The Sustainable Development Commission analysis confirmed that labels providing data about the ecological advantages or disadvantages of the products were unsuccessful in getting more shoppers to buy the more sustainable products (Maniates, 2010).

Nordin and Selke (2010) emphasized the need to differentiate the two distinct kinds of the social factors of sustainability: social equity and the consumer awareness and perceptions factor. Visual designers may have potential to motivate consumers with visual design to inspire sustainable consumer behavior change in this critical stage of the products' life (Jedlička et al., 2009). Ultimately, the success of the full implementation of recycling is subject to the consumers' comprehension and sustainable action (Nordin & Selke, 2010; Oki & Sasaki, 2000).

However, the unsustainable practices of the graphic design profession go beyond the ideological negative or lack of positive influence it may have on society. The material products of graphic design have a large impact on the environment as well: packaging, advertisements, flyers, magazines, and other mass-produced ephemera (Scalin, 2017). In 2014, total municipal solid waste (MSW) in the United States was 258 million tons that included durable goods (furniture), nondurable goods (paper, clothing, and packaging,) and other items such as food (EPA, 2016). To talk about the negative impact of print is also relevant because surveys showed that the majority of graphic designers still identified print as their main area of practice (Gavos, 2012). Over half of the annual waste discarded into the United States landfills is printed material (Northwest Product Stewardship Council, 2015). Besides generating solid waste, the print industry also pollutes water and air. Further, the global print industry is charged with raw material depletion and high-energy consumption related to non-renewable energies (Jedlička et al., 2009). Paper creates the highest concern of all printed materials, as the United States produces almost 69 million tons of paper per year (EPA, 2016). It is thus important for designers to realize that their work contributes to a global system that requires sustainable practices.

To research the institutionalized design ethical guidelines in regard to sustainability is both timely and pressing. Empirical research in graphic design is still at its infancy as "traditionally graphic design theory has privileged intuition and creativity over empirical research" (Bennett, 2006, p. 14). Additionally, graphic designers argued that calculating the impact of their design work would only bring even more restrictions on their creative process (Bennett, 2006). However, I argue that measuring the potential negative impact of graphic designers and mitigating the harm of the designed object and service on society and the environment would elevate rather than limit the significance of graphic design work.

The graphic design profession may include multiple different media and skills, which makes the graphic design field and training specialized and nuanced. The primary media graphic designers may use are print and digital which may include web and broadcast. According to Adrian Shaughnessy (2005) what ultimately defines the profession is the overarching goal to create a unique visual language, which brings balance between text (typography) and image (photography or illustration), and content and form. Marshall McLuhan (1964) gave voice to the power of the medium in which a designer chooses to produce their work:

> In a culture like ours, long accustomed to splitting and dividing all things as a means of control, it is sometimes a bit of a shock to be reminded that, in operational and practical fact, the medium is the message. This is merely to say that the personal and social consequences of any medium—that is, of any extension of ourselves—result from the new scale that is introduced into our affairs by each extension of ourselves, or by any new technology. (p. 7)

Furthermore, W. J. T. Mitchell (2005) indicated that "a medium is more than the materials of which it is composed. It is... a social practice, a set of skills, habits, techniques, tool codes, and conventions" (p. 10).

As there are many media involved in the graphic design profession, it is important to acknowledge that the social, ecological, and economic footprint of the media the graphic designer is applying to communicate their ideas. While the print media may have both large social and ecological footprints, the digital media may have less direct negative footprint on the environment but still have enormous social and environmental responsibility that is necessary in order to practice ethically. When discussing print media specifically, the term is understood as print design and is applied throughout this paper.

There are many specialized design career options for a graphic designer depending on the focus of the technological skillset, media, and methods of problem-solving that is acquired through their education and work experience. A graphic designer may work as an art director, advertising designer, book and magazine designer, illustrator, creative director, environmental graphics designer, interaction designer, motion designer, package designer, user experience designer (UX), user interface designer (UI), visual designer, or web designer which all have very specific attributes.

According to the recent US Department of Labor report, *Occupational Outlook Handbook* (2018), though most graphic designers are employed in publishing houses, public relations departments, advertising agencies, independent design studios, or as in-house graphic designers in larger corporations, in 2016 about 1 in 5 graphic designers were self-employed freelancers. This may be because while the most common work environment for a graphic designer is to be an in-house graphic designer, several companies may outsource their graphic design projects to freelancers or independent design studios. Today, in the midst of the technological and ecological transition, the public and therefore the market is increasingly responsive to social and environmental issues. Thus, it directly affects the demand and requirements graphic designers may face in their career. As such, there is a demand for sustainable graphic design education that prepares professionals to provide sustainable design services in each medium.

When graphic designers discuss the need to integrate ethical considerations into design practice, two main writings come to the surface: *First Things First: A Manifesto* by Ken Garland (1964), and *The Road to Hell* by Milton Glaser (2002). *First Things First: A Manifesto* (1964)—written by graphic designer Ken Garland and signed by twenty-two contemporary visual communicators—was a call for a more ethical practice in the field of graphic design. It pointed out some of the ethical challenges mainstream graphic designers face while working for commerce. The manifesto advocated for an educational reform, and to place larger public focus on cause related services that would improve greater society. The 1964 manifesto was significant because graphic designers for the first time publicly demonstrated awareness of the ramifications of their designs. Garland was driven by his social convictions, in which he disagreed with graphic design's entanglement with consumer and corporate culture. Garland (1964) wrote:

> We do not advocate the abolition of high-pressure consumer advertising: this is not feasible. Nor do we want to take any of the fun out of life. But we are proposing a reversal of priorities in favor of the more useful and more lasting forms of communication. (n.p.)

Garland's vision for graphic design was to embrace social and political issues and create meaningful designs that went beyond the tricks and gimmicks of a salesperson.

In *The Road to Hell*, Milton Glaser (2002) published a list of twelve common graphic design activities that required designers to misrepresent or to bend the truth in their everyday practice. Glaser (2002) used the metaphor of Dante's *Hell* to describe the graphic design profession. He explained that if graphic designers wanted to get to purgatory instead of hell, they must at least acknowledge their works' falsification. Although these writings brought awareness on the moral shortcomings of the commercial graphic design profession, they remained in the realm of the personal moral pursuit of activism. I argue that the only way graphic designers will be able to move toward a sustainable design is through institutionalizing main ethical professional standards in regard to social, environmental, cultural, and economic impacts. This may require future collaborations between different design disciplines, creative practice, manufacturing, and empirical research.

Furthermore, Shaughnessy (2005) wrote in his book *How to be a Graphic Designer, Without Losing Your Soul* that "Integrity in design is a bit like obesity in ballet dancers- you don't often see it" (p. 25). He explained that the reason for this is not because "designers lack honesty and decency; quite the opposite. Rather it is because preserving integrity in the remorseless climate of modern business is difficult" (p. 25). This statement again takes us back to the preliminary argument that graphic designers serve commerce, and therefore they should obey the needs and wants of the clients even if that is not in the best interest of the public or conflicts with their own personal moral values. The lack of autonomy graphic designers may feel over the design decisions they make may cause a detachment from the social and environmental responsibility their work carries.

Shaughnessy (2005) argued that the solution is for graphic designers to start standing up for the moral values and start negotiating ethical solutions with their clients: "By standing up for yourself, by having beliefs (creative and ethical), and perhaps most importantly of all, by questioning what you are asked to do as a designer, you can acquire self-respect, which is the first step on the path to earning the respect of clients and other designers" (p. 27). When Shaughnessy (2005) interviewed the famous contemporary graphic designer Neville Brody, about the necessity of integrating ethical considerations into the graphic design profession, Brody replied that "personal integrity in design is what differentiates the good from the bad" (p. 27). That brings up the following question: are there historic precedents of any relationship between moral responsibility with the arts and design?

Tolstoy (1995) explained that Alexander Gottlieb Baumgarten (1714–1762), the founder of aesthetics believed that man perceives beauty through its senses in nature, therefore the mission of art is to imitate and mimic nature. Other philosophers such as Moses Mendelssohn (1729–1786), and Ludwig Schütz (1838–1901) however, argued that the main goal of art is not only beauty but it is also to achieve moral perfection, as good is the moral will of man. Another aesthetic philosopher who contradicted this belief was Immanuel Kant (1724–1804). Kant's aesthetics were based on the premise that humans perceive themselves outside of the natural world; therefore, all their creations are artificial. This viewpoint created a duality not only between man and nature, but also between nature and art. Schiller (Tolstoy, 1995), one of Kant's followers, defined the purpose of fine art as the pursuit of beauty, without regard for usefulness. This short overview of aesthetics was necessary to understand the capstone relations of nature, art, and design. These conflicting beliefs illustrate the manifold philosophical grounds upon which art can be perceived. However, as graphic design originates from the fine arts, the debate whether design has a moral obligation to do good in the world is relevant. Because many graphic designers serve commerce, some graphic designers may feel morally isolated as the underpinning of graphic design is in the arts and not business.

Development of sustainable design and concepts, such as green design, ecological design. Design became aware of its environmental footprint in the late 1960s. Despite the awareness of the negative impacts of design, the scale of natural environment exploitation and pollution has been only growing. Brown and Schmidt (2014) wrote: "Human activity is changing the earth at a global scale... Of course, humans have been altering the earth to our advantage for thousands of years, but the planetary scale and influence of our impact is unprecedented" (p. 64). Theologian Thomas Berry suggested an ecozoic approach based on a "mutual –enhancing human-Earth relationship," rather than maintaining our current technozoic lifestyle that consumes its surroundings (Brown & Schmidt, 2014).

The environmental limit of human intervention into nature has been puzzling over the years. For instance, the Radical Environmentalism and

Deep Ecology ideological movements of the 1960s rejected any intervention into "nature," as they believed that any minor alteration of nature would cause irrecoverable harm to the ecosystem (Chiapponi, 1998, p. 109). To understand the connection between ecology and design, I will first review the three terms often attached to design: green, ecological, and sustainable. In the following, I examine the meaning behind each term. It is important to mention that these terms are used in all sorts of design areas, not specifically graphic design. The three terms appeared around the late '60s as the public became environmentally conscious due to scientific data reports showing the significant impact humans were having on the Earth's ecosystem by the current consumerist lifestyle.

Pauline Madge (1997) summed up the meaning of the three terms, which are often used interchangeably in graphic design. The ideology of "green design" (p. 329) dates to the late 1960s, but it was not until 1980 that the media popularized the issue. Increased media interest raised public awareness on green topics. The color green became a mainstream token and an advertising strategy. Green design did not reject either consumerism or the industrialized world. On the contrary, it boosted consumption under the new slogan: green. In 1988, John Elkington and Julia Hailes published the *Green Consumer Guide*. "Light green" became the political term of green consumerism, which raised opposition in many who believed in a more radical "dark green" approach of solving environmental problems. There was an urge to step beyond "Green Consumerism" (Madge, 1997, p. 330).

According to Madge (1997), the term "ecological design" (p. 331) was used from the late '60s onward. In the 1990s, there were many governmentally supported steps taken to reinforce global environmental standards and to include them into national policies. One of the examples of this was the European Union's Eureka program, where in 1991 a group of designers developed methods and processes to operationalize Eco-design. Furthermore, in the United Kingdom and the Netherlands, multidisciplinary research began to unify institutions with industry to develop and integrate life cycle models into the production chain.

The term sustainability nourished the idea of a system that helped to keep up a healthy well-being on Earth. In the context of design, sustainability considers the entire life cycle of products, which re-introduced the idea of long-life and durable products moving beyond recycling (Madge, 1997). Jedlička (2009), stated that the definition of sustainable development, which was coined by the World Commission on Environment and Development in 1987, is still wildly accepted and currently in use: "A sustainable development is development that meets the needs of the present without compromising the ability of future generations to meet their own ends" (p. 12).

Today, sustainable development has become one of the primary concerns and efforts of the United Nations. In September 2015, 193 world leaders signed the 17 Global Sustainable Development Goals (SDGs) of the 2030 Agenda for Sustainable Development at the historic United Nations Summit in New York (Transforming Our World: The 2030 Agenda for Sustainable Development, 2015). The document called for global investment and effort toward improving the life of all people, tackling climate change, and providing prosperity and peace by working in partnership with one another.

Graphic design ties with commerce. Graphic design from the beginning was concerned with promoting ideas in a visual manner. Graphic design—also referred to as visual communication—is a modified continuation of the traditional graphic arts, therefore the history of the traditional graphic design is as old as human beings. The cave paintings from Lascaux c. 15,000–10,000 B.C. are considered the earliest graphic art works (Meggs, 1998). The borderline between graphic design and art even today is elusive. Graphic arts gradually branched off from the other fine arts forms. As fine art was concerned with artistic expression, graphic art's concern was solving communication problems with visuals. As the printing press was adopted widely across Europe in the mid-1400s (Eskilson, 2012), graphic arts became a more functional tool, bringing information to the wider public.

However, the pivotal historical event and social change that started the process of bringing to life the graphic design profession was the British Industrial Revolution at the end of the 1800s and the early-1900s. Industrialization and mass production inflated material consumption to a greater scale (Assadourian, 2010). As Adams (2014) described, suddenly large quantities of identical products and services were available. The industrial revolution created an abundance of mass-produced items. In the overcrowded marketplace, manufacturers needed graphic artists to create visual-identities that made these similar mass-produced products immediately recognizable, memorable, and desirable to the public. Also, the industrial revolution brought many technological developments, notably for designers the 1875 Robert Barclay patent for the offset lithographic printing press that enabled printing on tin and metal plates. This paved the way for the development of packaging design (Meggs, 1998).

It is fair to say, that the graphic design profession not only has a link with the consumer culture, but also it is directly tied to the technological developments that accrue over time. Therefore, graphic design is a constantly evolving discipline that is highly responsive to new technology. This creates another contrast with other fine art forms, which may be more conservative with the adoption of new technology and more likely to practice and preserve traditional techniques than graphic design.

Among many who criticized the new emerging commercial arts and technical revolution was the British art historian John Ruskin (1819–1900), who wrote:

> All the stamped metals, and artificial stones, and imitation woods and bronze, over the invention of which we hear daily exultation—all the short, and cheap, and easy ways of doing that whose difficulty is its honour—are just so many new obstacles in our already encumbered road. They will not make us happier or wiser—they will extend neither the pride of judgement nor the privilege of enjoyment. They will only make us shallower in our understanding, colder in our hearts, and feebler in our wits. (Cramsie, 2010, p. 139)

According to Cramsie (2010) in this cultural climate of Britain, a successful British artist and designer William Morris (1834–1896) formed an opposite pole, by creating a new style; the Arts and Crafts movement. Many consider Morris's movement to be the forerunner of late twentieth-century environmental art and design. Morris recognized the high demand for mass-advertisement but advocated for art and design to keep its stylistic visual languages as hand-made, organic, and traditional arts and crafts. Morris created multi-disciplinary new stylistic principles for the arts called Art Nouveau. Jules Cheret (1836–1932), Leonetto Cappiello (1875–1942), Henri de Toulouse-Lautrec (1864–1901), Theophile Steinlen (1859–1923), Eugene Grasset (1841–1917), Alphonse Mucha (1860–1939), and Lucian Bernhard (1883–1972) were among the first celebrated designers who gained fame in Western society by creating a popular visual culture for the masses (Cramsie, 2010; Eskilson, 2012).

The First World War changed the landscape of Europe and its economy. Graphic design became a tool to communicate propaganda during wartime. James Flagg's (1877–1960) famous I want YOU for U.S. Army (1917) and Howard Christy's (1873–1952) well-known recruiting poster *Gee!! I Wish I Were a Man* (1917) illustrates the political temper of the era during which the posters were created. Between the first and second world wars, many styles emerged, such as Cubism, Dada, De Stijl, Purism, Russian Constructivism, Art Deco, Secession, and German Expressionism (Cramsie, 2010).

A significant milestone in the development of the graphic design history was 1919 when Herbert Bayer and Lászlo Moholy-Nagy (1895–1946) started to teach typography at the Bauhaus School in Weimar, Germany. The typography workshop became focused on brand identity, advertisement, and visual communication. The Bauhaus attempted to systematically connect the industry with the arts and design. German Expressionism continued to be the governing force in graphic design. Under the leadership of Walter Gropius (1983–1969), Johannes Ittens (1888–1967), Lyonel Feininger (1871–1956), Moholy-Nagy (1895–1946), Marcel Breuer (1902–1981), and Joost Schmidt (1893–1948) were among the many modern artists who taught at the modern school of Bauhaus. The term graphic design was created by the book and type designer William Addison Dwiggins (1880–1956) in 1922. From the 1920s, graphic designers and art directors were coordinating most of the design work (text and images) in publishing and advertising agencies. In 1920, the advertising industry in the United States grew rapidly. "Between 1914 and 1929, the annual dollar volume of advertising rose from $600,000 to nearly $3 billion" (Eskilson, 2012, p. 242). In the United States, many magazines appeared such as *Vogue*, *Seventeen*, *Vanity Fair*, and *Fortune* that enhanced the role of graphic designers in the consumer society. However, the political agenda was still a dominant aspect of the graphic design industry.

After the Second World War, economic prosperity allowed the focus of graphic design to shift from the war to corporate identities. Many companies wanted to create a unified visual look for their corporation to be more recognizable among the public. Saul Bass (1920–1996), Paul Rand (1914–1996), and Tom Geismar (b. 1931–) were among the first graphic designers to create corporate identities. These designs were created in the dominant style of the post-war era: the international style. The 1960s was the golden age of corporate identity and logo design.

In the United States, the international style was quickly followed by postmodernism. The postmodern style allowed designers to borrow from different styles and to combine them in an eclectic manner. In the early 2000s, there was a major shift in graphic design. As technology advanced, computer-based design emerged. Designs for print were created by computers, and manual applications were taken over by computer software (Photoshop, Freehand); therefore, the aesthetics of graphic design became a more digital aesthetics. However, the Digital Revolution, which created a new field in graphic design (digital and broadcast), only arrived after the late '90s (Eskilson, 2012). This historic overview shows how visual communication changed throughout human history, and how the tools and technologies used in the era shaped the development of the graphic design industry.

Sustainable Models in the Graphic Design Field

Modeling sustainable development helps professionals conceptualize and integrate sustainability into their practices. Most professions beyond graphic design model sustainability as residing at the balanced intersection of the three spheres of society, environment, and economy, with interdependent relationship in between these different spheres. These three spheres are often referred to as the "*triple bottom line* of sustainable development" (Elkington, 1998, p. 72). Elkington (1998) wrote about the importance of the share zones, an interdependent relationship in which "[s]ociety depends on the economy—and the economy depends on the global ecosystem, whose health represents the ultimate bottom line" (p. 73).

According to Cook (2008), all designed artifacts are embedded in a social environment, as they are the imperious work of humans, using raw materials from the natural environment. All three systems are interconnected and are dependent on each other's stability. Cook (2008) clarified that sustainability requires an understanding that artifacts are not natural systems, but human systems and therefore need clear ethical guidelines that avoid interfering with either the natural or the human systems. "Counterfeit naturalism" (Cook, 2008, p. 265) is when artifacts are treated as natural systems and therefore dealt with in ways that deny the ethical responsibilities of the designer.

Aaris Sherin (2008) modeled the concept of the triple bottom line as a series of overlapping spheres. While Elkington (1998) and Cook (2008) placed emphasis on the stability and interdependent relation between these spheres, Sherin's pointed out in her model that sustainability only occurs where Elkington's three principles intersect. Therefore, Sherin's model depicted the three pillars of sustainability as distinct spheres, and the overlapping area as sustainable practice.

Wendy Jedlička (2009) built her theory of sustainability on the triple bottom line as well, however, she organized the three different areas in a new relation. Jedlička explained that sustainable design requires “system thinking” (McNamara, 2009, p. 133). System thinking stresses the adoption of concepts of interconnectedness and interrelatedness of the world. A design, whether it is a book, a poster, or packaging, is a part of a single system, which is the environment. Jedlička’s model presented the interconnected and interdependent nature of design. What the designer creates is by all means connected to an economic system, to the society, and to the environment. A designed product cannot be disconnected from the environment to be sustainable. A designed product goes through these three layers at some point in its life cycle; therefore, a product must be satisfactory to all three layers of the system. For example, “A toxic material might appear to have a nice loop within the economic system yet affect workers in the societal system and have negative impacts on the environment” (Jedlička et al., 2009, p. 158).

Jedlička’s model contrasts the sustainable theory of Cook (2008). According to Jedlička (2009), the human system must be part of the natural environment to be sustainable. From this theoretical perspective, many natural design concepts emerged such as the cradle to cradle (McDonough & Braungart 2002) and biomimicry (Benyus, 1997). These concepts embrace the idea of the philosopher Mendelssohn and its followers, in which art is part of the natural world.

The Living Principles, the sustainability division of the American Institute of Graphic Arts (AIGA) , further refined this sustainability model. The Living Principles added “culture” as the fourth layer of sustainability. These sustainable principles—environment, people, economy, and culture—may guide the decision-making process of sustainability-conscious designers. The environmental layer includes moving away from production and manufacturing that impacts the natural environment and interrupts the eco-systems. It embraces eliminating activities from practices that may contribute to climate change or produce a large carbon footprint.

At the same time, it is important to engage in practices that will encourage preservation and restoration of natural resources. The social layer at AIGA focused on building a fair community for people, highlighting “poverty, violence, injustice, education, healthcare, safe housing, labor and human rights” (livingprinciples.org, n.p.). The third layer is the economy. This layer focused on profitability and monetary success, with emphasis on meeting humanity's basic needs. The fourth and last layer involved issues of culture. This layer is significant as any design product must be a product of its culture. Through culture, the identity of the community and place is articulated. Traditions and historic artifacts of a community are part of the cultural value of our society. According to AIGA, it is important to preserve cultural diversity in order to sustain human character.

While there are minor differences between these theoretical frameworks, they all rely on system thinking and a holistic view of production. Comparing Jedlička's with Sherin's model it becomes evident that in Sherin's model the three areas—the environmental, the economic, and the social—have independent existences that merely intersect. However, in Jedlička's model, these three areas cannot exist individually or separately—rather they are part of each other and dependent upon each other to function as a system. Furthermore, both Jedlička and Sherin's model considered three pillars of sustainability, while the AIGA's Living Principle model took more areas into consideration (such as the role of the individual, the planet, or businesses). This may obscure the relationship between the core pillars of sustainability (environment, society, and economy). Jedlička, by making clear the completely overlapping relationship between the elements, also defines the role of sustainable graphic designers within this system.

Lack of Standards

Dritz (2014) suggested that the core problem regarding sustainability in the graphic design industry derives from the absence of standards. Although "graphic designers are ready for a change" (Dritz, 2014, p. 36), there is lack of consistency in sustainable practices. Additionally, she mentioned that there is a shortage of sustainable education and information available for designers:

> The graphic design industry as a whole has not come to any consensus on the definition or expectation of the role of the sustainable graphic designer. This has created misunderstanding and potentially missed opportunities for graphic designers and the business they serve. (Dritz, 2014, p. 46)

Gavos (2012) surveyed graphic designers to ask them if a LEED Green Building type of certification in graphic design would be beneficial for them to move toward sustainable practices. Gavos' survey disclosed an overwhelming interest in LEED type education and certification in the field of graphic design. In line with Gavos, Carr (2009) advocated for introducing similar standards as LEED, provided by the U.S. Green Building Council (USGBC), to architecture. Carr (2009) also claimed that one of the main reasons for lack of standards in graphic design is that it does not "operate under a system of accreditation" (p. 1). Although LEED is a value-added credential, which is administered by the USGBC, this suggests that the graphics design industry might incorporate third-party licensure in order to establish some measure of accountability.

Autonomy deficit as service providers. As the literature indicated that graphic designers are "service providers" (Cramsie, 2010) rather than autonomous artists, their sovereignty in decision-making is limited. The mainstream design studios may accept work that benefits corporate clients but is not always in alignment with societal and ecological needs. The AIGA noted that "Private profit making is often at odds with public good" (Perkins, 2006, n.p.). If designers want to realize the power of their work and their position then they must have objective tools to negotiate sustainability in the intersections between corporations, the consumer, and the global impact of the designed work. While the AIGA encourages designers to "ask questions, express doubts, and propose alternatives. [They might do so by performing inquiries such as] is the message truthful? Is the service beneficial? Is the product useful, made well and produced in a sustainable way?" (Perkins, 2006, n.p.). Asking subjective questions without objective standards could jeopardize the client-designer relationship since the designer is a service provider for the large corporation. Thus, standards could help designers avoid conflicts because the concepts are already accepted by large professional design organizations.

Without standards, it becomes a difficult and personal process to determine which clients to accept and which to reject. This can become problematic for designers on several fronts. Designers might not want to seem overly critical of prospective clients and rejecting clients can have a huge economic impact on design firms. By suggesting that designers can be either profitable or principled, the AIGA implies that one cannot be both:

> Some designers consciously shift their activities away from for-profit clients and into the not-for-profit realm, into activism and cause-related marketing. Many designers have taken the leap to developing their own,

> non-commissioned projects. Design entrepreneurs working at a small scale have more latitude to explore new business models and practices. (Perkins, 2006, n.p.)

This suggests that designers who work for commission in the corporate global market can never fully be balanced between their ethical obligation and their professional duties.

The global market demands brand identities for consumers to be able to differentiate similar products and consumers are exposed to hundreds of advertisements, brands, and logos every day. The AIGA debated the position designers hold within the consumer market they serve and noted, "Our involvement in materialism and conspicuous consumption may even extend to the creation of artificial needs and the promotion of unnecessary products through advertising and marketing messages that are manipulative or deceptive" (Perkins, 2006, n.p.). Perkins' (2006) remark aligns with Garland's (1964), and Glaser's (2002) critique regarding the ethical barriers of graphic design profession because it serves business.

The entanglement with consumer culture is also detected throughout the historical evolution of other design disciplines. The main goal of design was to create the illusion of happiness and well-being and associate it with a specific brand and product. Assadourian (2010) explained, "In most countries today people are exposed to hundreds if not thousands of consumerist symbols every day. Logos, jingles, slogans…all these symbols of different brands routinely bombard people, influencing behavior even at unconscious levels" (pp. 8–9). The goal of graphic designers is to convince consumers to buy the product. Can graphic designers as visual communicators contribute to change current consumer behaviors to a sustainable consumer culture? Among many designers, Brian Dougherty (2008) urged his colleagues to do their share in transforming the industry into a sustainable one. Dougherty (2008) strongly believed communication must encourage the cultural shift for a sustainable life.

Yet, to transform the consumer culture we must investigate more about how human cultures form and how they shape human behavior. Assadourian (2010) explained that all humans are "embedded in a cultural system" (p. 3). Human beings grow into a range of "values, beliefs, customs, traditions, symbols, norms, and institutions" that becomes their "cultural reality," which people experience as a "natural" behavior (p. 3). Human norms, values, and traditions differ all around the globe. Cultures transform throughout history as well; they adjust to new circumstances.

Assadourian (2010) insisted that cultures can change and the culture of consumerism must change fundamentally for the sake of sustaining life on earth. He points out in his essay that:

> Transforming cultures is no small task. It will require decades of effort in which cultural pioneers—those who can step out of their cultural realities enough to critically examine them—work tirelessly to redirect key culture-shaping institutions: education, business, government, and the media, as well as social movements and long-standing human traditions. (p. 4)

According to Assadourian (2010), the solution would shift values, norms, and habits toward eco-system reconstruction. In addition, he argued that humans must reduce mainstream consumption to a minimum level. The remaining minimal consumption needs to be either durably or cradle to cradle designed. McDonough and Braungart (2002) modeled their cradle to cradle (C2C) design approach after cyclical ecological systems, in which organisms decompose after death to provide nourishment for the creation of new life, closing the loop of the environment (Jedlička, 2009, p. 235). This strategy opposed linear systems, or cradle to grave, where cradle is the birth of the design and the grave is the end of use, or the landfill.

The cradle-to-cradle approach of design thus suggested that materials must be either durable, transformable to different uses, or decomposable. In this way, it is modeled on natural systems that do not produce waste. One of the strategies of the cradle-to-cradle approach is biomimicry, which means to stimulate nature in the approach of design; bio refers to life, and mimesis refers to modeling or simulating. Both Assadourian (2010) and McDonough and Braungart (2002) clash with Chiapponi (1998), and Cook's (2008) ideas that considered design inherently artificial, therefore they did not believe that making design nature-like would provide a sustainable solution.

The Sustainable Development Commission confirmed that government and producer initiatives in the "choice editing" process affected consumer behaviors (Maniates, 2010, p. 119). Choice editing means to change the mainstream marketplace to a sustainable one by offering only sustainable choices for customers and therefore moving consumers to a more sustainable consumption (Maniates, 2010). This requires advocating changes from the key players who influence mass consumption. Although the main driver of consumption is economic, media, government, and education systems also have a great impact on consumers. For example, the government has a key role in applying tax and policies to motivate consumer behavior to a certain orientation. Governmental choice editing has occurred by considering safety factors and performance standards (Maniates, 2010). If sustainability is encoded at the institutional level, then it would not be left to the ethical choice or subjectivity of the individual graphic designer.

Although National Association of Schools of Art and Design (NASAD) has demonstrated a clear commitment to sustainable values in art and design education, standards for integrating sustainability into the design curriculum have yet to fully take shape. As a result, universal integration of sustainability-oriented standards and accreditation in design programs merits additional research. Also, as higher education institutions are gradually cycling toward accreditation review it may take time to integrate sustainable developments in design curriculum. Alain Findeli (2001) argued that most design schools lack courses that deal with design theoretical issues, teaching design with no philosophical, ethical, and sustainable approach. This has resulted in artists and designers lacking sufficient knowledge, responsibility, and insight for making ethical and sustainable artifacts. Also, as each division of manufacturing is so specialized and segmented, the design industry has lacked the vocabulary, knowledge, and, therefore, the ability and initiatives to collaborate within these separate but interconnected areas of the supply chain. David Orr (2002) argued that all current ecological issues are ramifications of design failures. Orr (2002) urged designers to view design from a completely new perspective and advocated for educational reform in the field of design toward a sustainably designed world. Similarly, Susan S. Szenasy (2012), an educator of design history and design ethics, also advocated for more sustainable practices in the design profession.

Current Resources and Approaches Supporting Sustainable Initiatives

Findeli (1994) researched the threshold of significance, in which he examined what differentiates the banal and the utopian objects from designed artifacts. He introduced the space of artifacts model, in which Findeli presented two different poles of the designed object spectrum: one pole was "purely instrumental" and the opposite was "purely symbolic" (Findeli, 1994, pp. 49–68). The threshold of significance includes the aesthetics, ethical responsibilities, and social, cultural, and environmental context of an object. According to Findeli (1994), there are two conditions of an artifact. First, a designed object's value must be greater than the "threshold of significance" (p. 53). Everything below this line is considered an object of "banality or uselessness" (p. 54)" The second condition is the budgetary and technological limitation of a design project. Everything above that is a utopian object. Therefore, to make an ethical design decision, a designer should evaluate the potential significance and ecological impact of a designed object (Findeli, 1994).

Medardo Chiapponi (1998) stated that: "The concept of nature has, since ancient times, always been connected to the idea of a monolithic and immutable genitive principle, which being outside and above human actions has therefore determined it" (p. 109). Which follows the philosophical view of Kant. According to Chiapponi (1998), the duality of a *natural* and *artificial* environment is inaccurate, as they are one entity. The technological development, just as human society, is a segment of the environment. Therefore, he opposed the concept of *radical environmentalism and deep ecology* since every human activity would alter the surroundings on some level. Chiapponi (1998) argued technology is not the cause of our environmental problems. He speculated that designers have detached their work from reality and the environment by over simplifying a complex system:

> As every designer knows, the tools to formalize reality, the model, the simulation, and the interventions on reality must be as simple as possible. There are apparently unsolved contradictions between the complexities of the environment regarded as system and the simplicity intrinsic to the design process. (p. 111)

To solve the artificiality of the design industry, it is necessary to look at design as part of an interconnected system. Life Cycle Assessment (LCA) measures sustainable effectiveness throughout the entire life cycle of a designed product. LCA gives credibility to the design, in that designers become accountable for their work as its impacts become measurable. Chiapponi (1998) urged designers to broaden their perspectives and methods in which they work by integrating knowledge and collaboration between segmented work phases of their products. LCA is the only way to track the environmental impact of design; therefore, it must be incorporated into the design process.

Russ (2010) urged design professionals to move the design industry toward a sustainable one. At the same time, he acknowledged a current lack of accurate data about sustainable materials and manufacturing for designers to work with. He wrote: "There are many definitions of sustainability and sustainable design; few are very satisfactory when it comes to actual applications" (Russ, 2010, p. 105). Russ further explained "While there is objective knowledge of human impacts on the environment and examples of design that has minimalized such impact, there is no objective "toolbox" on which designers may rely" (Russ, 2010, p. 67).

In the following, I will outline some of the main ongoing discussions regarding sustainability both in theory and practice in the field of graphic design. Many designers identified sustainable materials and best practices in the field of graphic design (Benson & Perullo, 2017; Boylston 2009; Dougherty, 2008; Chick & Micklethwaite 2011; and Sherin, 2008), and encouraged a more holistic system thinking that is rooted in the core of the ethical approaches of the profession (Fine, 2016; Jedlička, 2009; Sherin, 2013). Thus, they joined the broad ethical and sustainable discourse across design disciplines (Benyus, 1997; Findeli 2001; Fry, 2009; Manzini, 2014; McDonough & Braungart, 2002; Russ, 2010; Walker & Giard, 2013). Along with sustainable design, other approaches have emerged from design ethics such as human centered design and socially conscious design (Heller & Vienne, 2003; Resnick, 2016; Scalin, 2012; Shea, 2012; Simmons, 2011).

Chick and Micklethwaite (2011) explored methods to use design thinking and entrepreneurship to solve sustainability problems. They encouraged designers to solve these problems arguing designers must embrace a greater consciousness regarding their work's social and environmental impacts when designing new products and services. Chick and Micklethwaite (2011) developed a comprehensive method for sustainable designers to carve out a space in the global marketplace.

Sustainable toolkits. Graphic design practitioners have been developing environmentally friendly methods to reduce their ecological footprint. This section introduces these latest methods. Undoubtedly, there is still a lot to be done, but there are some initiatives that are already in place to help navigate through the sustainable design working process. These developments have addressed some of the main practical issues when adopting sustainable techniques into the graphic design practice. What follows is a review of published materials that have helped to establish sustainable graphic design practices, such as toolkits, charts, and resources available today for designers who seek to work sustainably.

Since most designers are still employed in print (Gavos, 2012), and most environmental impact is due to the print industry, this section examines the most common manufacturing processes and materials graphic designers use in the print industry. The review showcases extant scholarship relating to the printing process from an environmental perspective and studies on materials such as paper and inks; it also lists currently available resources for graphic designers.

The O2 International Network for Sustainable Design was founded in 1988 in Milan, Italy to advocate for nontoxic manufacturing and materials. Since then it has grown into an international network, partnering with over 70 countries. The O2 International Network organizes events, lectures, and workshops to teach sustainable design worldwide. Additionally, the AIGA has promoted sustainability by setting up a website that allows designers to locate and identify sustainable resources (livingprinciples.org, n.p.). The Paper Finder Tools, Renourish Paper Finder Tool, Re-Nourish Green Printer Tool, Living Principles Scorecard, and the Celery Design Sustainability Scorecard are among some of the helpful tools that assist designers toward sustainable design processes and products.

The latest progress includes work from Eric Benson and Yvette Perullo, co-founders and partners of *Renourich*, a non-profit organization. This project began as Benson's MFA Thesis, but it has since grown into an online resource that lets designers calculate in advance how they can reduce some of their negative impacts on the environment. Furthermore, Benson and Perullo (2017) published *Design to Renourish: Sustainable Graphic Design in Practice*, which instructed designers on integrating sustainability into their practice. However, these suggestions and calculations are far from being comprehensive since most current sustainability initiatives lack interdisciplinary input from other relevant sectors and industries.

Dougherty, a graphic designer and the creator of Celery Design Collaborative, wrote *Green Graphic Design* (2008), which helped to put theory in practice. He argued that the main problem in the print industry is that its products are disposed in the landfill rather than the recycling facility. Additionally, its manufacturing process requires a large amount of natural resources. Dougherty attempted to target and eliminate all materials from the graphic design industry that are destined to have a dead end. He suggested designers work exclusively with design materials and processes that have a sustainable profile. Dougherty introduced a chart, originally created by Michael S. Brown, called the "Sustainability Toolkit and Scorecard" (Dougherty, 2008, p. 186). His chart aimed to help graphic designers to choose the right materials for their work and determine the ultimate destinations of those materials. The scorecard is easy to use and defined materials from an ecological perspective. These measurements presented segments of the process that concern the environmental impact of the materials, but it failed to reveal the full impact of the entire design process. To have a more integral view on the sustainable impacts, graphic designers might create a holistic chart that measures the environmental impact of every work phase involved in the process of the product and service lifecycle.

The Status of Sustainability in Graphic Design Education and Professional Practice

The National Association of Schools of Art and Design (NASAD) and the American Institute of Graphic Arts (AIGA) are both institutional bodies that mention sustainability as a standard and essential design practice for their members. For instance, the NASAD guidelines recommended discussing matters of lifespan and sustainability in the classroom. Specifically, it mentioned that undergraduate design students should have the "ability to justify the use of resources and identify long-term consequences of design action in their solutions to problems" (NASAD Handbook 2017–18, 2018, p. 116). The document endorsed all three pillars of sustainability as a fundamental foundation of good practice. It drew attention to the importance of exercising "critical judgment about the student's own design and the design of others with regard to usefulness, usability, desirability, technological feasibility, economic viability, and sustainability in terms of long-term consequences" (NASAD Handbook 2017–18, 2018, p. 120). Furthermore, the NASAD Handbook 2017–18 (2018) also suggested developing students' "functional knowledge of …ethics, intellectual property, labor issues, and decisions associated with ecological and social responsibility and sustainability" (p. 122). These guidelines firmly demonstrate NASAD's strong commitment to a comprehensive design education that includes the core principles of sustainable design.

The American Institute of Graphic Arts (AIGA) encourages graphic designers to take ownership of their ethical obligations. In 2010, the AIGA published its Standards of Professional Practice, in which it outlines some of the main ethical obligations of its members. Item 7.3, added in 2011, declared the designer's responsibility to society and the environment: "A professional designer shall consider environmental, economic, social, and cultural implications of his or her work and minimize the adverse impacts" (AIGA, 2010, n.p.). While the guideline does not explicitly use the word sustainability, it does refer specifically to the three pillars of sustainability, which are the social, environmental, and economic systems in our interconnected world (Elkington, 1998). However, this point does not go into any further standards or details for implementation of sustainable practices. It is the responsibility of the graphic design practitioner to apply their judgment to interpret this guideline into her practice.

Some graphic designers are searching to reduce their negative impact on society and the environment. However, Thomas Russ (2010) also posed the question, “as the designer undertakes a design that is intended to meet some degree of sustainability but that has no objective standard on which to rely, what will guide the process?” (p. 67). Russ (2010) argued professional institutions must take the lead and define its ethics regarding sustainability. This review indicates that much more work is needed in the field of sustainable graphic design education. However, embedding social and environmental ethics into graphic design students’ practice is a meaningful place to start.

The State University of New York at Cortland’s Cultural and Intellectual Climate Committee (CICC) invited graphic design students from the college’s Digital Illustration course to create a socially and environmentally conscious poster. The assignment was to explore the theme “Care, Crisis, Climate, and Debt.” Students were encouraged to think critically, engage in discussions, and conduct in-depth research on the chosen issue prior to beginning their designs. After many brainstorming sessions, students created thought provoking posters that reflected their point of view on health care, student loans, criminal justice, inequality, and climate change. This school assignment concluded with an on-campus public exhibition, showcasing all thirteen student posters. Here are some examples of graphic design student project, that are a good example of the providing students an opportunity to advocate for a social or environmental cause, enhances their motivation in excelling in their disciplinary skills. While learning disciplinary skills, also developing critical thinking and practicing socially and environmentally aware design (Figs. 1, 2, 3, 4, and 5).

Fig. 1 Student project by MATTHEW OKERAYI, fall 2019, media: digital print (*Source* Permission from students was obtained to publish their posters)

Fig. 2 Student project by BROOKE HOLLISTER, fall 2019, media: digital print (*Source* Permission from students was obtained to publish their posters)

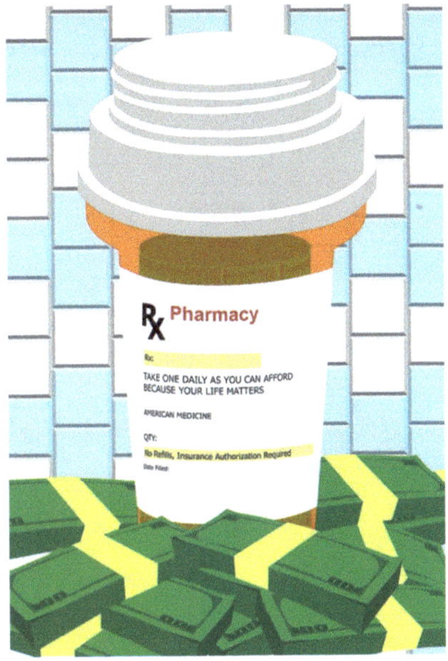

Fig. 3 Student project by ALEX GENTNER, fall 2019, media: digital print (*Source* Permission from students was obtained to publish their posters)

Fig. 4 Student project by FRANCIS FRUEHAN, fall 2019, media: digital print (*Source* Permission from students was obtained to publish their posters)

Fig. 5 Student project by COURTNEY MAURIN, fall 2019, media: digital print (*Source* Permission from students was obtained to publish their posters)

Bibliography

Adams, S. (2014). *Learning graphic design history*. Lynda.com. Retrieved from https://www.lynda.com/Graphic-Design-tutorials/Learning-Graphic-Design-History/166781-2.html.

American Institute of Graphic Arts (AIGA). (2010). *AIGA standards of professional practice*. Retrieved from https://www.aiga.org/standards-professional-practice.

American Institute of Graphic Arts (AIGA). (2015). Retrieved from http://www.aiga.org/.

Assadourian, E. (2010). The rise and fall of consumer cultures. In L. Starke & Mastny (Eds.), *State of the world: Transforming cultures from consumerism to sustainability* (pp. 3–23). New York, NY: W. W. Norton.

Bennett, A. (2006). *Design studies: Theory and research in graphic design*. New York: Princeton Architectural Press.

Benson, E., & Perullo, Y. (2017). *Design to renourish—Sustainable graphic design in practice*. Boca Raton, FL: CRC Press, Taylor & Francis.

Benyus, J. M. (1997). *Biomimicry: Innovation inspired by nature* (1st ed.). New York, NY: Morrow.

Bierut, M. (1994). *Looking closer: Critical writings on graphic design*. New York, NY: Allworth Press.

Boylston, S. (2009). *Designing sustainable packaging*. London: Laurence King.

Brown, P., & Schmidt, J. (2014). Living in the Anthropocene: Business as usual, or compassionate retreat? In R. Orr (Ed.), *State of the world: Governing for sustainability* (pp. 63–71). Washington, DC: Island Press.

Bucci, D. Z., & Forcellini, F. A. (2007). Sustainable packaging design model. In G. Loureiro & R. Curran (Eds.), *Complex systems concurrent engineering: Collaboration, technology, innovation, and sustainability* (pp. 363–370). London: Springer-Verlag.

Buell, L. (2005). *The future of environmental criticism: Environmental crisis and literary imagination*. Malden, MA: Blackwell.

Carnegie Classification of Institutions of Higher Education. (2017). *Institution Lookup*. Retrieved from http://carnegieclassifications.iu.edu/lookup/lookup.php.

Carr, E. (2009). Applying LEED principles to graphic design. *AIGA Center for Sustainable Design*, 10/1.

Carroll, J. (2012). Foreward. In K. Verghese, H. Lewis, & L. Fitzpatrick (Eds.), *Packaging for sustainability* (pp. v–vi). London: Springer.

Carson, D., & Blackwell, L. (1996). *The end of print: The graphic design of David Carson*. San Francisco, CA: Chronicle Books.

Celery Design Collaborative. (2015). Retrieved from http://www.celerydesign.com/eco-tools.

Chan, J. (2016, June). *Afterthought to precondition re-engaging design ethics from Technology Sustainability and Responsibility*. 2016 Design Research Society Conference. Brighton, UK.

Chiapponi, M. (1998). Environmental design and industrial design: Integrating knowledge around urgent issues. *Design Issues, 14*(3), 74–84.

Chick, A., & Micklethwaite, P. (2011). *Design for sustainable change: How design and designers can drive the sustainability agenda*. New York, NY: Bloomsbury Academic.

Chick, A. (2012). Design for social innovation: Emerging principles and approaches. *Iridescent, 2*(1), 52–64.

Communication Arts. (2016). 57/1.

Cook, N. (2008). Design and responsibility: The interdependence of natural, artificial, and human systems. In *Philosophy and design: From engineering to architecture* (pp. 259–269). Dordrecht, NL: Springer.

Cezzar, J. (2015). *What is graphic design?* AIGA. Retrieved from http://www.aiga.org/guide-whatisgraphicdesign.

Chafetz, J. S., Lorence, J., & Larosa, C. (1993). Gender depictions of the professionally employed: A content analysis of trade publications, 1960–1990. *Sociological Perspectives, 36*(1), 63–82.

Coffey, A. (2013). Analyzing documents. In U. Flick (Ed.), *The Sage handbook of qualitative data analysis* (pp. 367–379). Thousand Oaks, CA: Sage.

Cramsie, P. (2010). *The story of graphic design: From the invention of writing to the birth of digital design*. New York: Abrams.

Crawford, T. (2005). The graphic design business book. New York: Allworth Press.

Davis, M. (2012). *Graphic design theory*. New York: Thames & Hudson Inc.

Dresner, S. (2002). *The principles of sustainability*. Abingdon, Oxon: Routledge.

Dritz, A. (2014). *Closing the sustainability gap: The emerging role of sustainable graphic designer* (Master thesis Minneapolis College of Art and Design). Retrieved from http://amydritz.prosite.com/.

Dominic, C. A. S., Östlund, S., Buffington, J., & Masoud, M. M. (2015). Towards a conceptual sustainable packaging development model: A corrugated box case study packaging technology and science. *Packaging Technology and Science, 28*, 397–413.

Dougherty, B. (2008). *Green graphic design*. New York, NY: Allworth Press.

Edwards, A. (2005). *The sustainability revolution—Portrait of a paradigm shift*. Gabriola, BC, Canada: New Society Publishers.

Elkington, J. (1998). *Cannibals with forks: The triple bottom line of 21st-century business*. Gabriola Island, BC, Canada: New Society Publishers.

Ensure sustainable consumption and production patterns. Retrieved from http://www.un.org/sustainabledevelopment/sustainable-consumption-production/.

Eskilson, S. (2012). *Graphic design: A new history*. New Haven, CT: Tale University Press.

Esslinger, H. (2012). *Design forward: Creative strategies for sustainable change*. Stuttgart, Germany: Arnoldsche Verlagsanstalt.

Field, C. B., & Intergovernmental Panel on Climate Change. Working Group II. (2014). *Climate change 2014: Impacts, adaptation, and vulnerability*. Cambridge, UK: Cambridge University Press.

Findeli, A. (2001). Rethinking design education for the 21st century: Theoretical, methodological, and ethical discussion. *Design Issues, 17*(1), 5–17.

Findeli, A. (1994). Ethics, aesthetics, and design. *Design Issues, 10*(2), 49–68.

Fine, P. C. (2016). *Sustainable graphic design: Principles and practices*. New York, NY: Bloomsbury Academic.

Fisher, T. (2010). *Designing for re-use: The Life of consumer packaging*. London, UK: Earthscan.

Florman, S. (1987). *The civilized engineer* (1st ed.). New York, NY: St. Martin's Press.

Frascara, J. (2004). *Communication design—Principles, methods, and practice*. New York, NY: Allworth Press.

Frascara, J. (2006). Graphic design: Fine art or social science? In A. Bennett (Ed.), *Design studies: Theory and research in graphic design*. New York, NY: Princeton Architectural Press.

Fry, T. (2009). *Design futuring: Sustainability, ethics, and new practice*. New York, NY: Berg.

Fuad-Luke, A. (2009). *Design activism: Beautiful strangeness for a sustainable world*. London: Earthscan.

Gavos, R. (2012). *The sustainable design office: LEED-type certification* (Master thesis Texas A&M University-Commerce).

Garland, K. (1964). *First things first: A Manifesto*. London, UK: Goodwin Press Ltd.

Garland, K. (1966). *Graphics handbook*. New York, NY: Studio Vista.

Gibboney, R. K. (2013). *Community as client: Defining social design as a means of designing for good*.

Glaser, M. (2002). The Road to Hell. *Metropolis*.

Gomez-Palacio, B. (2009). *Graphic design, referenced: A visual guide to the language, applications, and history of graphic design*. Beverly, MA: Rockport Publishers.

Gowdy, J. (2014). Governance, sustainability, and evolution. In R. Orr (Ed.), *State of the world: Governing for sustainability* (pp. 31–39). Washington, DC: Island Press.

Greenwood, J. (1994). Action research and action researchers: Some introductory considerations. *Contemporary Nurse*, 3(2), 84–91.

Groth, C. (2006). *Exploring packaging design*. Clifton Park, NY: Thomson Delmar Learning.

Hawken, P., Lovins, A. B., & Lovins, L. H. (1999). *Natural capitalism: Creating the next industrial revolution*. Boston, MA: Little, Brown and Co.

Heller, S., & Vienne, V. (2003). *Citizen designer: Perspectives on design responsibility*. New York, NY: Allworth Press.

Heller, S., & Ilić, M. (2012). *Stop think go, do: How typography & graphic design influence behavior*. Beverly, MA: Rockport Publishers.

Heller, S. (2014). *Design literacy: Understanding graphic design*. New York, NY: Allworth Press.

Jedlička, W. (2009). *Sustainable graphic design: Tools, systems and strategies for innovative print design*. Hoboken, NJ: Wiley.

Jedlička, W., Amel, E., & Baumeister, D. (2009). *Packaging sustainability: Tools, systems, and strategies for innovative package design*. Hoboken, NJ: Wiley.

Jobling, P. (2003). Lavin, Maud. Clean new world: Culture, politics and graphic design (MIT Press, 2001). *Journal of Design History, 16*(3), 260–262.

Johnson, A. (2014). *Packaging for sustainability*. Hoboken, NJ: Wiley-Blackwell.

Kadas, S., & Britten, B. (2017). *Exploring the concept of sustainability within the GD USA magazine*. Unpublished manuscript.

Kiron, D., Unruh, G., Reeves, M., Kruschwitz, N., Rubel, H., & ZumFelde, A. M. (2017). Corporate sustainability at a crossroads. *MIT Sloan Management Review, 58*(4).

Klöpffer, W., & Grahl, B. (2014). *Life cycle assessment: A guide to best practice*. Hoboken, NJ: Wiley.

Laszlo, C. (2003). *The sustainable company: How to create lasting value through social and environmental performance*. Chicago, IL: Shearwater Books.

Laszlo, C. (2008). *Sustainable values: How the world's leading companies are doing well by doing good*. Stanford, CA: Stanford Business Books.

Lavin, M. (2001). *Clean new world—Culture, politics, and graphic design*. Cambridge, MA: MIT Press.

Lee, G. (2002). *Selling the internet: An analysis of advertisements for the internet and related products in "Time" magazine, 1995–2000* (Doctoral dissertation). Retrieved from ProQuest. http://search.proquest.com/docview/305508516?accountid=2837.

Lupton, E., & Phillips, J. (2008). *Graphic design: The new basics*. Baltimore, NY: Princeton Architectural Press.

MacIntyre, A. J. (2003). *The power of institutions: Political architecture and governance*. Ithaca, NY: Cornell University Press.

Madge, P. (1993). Design, ecology, technology: A historiographical review. *Journal of Design History, 6*(3), 149–166.

Madge, P. (1997). Ecological design: A new critique. *Design Issues, 13*(2), 44–54.

Maniates, M. (2010). Editing out unsustainable behavior. In L. Starke & Mastny (Eds.), *State of the world: Transforming cultures from consumerism to sustainability* (pp. 119–126). New York, NY: W. W. Norton.

Manion, M. A. (2010). *The Wiley encyclopedia of packaging technology*. Middletown, CT: American Library Association.

Manzini, E. (1992). Prometheus of the everyday: The Ecology of the artificial and the designers' responsibility. *Design Issues, 9*(1), 5–20.

Manzini, E. (1994). Design, environment and social quality: from "existenzminimum" to "quality maximum". *Design Issues, 10*(1), 37–43.

Manzini, E. (2003). Hong Kong as "laboratory of the future". *Design Issues, 19*(3), 59–70.

Manzini, E. (2014). Making things happen: Social innovation and design. *Design Issues, 30*(1), 57–66.

Margolin, V. (1998). Design for a sustainable world. *Design Issues, 14*(2), 83–92.

May, T. (2011). Documentary research: Excavation and evidence. In *Social research: Issues, methods and process* (pp. 191–218). Maidenhead, UK: McGraw-Hill Education.

McDonough, W., & Braungart, M. (2002). *Cradle to cradle: Remaking the way we make things* (1st ed.). New York, NY: North Point Press.

McGee, T., & Baumeister, D. (2009). Biomimicry. In W. Jedlička (Ed.), *Packaging sustainability: Tools, systems, and strategies for innovative package design* (pp. 158–223). Hoboken, NJ: Wiley.

McLuhan, M. (1964). *Understanding media: The extensions of man*. New York, NY: McGraw-Hill.

McLuhan, M., & Fiore, Q. (1967). *The medium is the massage*. New York: Bantam Books.

McNamara, C. (2009). System thinking. In W. Jedlička (Ed.), *Packaging sustainability: Tools, systems, and strategies for innovative package design* (pp. 133–140). Hoboken, NJ: Wiley.

Meggs, P. B. (1998). *A history of graphic design* (3rd ed.). New York, NY: Wiley.

Meyer, J. M. (2015). *Engaging the everyday: Environmental social criticism and the resonance dilemma*. Cambridge, MA: MIT Press.

Micklethwaite, P., & Chick, A. (2005). Remarkable Pencils Ltd: Breaking out of the green niche. *Design Management Review, 16*, 23–28.

MIT Sloan Management Review and Boston Consulting Group. (2012). Environment; nearly a third of companies say sustainability is contributing to their profits, says MIT sloan management review-Boston consulting group report. *Business & Finance Week*, 798.

Mitchell, W. J. T. (2002). Showing seeing: A critique of visual culture. *Journal of Visual Culture, 1*(2), 165–181.

Mitchell, W. J. T. (2005). *What do pictures want: The lives and loves of images?* Chicago, IL: University of Chicago Press.

Molleda, J. C., & Laskin, A. V. (2005). *Global, international, comparative and regional public relations knowledge from 1990 to 2005: A quantitative content analysis of academic and trade publications*.

Morton, T. (2007). *Ecology without nature: Rethinking environmental aesthetics*. Cambridge: Harvard University Press.

NASAD Handbook. (2018). *NASAD*. Retrieved from https://nasad.arts-accredit.org/accreditation/standards-guidelines/handbook/.

Nederhof, A. J., & Meijer, R. F. (1995). Development of bibliometric indicators for utility of research to users in society: Measurement of external knowledge transfer via publications in trade journals. *Scientometrics, 32*(1), 37–48.

Nordin, N., & Selke, S. (2010). Social aspect of sustainable packaging. *Packaging Technology and Science, 23*, 317–326.

Northwest Product Stewardship Council (NWPSC). (2015). *The problem: Volume, waste, cost, design*. Retrieved from http://productstewardship.net/products/packaging.

O2 International Network for Sustainable Design. (2015). Retrieved from http://www.o2.org/.

Oki, Y., & Sasaki, H. (2000). Social and environmental impacts of packaging (LCA and assessment of packaging functions). *Packaging Technology and Science, 13*, 45–53.
Orr, D. W. (2002). *The nature of design: Ecology, culture, and human intention*. New York, NY: Oxford University Press.
Oxford English Dictionary (OED). (2017). Retrieved from https://en.oxforddictionaries.com/definition/us/sustainability.
Pantzar, M. (1997). Domestication of everyday life technology: Dynamic views on the social histories of artifacts. *Design Issues, 13*(3), 52–65.
Pantzar, M. (2000). Consumption as work, play, and art: Representation of the consumer in future scenarios. *Design Issues, 16*(3), 3–18.
Perkins, S. (2006). *Ethics and social responsibility*. The Professional Association for Design Retrieved from www.aiga.org/ethics-and-social-responsibility/.
Poynor, R. (1999). The first things first revisited. *Émigré, 51*.
Renner, M., & Prugh, T. (2014). Failing governance, unsustainable planet. In R. Orr (Ed.), *State of the world: Governing for sustainability* (pp. 3–20).Washington, DC: Island Press.
Re-nourish. (2015). Retrieved from http://www.re-nourish.com/?l=home.
"Responsible Design". (2016, October). *Graphic Design USA, 4*, 28–47.
Resnick, E. (2016). *Developing citizen designers*. New York, NY: Bloomsbury Academic.
Robertson, M. (2014). *Sustainability principles and practice*. Abingdon, Oxon: Routledge.
Rowledge, L. R., Barton, R. S., & Brady, K. S. (1999). *Mapping the journey: Case studies in strategy and action toward sustainable development*. Sheffield: Greenleaf.
Russ, T. H. (2010). *Sustainability and design ethics*. Boca Raton, FL: CRC Press, Taylor & Francis Group.
Scalin, N. (2012).*The design activist's handbook—How to change the world (or at least your part of it) with socially conscious design*. Cincinnati, OH: How Books.
Scalin, N. (2017). Foreward. In *Design to renourish—Sustainable graphic design in practice* (pp. vii–viii). Boca Raton, FL: CRC Press, Taylor & Francis Group.
Selke, S. (1994). *Packaging and the environment*. Lancaster, PA: Techonomic Publishing Company, Inc.
Shaughnessy, A. (2005). *How to be a graphic designer, without losing your soul*. New York, NY: Princeton Architectural Press.
Shea, A. (2012). *Designing for social change: Strategies for community-based graphic design* (1st ed.). New York, NY: Princeton Architectural Press.
Sherin, A. (2008). *SustainAble: A handbook of materials and applications for graphic designers and their clients*. Beverly, MA: Rockport Publishers.

Sherin, A. (2013). *Sustainable thinking: Ethical approaches to design and design management*. New York, NY: Bloomsbury Academic.

Simmons, C. (2011). *Just design—Socially conscious design for critical causes*. Cincinnati, OH: How Books.

Singer, P. (2002). *One world: The ethics of globalism*. New Haven, MA: Yale University Press.

Sustainable Packaging Coalition® (SPC). (2015). Retrieved from http://www.sustainablepackaging.org/.

"Sustainable Design Dictionary". (2017). Retrieved from http://www.aiga.org/sustainable-design-dictionary/.

Szenasy, S. S. (2012). Reflections on sustainable design. *Journal of Interior Design, 37*(7), 10.

"The Copenhagen Letter". (2017). Retrieved from https://copenhagenletter.org/.

Tolstoy, L. (1995). *What is art?* London, UK: Penguin Books.

Triggs, T. (2002). Review of *Clean New World: Culture, Politics and, Graphic Design. Design Issues* , *18*(3), 93–95. Retrieved from http://www.jstor.org/stable/1512071.

Triggs, T. (2009). Designing graphic design history. *Journal of Design History, 22*(4), 325–340.

Triggs, T. (2010). Graphic design history: Past, present, and future. *Design Issues, 27*(1), 3–6.

United Nations Environment Programme (UNEP). (2015). *Global partnership on waste management*. Retrieved from http://www.unep.org/gpwm/Background/tabid/56401/Default.aspx.

United Nations Framework Convention on Climate Change. (2016). Retrieved from www.unfccc.com.

United Nations World Commission. (1987). *Our common future*. Retrieved from http://www.un-documents.net/our-common-future.pdf.

United States Department of Labor. (2018). "Graphic Design," *Occupational Outlook Handbook*. U.S. Bureau of Labor Statistics. Retrieved from https://www.bls.gov/ooh/arts-and-design/graphic-designers.htm#tab-1.

United States Environmental Protection Agency (EPA). (2015). Retrieved from http://www.epa.gov.

United States Environmental Protection Agency (EPA). (2016). *Advancing sustainable materials management: 2014 fact sheet*. Retrieved from http://www.epa.gov.

Verghese, K., Lewis, H., & Fitzpatrick, L. (2012). *Packaging for sustainability*. London, UK: Springer.

Vermaas, P. (2008). *Philosophy and design: From engineering to architecture*. Dordrecht, NL: Springer.

Walker, S., & Giard, J. (2013). *The handbook of design for sustainability*. New York, NY: Bloomsbury Academic.

Micro and Macro Consequences of Debt and the Possibility of Forgiveness

Can Household Debt Cause a Financial Crisis?

Joëlle Leclaire

Financial crises are caused by a run up of bad business debt. The devaluation of this bad debt causes bank/financial institution losses or failures which has a contagion effect across the financial sector. Even in the case of international financial crises, bad business debt run up is at least partly the culprit. Problems of currency inconvertibility either cause a crisis or add fuel to the fire. Business debt is incurred to undertake investment, to cover payroll, to cover regular working capital expenses, to pay interest and/or dividends, or, to buy-back publicly traded shares and makes a public company private.

As Minsky explained, as the economy grows, businesses will take on greater levels of debt to cover riskier positions. When the prevalence of Ponzi firms (firms indebting themselves to pay interest on their existing debt) is high enough, the economy will fall into a financial crisis (Minsky 1992, 6). About thirty years ago, households started increasing their use of debt to cover consumption and mortgage expenses. This movement was led by banks/financial institutions having better access to consistent

J. Leclaire (✉)
College at Buffalo, State University of New York, Buffalo, NY, USA
e-mail: leclaijj@buffalostate.edu

B. C. Wilson, *Care, Climate, and Debt*,
https://doi.org/10.1007/978-3-030-96355-2_7

borrower information, changes in legislation creating secondary markets for household debt, stagnating wages and salaries, and, changing feelings about debt by households. The question we now ask ourselves is whether greater levels of household debt can also have the effect of causing a financial crisis. If they can, how do they cause a financial crisis?

The purpose of this chapter to bring forward the main ways in which household debt matters to financial stability. We will use four frameworks to study the role of household debt in economic and financial stability. These include first is the American Post Keynesian approach, the Cambridge post-Keynesian school, the Theory of the Monetary Circuit approach (TMC), and Modern Monetary Theory (MMT). What we find is that together these analytical frameworks help us see that household debt can cause financial crises via five main channels and their interrelationships. The four primary channels are (1) reductions in consumption, (2) increased leverage of financial institutions, (3) declines in the rate of return on mortgage and other debt held by banks and other financial institutions, (3) reductions of the rate of return on the production of goods and services, and job creation, and, (4) a decline in the overall well-being of households. How do we effectively stop household debt from threatening financial stability? We will discuss how public policy can address the reasons why households incur growing levels of debt and how dealing with those reasons will make greater financial stability possible.

Four Approaches to Household Debt's Role in Financial Crisis

Four schools of thought deal with the relationship between household debt and financial crisis. These are the American Post Keynesian approach, the Cambridge post-Keynesian school, the Theory of the Monetary Circuit (TMC) school, and, Modern Monetary Theory (MMT). Each of these schools provide a model for explaining the connection between households, their debt, and the financial well-being of the system as a whole. No single school seems to capture all the elements that need to be considered to fully understand the issue, but together, these hit the top targets. The American Post Keynesian framework places emphasis on stable positions between the financial sector balances, institutional factors including legislation and securitization, normative factors such as households feeling better about increasing debt, and, income inequality pushing households to increase debt. The Cambridge post-Keynesian school highlights the importance of a steady connection between wages and profits, between investment and the rate of growth of output, debt and income transfer, and, crisis caused by uneven investment in future relative to current output. The Theory of the Monetary Circuit (TMC) expresses the need for bank loans for be repaid after the wage bill and working capital is covered, the link between more financialization and higher levels of liquidity preference, and, how liquidity preference can cause financial crisis. Finally, Modern Monetary Theory (MMT) shows that liquidity preference can be offset by government spending, develops links to the other schools, and explains how government spending, taxes, and bonds interact to create moving equilibrium states that can secure financial stability for the household and potentially also for the system as a whole.

Causes of Financial Crisis: American Post Keynesian Approach

Some of the best features of the American Post Keynesian school are its' reliance on the financial sector balances, institutions, norms, and income inequality to explain financial stability. It provides clarity and connection between what we see happening all around us in the real world and what is going on in finance. Figure 1 shows us the increase in household debt.

It's clear from the chart that household debt has increased at greater amplitude starting about 30–35 years ago. The trend reversed for a short time in 2008 due to the financial crisis of that year, and then continued on course from 2013 on. What we are trying to understand is how this increase in household debt may be increasing systemic financial fragility. Does it pose a new problem that we need to address to make sure the financial system stays strong and resilient in the service of households, job creation, and well-being?

This massive run up of household debt is hidden in a model used by American Post Keynesians called the Financial Sector Balances. In the Financial Sector Balances model, we see the financial side of the economy divided into its three main components: the private sector, the government, and the external sector. Each sector is expressed as "net assets" which means the model shows total assets minus total liabilities for each sector individually. In finance each existing liability is associated with an asset so net assets for each sector net out between one another for all sectors. For example, if the external sector equals zero, then private

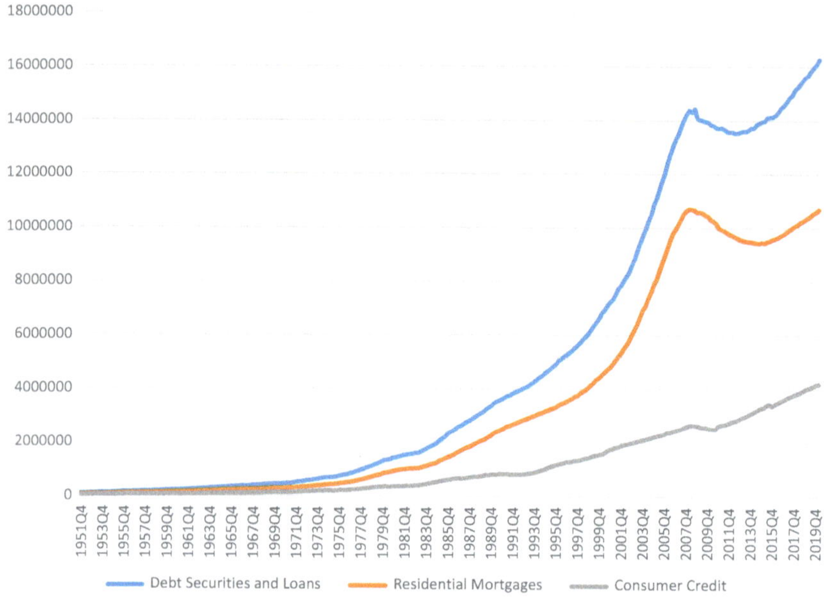

Fig. 1 Outstanding household debt 1951Q1–2020Q1 (millions of dollars, seasonally adjusted) (*Source* Federal Reserve 2020, Table D3: Debt Outstanding by Sector, retrieved 6/13/20 and author's calculations)

sector net assets are perfectly matched by government sector net liabilities. Conversely, if the external sector equals zero again (for simplicity), then private sector net liabilities equal government sector net assets. The sum of all the sectors together (the private, government, and external sectors) must equal zero. That is not a choice, or a desired hypothetical option, but a real-world accounting fact. Figure 2 shows how this looks when it is expressed as a chart.

Looking at this chart you see right away that the government has a net liability position which is offset by net assets in the private and/or external sectors. This is the case for most of the last 60 years in the US, with one exception (1998–2001) (cf. Leclaire 2008 for a discussion of why this exception occurred). American Post Keynesians use this model to show that if government net deficit spending is reduced, then this must be offset by a reduction in net assets in the private sector and/or the external sector. It shows that the financial system adjusts automatically

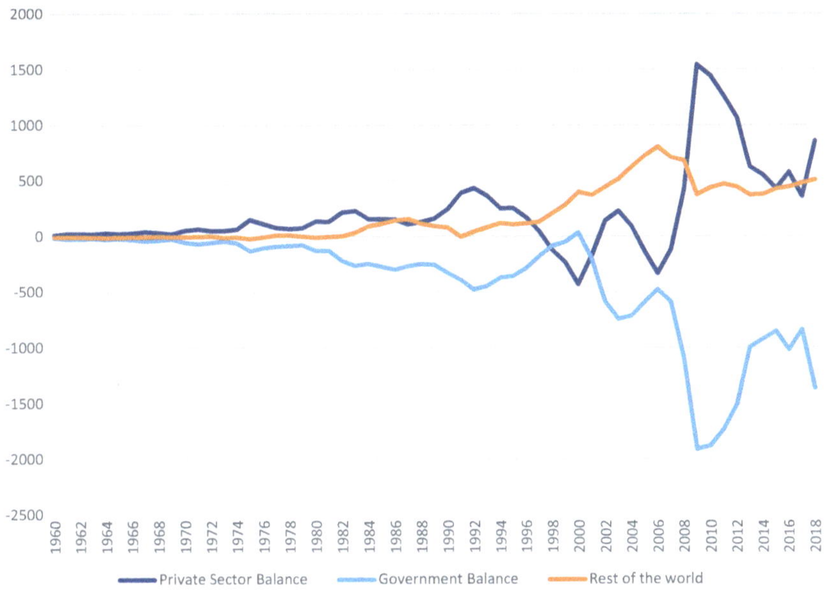

Fig. 2 US financial sector balances 1960–2018 (billions of USD, seasonally adjusted) (*Source* BEA 2020a. Table S.2.q. and author's calculations 6/13/2020)

for changes in net assets/liabilities in all sectors and between the three sectors. Whether changes in positions are deliberate policy choices, such as unfortunate deficit reduction bills passed by Congress, or the result of general economic growth, such as the expansion leading up 2020, financial sector values adjust automatically to maintain a zero balance for all three sectors.

How is household debt a part of this model and how can the model explain whether growing household debt will create a financial crisis?

The household is part of the private sector balance. This sector contains the net assets/liabilities of all households and businesses. The following chart splits up the net balance of the household and business for the last 60 years.

Figure 3 clarifies that typically households have net assets and businesses have net liabilities. There have been some changes in that position, the most obvious one being in 2002–2015, with many states occurring

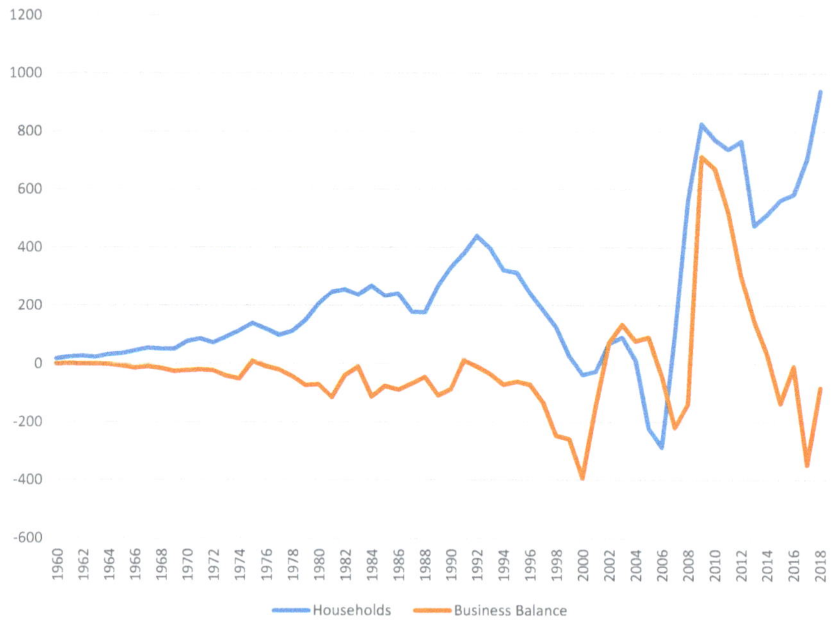

Fig. 3 US household and business sector balances 1960–2018 (billions of dollars, seasonally adjusted) (*Source* BEA 2020a. Table S.2.q. and author's calculations 6/13/2020)

in that interim period. From 2002 to 2004, and 2009–2015 both households and businesses had net assets. From 2004 to 2007, both had net liabilities. It would be interesting to tease out the reasons why these different situations happened, but our main goal is to see how household debt could cause a systemic financial problem. In this pursuit, we note that the household in this chart is net assets/liabilities. It is the sum of household assets minus household debt. Therefore, as household debt increases, it will affect the overall financial system via its effect on the household position which could increase or decrease when household debt increases. For example, household debt may increase as a household uses a mortgage to purchase a new house, but the value of the house also increases household assets so it's not clear whether an increase in household debt increases or decreases household net assets for the sector as a whole. Net household assets have skyrocketed since 2007, so the value of assets far exceeds the value of debt for all households taken together.

What we really do not want to see is households having a net liability position. Plus, if the private sector balance were negative (a net liability position), it would mean that households and/or businesses were supporting larger government surpluses and/or external surpluses. This is a very precarious and unsustainable position which directly results in financial crisis. Right now, even though household debt is skyrocketing, the value of household assets is still greater and is offset mainly by government deficits. We are living a very sustainable position, at the moment, from a macro-financial perspective. However, this macro position depends on underlying groups acting within existing institutions. As soon as those institutions and/or actions change, then so does the macro result we see.

Institutional Factors: Legislation and Securitization

Are there any risky institutional changes or actions that could threaten the stability we are experiencing at the macro-financial level? American Post Keynesians say yes and point to legislative changes and the rise of securitization as very disruptive developments. Significant legislative changes include the Tax Reform Act of 1986, a 1992 Securities and Exchange Commission (SEC) administrative ruling on Special Purpose Vehicles (SPVs), the Gramm-Leach Bliley Act of 1999, and, current legislation on real estate and its depreciation. Increased securitization of home mortgages has also increased financial instability. All of the legislative changes and the resulting rise in securitization deal with the major vehicle of household debt; mortgages and home equity lines of credit. Because more household debt (and its securitization) increases the leverage of financial institutions making up the financial structure, financial instability is increased.

Three big changes in legislation, in concert with existing real estate legislation form the background for financial instability that led to the 2008 financial crisis and threatens our current systemic stability. The first of these is the Tax Reform Act of 1986. By removing the tax deductibility of interest payments with the exception of mortgage interest, the 1986 act provided incentive for households to hold any debt in the form mortgage or home equity lines of credit (HELC) (Cynamon and Fazzari 2013, 144; Barba and Pivetti 2009, 115). Pushing household debt away from higher interest forms of revolving and non-revolving debt into lower interest mortgage and HELC debt allowed households to increase debt levels for a given interest payment (Barba and Pivetti 2009, 115). Figure 1 shows this movement very clearly starting in 1986.

The second and third legislatives changes that brought about greater systemic instability were a 1992 administrative ruling regarding SPVs, and the Gramm-Lech Bliley Act of 1999. You can even see the impact of these changes on the slope of residential mortgages in Fig. 1! In 1992, an administrative ruling by the Securities and Exchange Commission, Rule 3a-7, made SPVs distinct from investment companies. They do not need to follow the same rules and are not subject to the same scrutiny as investment companies, even though they act in the same way (Kregel 2013, 92; Federal Register, 2020). This made holdings of mortgage bundles in SPVs more profitable than holding them on bank balance sheets. Banks sell bundled mortgages to SPVs in exchange for cash. SPVs hold the mortgage bundles as assets and sells obligations to investment firms that manage retirement and/or financial wealth portfolios. These obligations are called Collateralized Mortgage Obligations (CMOs) and their return depends on the return to the underlying mortgages, which in turn rely on the household making payment on their mortgage. Household mortgage debt becomes **many times** more profitable when it is handled in this way! Not only do banks make money, but so do the SPVs, the financial investment firm, and the households who ultimately hold the CMO in their retirement/and/or financial wealth portfolio (Wray 2013, 79). It is easy to see that this is also quite problematic if households fail to be able to make mortgage payments. The whole Jenga tower could fall as it did in 2007–2008.

The Gramm-Leach-Bliley Act of 1999 rescinded protections that had been put into place in 1936 by the Glass-Steagall Act as a response to the Great Depression. These protections stopped commercial banks from engaging in investment bank behavior because legislators believed that those actions were an important factor in causing the Great Depression. Legislators in 1999 believed that this law was antiquated. They removed the restriction, and the economy grew as commercial banks essentially created securities out of home mortgages (via SPVs) and used the proceeds from the sale of those securities to invest in the stock market. Through the creation of SPVs commercial banks use customer deposits to leverage stock market investments, something that had been reserved for investment banks only. This adds a great deal of potential instability to our financial system! Household mortgage debt is a prime vehicle for three or four layers of financial growth. When household debt falls, then so will the value associated with the other layers that depend on it.

Normative Factors: Households Increase Debt

From the household perspective, there are a number of reasons why increasing debt became more appealing. Household saw "normal" consumption levels grow, they noticed that people increased debt and suffered no deleterious consequences, and mortgage refinancing was more often used to increase available money for consumption. It seems cliché to think that media advertising, product placement, and what your friends have should influence household consumption today, given our cynical nature, but it they do. Households make consumption decisions by looking at their social reference group, as well as real, virtual, and media-based patterns (Cynamon and Fazzari 2013, 139, 145). Since the late 1970s, despite stagnant wages and greater socio-economic inequality, the "normal" amount of consumption was growing. In order to reach these higher levels of consumption, when wages were not growing, households increased debt starting in the mid-1980s (Cynamon and Fazzari 2013, 133, 143; Wray 2013, 69). Consumption grew for all quintiles, even though only the top income quintiles experienced increased income to finance that new consumption. Lower income quintiles financed growing consumption with debt (Cynamon and Fazzari 2013, 129; Wray 2013, 82). These households were encouraged by others increasing debt to finance consumption and seemingly not having any problems. By 2000, it became "normal" to increase consumption to what could be financed by mortgage debt in particular (Wray 2013, 69; Drechsel-Grau and Schmid 2013, 7). In 2020, we also see mortgage refinancing as a vehicle to increasing household consumption.

Cambridge Post-Keynesian School

Cambridge post-Keynesians look at the ratio of profits of wages to determine economic and financial stability. Specifically, in the 1950s, it was determined that real wages needed to grow in line with productivity in order for employment to remain constant and growth to be sustainable (Kaldor 1955–1956, 83). This state of affairs, where real wages grow in tandem with productivity, and employment and growth are stable as a result, is called the "golden rule" (Hein and Truger 2017, 422–423; Setterfield 2013, 160–162; Barba and Pivetti 2009, 122–124; Hudson 2012, 185; Kaldor 1955–1956, 83). In 2013, Setterfield indicated that the gap between real wages and productivity that had been violating the golden rule since the late 1970s was being filled by household debt. This prevented the economy from immediately experiencing a crisis in employment and growth, but it put us with an unsustainable growth path (Setterfield 2013, 160–162, 169).

Whenever real wages fall short of increases in productivity, unemployment grows. It grows because in real terms, workers cannot purchase the proceeds of production on their real wages. Part of their production is redirected toward capitalists who it is assumed do not consume. Another way of looking at it is that aggregate demand for the products fall when real wages fall. In reality, in the US and most developed countries, we have falling real wages since the 1970s. Real wages have fallen because productivity gains have not been incorporated into higher real wages. Usually, unions fight for many worker protections, and they also fight for real wage increase as workers produce more output. However, union busting legislation and a decline in the rate of unionization (because people did not think unions were helpful), have resulted in lower living standards for most workers in the US and across the developed world. As real wage income fell, household debt increased to fill the demand gap. Workers used debt to continue to increase their consumption so aggregate demand for products grow in line with productivity and prevent, for the most part, higher levels of unemployment and economic and financial crisis (Setterfield 2013, 169; Barba and Pivetti 2009, 126–128; Lavoie and Stockhammer 2013, 3–4). Figure 4 show the profit to wage share for the US 1947Q1 to 2020Q1. It's clear that the ratio of profits to wages grew in the early 1970 and has now reached unprecedented levels, now almost 50%. This means that profits and wages share about equal proportions of the total real output. The problem with that of course if that there are much fewer owners of profits than there are wage earners so income inequality is currently quite severe. Growing household debt here conceals serious economic inequality and delays economic and financial crisis.

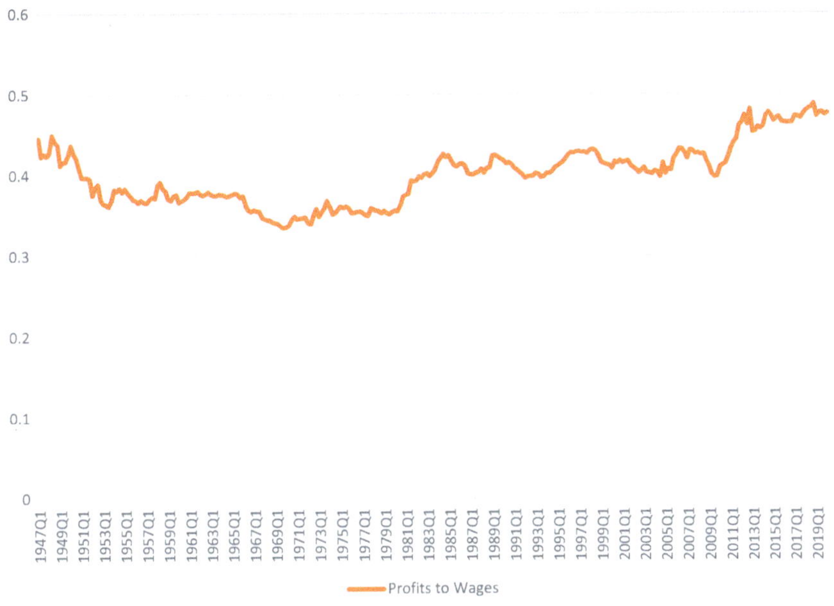

Fig. 4 US profit share to wage share 1947Q1 to 2020Q1 (*Source* BEA 2020b, Table 2.1 and author's calculations)

Investment and the Rate of Growth of Output and Debt and Income Transfer

Firm investment depends on achieving a rate of return. When households refrain from consumption in order to make their interest and/or debt payments, then firms don't sell as much of their output as they expected. This reduces the rate of return on investment in producing real goods and services. When households spend less on consumption goods because they have to pay higher debt service payments, and if they eventually also spend less on consumption goods because their income is not growing in line with the products they produce, then we can see right away that if household consumption were ever to need to be limited to income, or income less debt payments, that the rate of return on consumption goods and services would be radically lowered. It is currently lowered by the debt service payment but because debt is used to make up the deficient income, firms still capture a large art of their pre-household debt returns.

If household debt becomes unsustainable, then the returns to firms would fall by both the income gap (now filled by debt), the debt service payment (interest on debt), and even potentially the household debt payment. The returns to production would fall but the returns to holding debt could increase for a while then fall if households default on their debt because they cannot find employment and/or sell assets to make payment (cf. Setterfield 2013, 172; Kaldor 1955–1956, 97–99; Palley 1994 372; Barba and Pivetti 2009, 128). Firms that produced goods and services could suffer at the hands of firms that sold debt, but this income transfer would be temporary, overshadowed by the household's inability to find employment eventually.

Crisis caused by uneven investment in future relative to current output.

Kaldor, a major economist of the Cambridge tradition expressed the concern that if firms invested too much in future rather than current production, that this could lead to an effective demand crisis. In this context, if productive firms invest too much in other sectors like the FIRE sectors (Finance, Insurance, Real Estate), then they effectively reduce the production of goods and services now (Hudson 2012, 461; Wray 2013, 82). Fewer workers are needed to produce this lower level of goods and services and thus employment effectively falls (Kaldor 1955–1956, 97–99). The redirection of investment away from current production and toward future output, or other non-productive sectors can lead to a breakdown of the investment process that creates unemployment and lower rates of return. Increased household debt redirects household income toward debt service and/or debt payment which are non-productive industries. This movement reduces the rate of return to productive investment.

Circuit Approach

The circuit approach considers the economy and financial systems as an integrated whole. The circuit operates as follows. Firms incur bank debt in order to produce. They use bank loans to pay wages and working capital. Worker households return the wage bill to firms as they buy products. If a household saves, they also return the wage bill to financial firms, buying financial assets. As firms receive the proceeds of production or of the sale of financial assets, they can use them to pay off their loans with the banks. In this context, financial crisis happens when households decide to save in the form of cash, rather than buying financial assets. This prevents firms from recapturing the wage bill in its entirety, thus loans cannot be repaid and banks incur losses. Household debt both allows greater levels of consumption and/or purchases of financial assets so it temporarily increases the flow to firms and their capacity to repay bank loans (cf. Seccareccia 2013, 283). However, as more money is hoarded as cash, the return to production and employment falls, as does the return to financial firms. Household debt then leads to a reduction in the rate of return to production, employment, and, possibly even finance eventually as liquidity preference rises.

Bank Loans and the Wage Bill

In the Theory of the Monetary Circuit (TMC), the wage bill gets spent on all the other components of income. Income in all sectors originally comes from the wage bill which is borrowed from the bank (Lavoie 2014, 269–270; Seccareccia 2013, 280–281; Wray 1993, 547–550; Graziani 1989, 4–55; Rossi 2006, 124; Leclaire 2019). Figure 5 is a physical representation of the circuit in time using actual US data. It shows the various expenditure categories of employee income. These include taxes, nonfinancial income, financial income, rest of world, and saving.

As shown in the Fig. 5, financial expenditures outstrip spending in the nonfinancial sector. Employee Saving is the largest (and growing) category. From the circuit perspective, employee saving is the offset of firm profits (Graziani 1989, 7; Seccareccia 2013, 281; Lavoie 2014, 269–270; Wray 1993, 550; Leclaire 2019). One can look at employee saving as the total flow of profit, which is growing as depicted. For the circuit to close, all bank loans must be repaid and this include profits and household saving. If profit or household saving exist, then not all bank loans have been repaid, and the circuit is not closed (Rossi 2006, 128, 130–131; Graziani 1989, 19; Bellofiore and Passarella 2016, 244; Parguez and Seccareccia 2000, 105; Leclaire 2019). From the depiction above, the circuit never closes because employee saving/profits always exist.

Financialization and Liquidity Preference

Household liquidity preference, which shows up as households wanting to save cash when faced with uncertainty, stops firms from paying off their loans, and this can cause a financial crisis if it becomes widespread enough. Household debt payment reduces the return to nonfinancial firms because

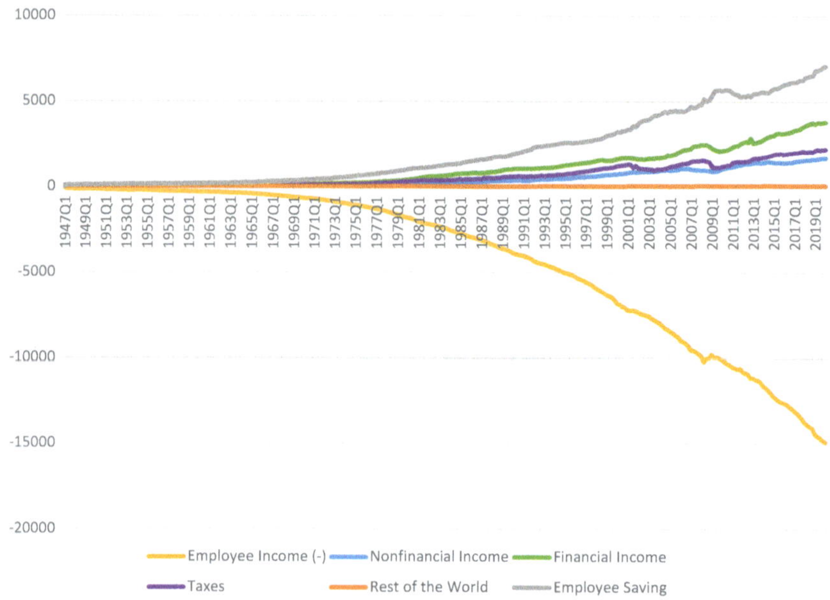

Fig. 5 US Employee Income distributed between Nonfinancial Income, Financial Income, Taxes, the Rest of World, and, Employee Saving 1947Q1 to 2020Q1 (Billions of USD) (*Source* BEA 2020b, Table 2.1 and author's calculations)

instead of buying goods, households pay down debt, and unemployment may increase as a result. The uncertainty can push households to increase their cash hoards, which results in an inability of firms to pay off their loans, eventually leading to financial crisis. Firms are dependent on household debt.

Modern Monetary Theory

Modern Monetary Theory (MMT) offers an alternative way for firms to get the money they need to pay off their loans without relying on varying levels of certainty of households. Net government spending increases the amount of money in the economy and this money can be captured by firms to repay their debts and restart the loan-production cycle again (cf. Wray 1998, Graziani's model as discussed in Bellofiore and Passarella

2016, 245). Government deficit spending works to stabilize the economy from two sides. First, it allows firms to repay bank loans with government money. Second, it can help reduce the liquidity preference of households, stopping them from wanting to hold cash because they fear not being able to pay their bills. The way it does this is by using the government deficit spending to provide goods and services that household commonly require and indebt themselves to buy such as health care, education, childcare, eldercare, and housing. Instead of household debt supporting the profits of firms, net government spending can do so while improving the well-being of households and firms in the process.

Summary: Similarities and Policy Solutions

From what we have seen, household debt can indeed lead to financial crisis through five distinct but interrelated channels. It is due to the combined efforts of four groups of economists that we are able to understand this process from household debt to crisis more clearly and possibly even protect ourselves from future crises. All the traditions express that household debt can increase consumption as households increase debt, but it can also decrease consumption as debt and/or interest payments increase. Thus, household debt affects consumption, and through consumption affects systemic financial stability. The American Post Keynesian school shows us that household debt and its securitization increases the leverage of financial institutions. The same group in concert uses institutional analysis to show that household debt affects the rate of return on mortgages and other debt held by financial institutions. Therefore, its' growth affects systemic financial stability. The Cambridge framework and the Theory of the Monetary Circuit provide an analysis where increased household debt reduces the rate of return on production of goods and services, which can lead to financial crises. Finally, Modern Monetary Theory shows that household debt reduces the well-being of households and that instead of allowing debt to increase, the government should use deficit spending to increase the stability of the household's financial position by improving the provision of basic services to eliminate reasons why households typically incur debt. The conclusion we come to as a result of this analysis is yes, household debt can cause a financial crisis. However, we also find that removing the causes of household debt can stabilize the economy to the households' main benefit.

References

Barba, Aldo and Massimo Pivetti. 2009. 'Rising Household Debt: Its Causes and Macroeconomic Implications—A Long Period Analysis'. *Cambridge Journal of Economics* 33: 113–137.

Bellofiore, Riccardo and Passarella, Marco V. 2016. 'Introduction: The Theoretical Legacy of Augusto Graziani'. *Review of Keynesian Economics* 4 (3): 243–249.

BEA. 2020a. 'Table S.2.a. Selected Aggregates for Total Economy and Sectors'. Bureau of Economic Analysis. Accessed 6/12/2020b. Bea.gov.

BEA. 2020b. 'Table 2.1. Personal Income and its Disposition'. Bureau of Economic Analysis. Accessed 6/12/2020c. Bea.gov.

Cynamon, Barry and Steven Fazzari. 2013. 'The End of the Consumer Age'. In *After the Great Recession: The Struggle for Economic Recovery and Growth*, edited by B. Cynamon, S. Fazzari, and M. Setterfield, 129–155. New York: Cambridge University Press.

Drechsel-Grau, M. and K. Schmid. 2013. 'Habits and Envy: What Drives the Consumption Behavior of U.S. Housholds?' IMK Macroeconomic Policy Institute Working Paper 123, October, 10pp.

Federal Register. 2020. https://www.federalregister.gov/documents/2011/09/07/2011-22772/treatment-of-asset-backed-issuers-under-the-investment-company-act (retrieved 8/6/2020).

Federal Reserve. 2020. 'Table D3: Debt Outstanding by Sector'. Z.1. Financial Accounts of the United States, Board of Governors of the Federal Reserve System. Accessed 6/13/20. Federalreserve.gov.

Graziani, Augusto. 1989. 'The Theory of the Monetary Circuit'. *Thames Papers in Political Economy* (Spring): 1–26.

Hein, Eckhard and Achim Truger. 2017. 'Opportunities and Limits to Rebalancing the Eurozone via Wage Policies'. *PSL Quarterly Review* 70 (283): 421–447.

Hudson, Michael. 2012. *The Bubble and Beyond: Fictitious Capital, Debt Deflation and the Global Crisis*. Dresden: Islet.

Kaldor, Nicholas. 1955–1956. 'Alternative Theories of Distribution'. *The Review of Economic Studies* 3 (2): 83–100.

Kregel, Jan. 2013. 'Trying to Serve Two Masters: The Dilemma of Financial Regulation'. In *After the Great Recession: The Struggle for Economic Recovery and Growth*, edited by B. Cynamon, S. Fazzari and M. Setterfield, 86–103. New York: Cambridge University Press.

Lavoie, Marc. 2014. *Post-Keynesian Economics: New Foundations.* Northampton: Edward Elgar.

Lavoie, Marc and Engelbert Stockhammer. 2013. 'Wage-Led Growth: Concept, Theories and Policies'. In *Wage-Led Growth: An Equitable Strategy for*

Economic Recovery, edited by Marc Lavoie and Engelbert Stockhammer, 13–39. New York and London: Palgrave Macmillan and International Labour Organisation.

Leclaire, Joelle. 2008. *The Great Deficit Debacle: Causes and Consequences of American Federal Budget Surpluses and Deficits*. Saarbrucken: VDM Verlag.

Leclaire, Joelle. 2019. 'Linking the Real and Financial Sectors of the Economy: The Major Contribution of Post-Keynesians'. In *Finance, Growth and Inequality*, edited by L.P. Rochon and V. Monvoisin, 285–300. Cheltenham: Edward Elgar.

Minsky, Hyman. 1992. 'The Capital Development of the Economy and the Structure of Financial Institutions'. Hyman P. Minsky Archive, Levy Economics Institute Paper 179, 33pp.

Palley, Thomas. 1994. 'Debt, Aggregate Demand, and the Business Cycle: An Analysis in the Spirit of Kaldor and Minsky'. *Journal of Post Keynesian Economics* 16 (3): 371–390.

Parguez, Alain and Mario Seccareccia. 2000. 'The Credit Theory of Money: The Monetary Circuit Approach'. In *What Is Money?*, edited by John Smithin, 101–123. New York: Routledge.

Rossi, Sergio. 2006. 'The Theory of Money Emissions'. In *A Handbook of Alternative Monetary Economics*, edited by P. Arestis and M. Sawyer, 121–138. Cheltenham, UK and Northampton, MA, USA: Edward Elgar.

Seccareccia, Mario. 2013. 'Financialization and the Transformation of Commercial Banking: Understanding the Recent Canadian Experience Before and During the International Financial Crisis'. *Journal of Post Keynesian Economics* 35 (2): 277–300.

Setterfield, Mark. 2013. 'Wages, Demand, and U.S. Macroeconomic Travails: Diagnosis and Prognosis'. In *After the Great Recession: The Struggle for Economic Recovery and Growth,* edited by B. Cynamon, S. Fazzari and M. Setterfield, 158–181. New York: Cambridge University Press.

Wray, L. Randall. 1993. 'Money, Interest Rates, and Monetarist Policy'. *Journal of Post Keynesian Economics* 15 (4): 541–569.

Wray, L. Randall. 1998. *Understanding Modern Money: The Key to Full Employment and Price Stability*. Cheltenham, UK and Northampton, MA, USA: Edward Elgar.

Wray, L. Randall. 2013. 'Minsky's Money Manager Capitalism: Assessment and Reform'. In *After the Great Recession: The Struggle for Economic Recovery and Growth*, edited by B. Cynamon, S. Fazzari and M. Setterfield, 61–85. New York: Cambridge University Press.

Squid Game and Student Debt Resistance: A Politics of Self-Care, Creativity, and Collective Action in the Neoliberal University

Caroline K. Kaltefleiter, Julian S. Ponirakis, and Jacob T. Robinson

Introduction

We shouldn't be suffering to obtain a degree. I'm the only person in my household to get a bachelor's degree. I shouldn't have to worry about

C. K. Kaltefleiter (✉)
State University of
New York College at Cortland, Cortland, NY, USA
e-mail: caroline.kaltefleiter@cortland.edu

J. S. Ponirakis
State University of New York College at
Geneseo, Geneseo, NY, USA
e-mail: jsp11@geneseo.edu

J. T. Robinson
State University of New York College at Cortland, Cortland, NY, USA
e-mail: jacob.robinson03@cortland.edu

B. C. Wilson, *Care, Climate, and Debt*,
https://doi.org/10.1007/978-3-030-96355-2_8

> paying everything back. I want a better future for myself and not be in the lower class for the rest of my life. Will I ever pay this student loan off? It feels like a game, and right now, I'm losing.
>
> Kaitlyn, College Senior

> All of you in this room are living on the edge with debts you cannot pay off.
>
> Squid Game

The South Korean popular survival show *Squid Game* situates our discussion of student debt and the financialization of higher education. Debt is the primary motivator for characters in the Netflix hit series, a dystopian drama set in which 456 participants who are heavy in debt fight to the death—literally—for a chance at a life-changing windfall of 45.6 billion won or 40 million dollars (Kim 2021). Audiences make comparisons of *Squid Game* to the *Hunger Games* trilogy because the characters exist in a setting that if they lose, they die. The landscape of both programs equates to a continuum of competition, debt, life, and death. In the case of *Squid Game*, the prize money goes up when another play dies, "so the higher the prize money paired with less competition means *Squid Game* characters choose to kill other players" (Williams 2021). In both shows, the winners walk away with or amass a fortune through killing others, eliminating competition, and forging an understanding of collateral damage in everyday life. And now, Netflix has announced a "real life" *Squid Game* competition series where contestants "compete in heart-stopping games to become the sole survivor and walk-away with life-changing cash prices" (Wong 2022).

Meanwhile, the fictional show's popularity transcends its country of origin. As early viewers of the series, we saw connections with sentiments about debt anxieties and everyday life articulated in our research. *Squid Game* illuminates a sense of desperation as debt threatens to consume them. The show reflects class divisions and offers viewers, particularly college students, a vehicle to investigate debt culture and social mobility. The Loyola Marymount University student paper ran a satirical headline, "LMU to replicate *Squid Game*, giving students a chance to cancel their debt." In this spoof article, Ramirez (2021) writes,

> As a response to many students' cries for student loan debt forgiveness and to "live decently," The University has decided to replicate the premise of

> *Squid Game* for any student who wishes to put their life on the line for a chance to not be thousands of dollars in debt before they've even started life. Like *Squid Game*, the competition will include five children's games.

This section of the LMU newspaper is titled "The Bluff" and functions as an intertextual reference to the game of poker and recognition of the high stakes of student loan debt. As the late David Graeber (2014) notes, "student loans are destroying the imagination of youth...If there's a way of a society committing mass suicide, what a better way than to take the youngest, joyous people and saddle them with $50,000 of debt, so they have to be slaves" (qtd. in Kelly 2013).

The catastrophic social, cultural, and economic conditions of student debt warrant critical analysis. This chapter will contextualize the student loan crisis within a framework of neoliberalism and the university. Drawing upon the works of Zygmunt Bauman and Henry Giroux, we will examine the politics of disposability and the burdens of debt linked to psychological scars and suicidal ideations among young people. Further, through the theoretical framework of Eric Fromm and Michel Foucault, this chapter delves into the notion of (self)care, creativity, and collective actions as forms of resistance.

We come to this work as a collective, teacher and students. Our everyday life experiences and discussions shape each other's work and constitute collective knowledge that culminates in our writing. We employ a narrative approach that includes historiography and ethnographic methods such as semi-structured interviews and textual analysis. We explore narratives of those struggling financially and psychologically with student loan debt. As such, we detail experiences and reflections about student debt, illuminating platforms used to speak about, and thus make visible connections to projects of debt resistance and calls for student actions within the university. Finally, we acknowledge those who participated in this work as narrators, and co-researchers on this journey of debt resistance.

Neoliberalism and Financialization: Universities as Capital Enhancing Markets

> Under neoliberalism, the collective good—a disposition grounded in the idea that society improves together—is being subverted as self-reflection and collective empowerment are reduced to self-promotion and self-interest.
>
> Giroux (2004, xv)

The desire to attend college and to become a contributing member of society remains costly for students and their families, and many leave with exorbitant debt. In the United States, student loan debt has grown significantly over the last several decades. The Federal Reserve estimates that in the second quarter of 2021, Americans owed over $1.73 trillion in student loans. The record-breaking total marks an increase of 3% compared to quarter two of 2020—despite a lengthy pause on federal student loan interest rates and the elimination of 9.5 billion dollars federally held student loans by the Biden Administration (Hess 2021). As this essay goes to print, the United States Department of Education has approved another $8 billion in public service loan forgiveness with more announcements of student loan cancellation expected later this year (Camera 2022). This may be good news as college graduates from the class of 2020 borrowed $29,927 on average. That's nearly $5,000 more than borrowers than the class of 2010 had to shoulder—representing a 20% increase in the amount students borrow (Kerr and Wood 2021). The decades-long increase in student debt is even more noticeable when compared to decades prior. Hess (2021) notes, "Americans owed roughly $905 billion in student loans, which means that US student debt has increased by more than 91 percent in the past decade." Given such extreme increases, one must ask what contributed to such escalation? To that, we turn to a discussion of how neoliberalism functions as a driving force behind the student loan crisis.

Cassell and Nelson (2013) suggest that neoliberalism functions as an "invisible hand in free-market, private-interest-driven economics grounded in fear, surveillance and economic deprivation. In *Squid Game*, the VIPs function as a material representation of neoliberalism who hide behind their gold masks and connect to a superstructure of cultural embodiment. Catherine Rottenberg (2018) asserts that neoliberalism "is not merely an economic system or a set of policies that facilitate privatization and market deregulation" (7). In higher education, neoliberalism emerges as a political ideology that recasts individuals as capital-enhancing agents. Students, couched as consumers, are the core of the marketization of higher education wherein "The overarching narrative neoliberalism, and of the student loan crisis is that of 'pay to play.' Many college students will bear a larger cost to obtain a post-secondary education. That cost is even greater for students of color" (Levy 2017, 18). Neoliberalism's impact on public education is "widely recognized and well-illustrated by the growing budget crises plaguing public universities and colleges, and through changing structures of academia throughout the US and western world" (Seis 2021, 44). These structural changes account for what Harvey (2008) describes as the financialization of everything. He articulates advancements in financial instruments and activity as central to the expansion of neoliberalism, freed from the regulatory constraints and barriers, and a wave of financial services that produced sophisticated global interconnection; neoliberalism as such then is the financialization of everything (Harvey 2008, 33). The financialization of everything provides a framework to examine higher education. Institutions hawk their wares as "student-centered." Universities become cultural malls with faculty serving as retail assistants, neatly cataloging and folding information about programs into open house events. More emphasis is placed on free college t-shirts and water bottles than on comprehensive curriculums to prepare the next generation of leaders and problem-solvers (Kaltefleiter 2022).

The Great Recession of 2008 marks the acceleration and financialization of the student loan crisis. Federal and state governments made deep cuts to higher education funding. From the start of the Great Recession in 2008 through 2018, college costs and debt increased substantially. Despite more economic stability during those ten years, state and federal funding for higher education did not return to pre-2008 levels. As Hess (2021) points out, "In 2018, state funding for two-and-four-year public colleges was over $7 billion less than it was in 2008." The COVID-19 global pandemic charts new ground in terms of student loan accruals and possible debt cancellation. It is beyond the scope of this chapter to take up college debt in a post-pandemic society; however, future research will address such issues. The increase in student debt is not merely due to a reduction in state funding. Rather, the confluence of a weak economy, starting with the 2008 recession, the labor market contributed to enrollment increases at public or private colleges and universities that left many students without a placement. Forced out of the normal pathways to college, students turned to for-profit institutions. At its peak, "the for-profit sector accounted for a little bit more than 10% of all enrollment, but about a quarter of Pell Grants, about a third of student loans and more than half of defaults" (ibid.). Even now, in the flux of the enrollment fallout of the pandemic, demand for seats at more selective institutions remains high. Scarcity leads to both predatory recruiting and lending. As Kirstein (2020) asserts, "The wealthy can pick their university, but poor and working-class students are denied access or carry so much debt that adult life begins in bondage to predatory creditors (19). Thus, certain groups, particularly debt students of color, whose futures remain bleak despite discussions of diversity equity and inclusion (Levy 2017). Colleges and universities are at the helm of this demise. Higher learning institutions become platforms that act as conduits between investment firms, hedge funds, and endowments that extract capital, labor, and future wealth from students whose professional careers have not yet started through the issuance of student loans. The impact of student debt is devastating. Young people in their late 20s and early 30s today are one-third less likely to own a house than their parents were at the same age. Further, the homeownership rate among young black Americans has fallen below 30 percent, its lowest rate in 60 years (Thompson, 2020).

Student loan debt begins with promissory documents. Signing a student loan promissory note is akin to the release form signed by players of *Squid Game*, wherein risk and payment are acknowledged. As such, indebtedness obscures the manufacture of consent through modes of capitalist production. Here, capitalism (re)distributes necessary labor and creates a value system cloaked in commodity fetishism (e.g., degree collecting and credentialing) and obscures the reality of exploitative social relations and a culture of oppression. Seis (2021) asserts, "Refashioning the public university to serve the needs of capital and the markets is a grand-scale project aimed at reconfiguring the nature of knowledge, civic engagement, agency, and moral and social responsibility" (Ibid.). In the end, capitalism is never satiated as education sacrifices the young on the altar of the neoliberal university.

Debt Anxiety: Dreams Disrupted and Deferred

> I see debt as an excuse to hold someone back from their goals in life.
> Shannon, College Junior

Before the COVID-19 global pandemic, personal financial concerns ranked as a top stressor for adults in the United States (APA 2016). Young adults report some of the highest levels of stress about money (Heckman et al., 2014; Tran, Mintert, Llamas, & Lam, 2018). Financial stressors include living expenses, tuition, educational expenses, student loan debt, work-school-life balance, financial pressures from family, and uncertain employment after graduation (Heckman et al., 2014; Tran, Mintert, Llamas, & Lam, 2018; Wisconsin HOPE Lab, 2018).

The student loan crisis requires us to examine a growing mental health crisis concurrent with worsening material conditions among young people. As Bassi (2020) observes, "The unprecedented financial burden of tuition and fees, coupled with uncertainty about employment, post-graduation are major contributors to the rise of anxiety and depression among university students (p. 31). The American College Health Association (ACHA) reports that well over half of college students (61.9%) report "overwhelming anxiety" in the past year; more than a quarter (26.5%) describe that past-year anxiety has influenced their academic performance, and nearly one in five (19.7%) characterize their anxiety as reaching clinical levels for which they received a diagnosis or were treated by a professional (ACHA, 2017). Moreover, a gender difference is notable, as the estimated rate of "overwhelming anxiety" for female college students (67.7%) far exceeds that of male students 47.4%; (ACHA, 2017; Tran, Lam, & Legg 2018). During the COVID-19 pandemic, over 71% of students indicated a rise in stress and anxiety, including financial stress (Son et al. 2020). And most alarming, one in nine borrowers with $80,000 to $150,000 in student debt contemplated ending their lives (Wang 2019).

The escalating student mental health crisis in higher education can be understood then as not a problem of the individual per se but rather as a manifestation of the pathology of normalcy in which capitalism is the problem, and external capitalist social relations become embedded in college students' lives. Internalized capitalism within higher education leads to further competition between institutions and pointedly between students themselves. Their decision-making and labor are "increasingly painstaking because of the fear and anxiety of failing, of feeling worthless, amid the accumulation of significant debt (Bassi 2020, 34). One of our narrators expressed fear and anxiety associated with the impact of generational poverty and debt,

> Debt was always scary to me. I think the debt my parents struggled with and their anxiety transferred to me subconsciously. The only thing I knew was to avoid debt. Coming out of high school, I got into a decent university but received a poor financial aid package that did not accurately represent my parent's financial situation.

Another narrator discussed debt paralysis in which one becomes stagnant and unable to move forward with life goals due to anxiety brought on by debt, commenting,

> The debt scared me to the point that I did not attend that school, and it sent me down a vortex in terms of finding myself in a career, which I'm just now trying to crawl out from. I feel like a failure. It's [debt] also that nagging weight on your shoulders that you seemingly can never get out from.

The confluence of financial burdens and a lack of purpose illuminates a crisis of the future and dreams disrupted. Giroux (2013) notes, "Youth is no longer the place where society reveals its dreams but where it increasingly hides its nightmares. As one of our narrators remarked,

> It's already impacting me. I can't deal with my financials anymore because I try to drop out of school each time I look at my loans. I'm terrified to dig myself into a hole I can't climb out. This debt cycle has become a very dark place for me and sends me into weeks of depression. I understand now why the suicide rate among those with student loan debt is on the rise.

Giroux (2013) asks us to consider the impact of social bonds, given financial status and ability. He notes, "Social bonds have given way to the collapse of social protections and the welfare state" (107). The emphasis is now on individual solutions and problems (Bauman 2007, 14). The consequences of this shift under neoliberalism span demographics. Bauman (2004) suggests that the plight of outcast(s) may embrace an entire generation, and today's youth "have been cast in a condition of liminal drift—with no way of knowing whether it is transitory or permanent" (76). Bauman (2004) shines a light on the phenomenological conditions of college students in pursuit of vanishing dreams where they fear lack of purpose and worthiness in as such, "To be declared redundant means to have been disposed of because of being disposable" (p. 12). He continues,

> Part of the problem is there is no compartment reserved for 'human waste' (more to the point, wasted humans). Even if the threat hanging over *biological survival* is dealt with and fought back against effectively, such a no-mean feat would nowhere near the assurance of social survival. (Bauman 2004, 13)

Higher education plays a role in the game of social survival and financial markets. Four years in college is a waiting game—waiting for one's turn to join the marketplace, accruing debt, and weighing opportunity costs. The passage of time "is recorded on the debit side of human life projects, it brings losses, not gains. Moreover, the passage of time "portends the waste of opportunities that ought to have been grasped and consumed as they came (Bauman 2004, 109). The university experience becomes a holding pen and detains the next cohort until ready for release on the market. *Squid Game* illuminates this phenomenon where contestants face imprisonment in a liminal space between life on the outside and an inside competition of life and death. Students, too, oscillate between desire and fear, anticipation and uncertainty, failure, and mounting losses equated in debt and opportunities lost. Upon graduation, student loan payments come due, leaving some students to express going through what one student called "living hell." As one other student wrote,

> I received my degree in the mail. I never marched in a cap and gown. There was no celebratory dinner. No "congratulations" or "good job." There was nothing. Then I found out I had student loans with a total amount of $75,000. I had my wages garnished, taking $400 a month of my income (qtd. in O'Connell 2021)

Some students expressed frustration with bursar and financial aid offices and a lack of flexibility in paying off accounts, adding another barrier to employment and creating additional stress. One of our narrators recounted this catch-22.

> I still have some "debt"—I owe the college beyond my loans because my financial aid did not cover my previous semester. I graduated last month, and I still can't receive my transcript or diploma until I pay my balance of $1,000 to the college. I need a job to pay off my debt, but I cannot find work sufficient to pay off my debts without these documents.

The barriers of student debt leave some students deciding to attend graduate school, taking on more debt to defer their loans just to escape collection agencies and loan companies (Lustig 2021). Here, we return to *Squid Game* and an episode titled "Hell." In this installment, we learn about the financial circumstances of the characters, some of which are so horrific that contestants prefer to go back to wagering their lives to pay off their debts. A character notes, "I don't have a home to go back to–In here, I stand a chance, at least. I've got nothing out there." As (Abdelmahmoud 2021) writes, "These are desperate people, willing to do anything to get out of hell. Their desperation becomes familiar to viewers whose household debts are snowballing and includes student debt."

In short, we cannot dismiss the desperation and mental health implications of financial stress for college students, and the fact that general anxiety may be among the most proximal health correlates of financial stress (Son et al. 2020).

The Debt Card or Invitation Card: Circle | Triangle | Square

> The debt card made me feel like I had an imaginary rock and chain at my foot. It's always there and will keep dragging and haunting me unless I start paying it off.
>
> James, College Senior

The invitation card to join the *Squid Game* is a central part of the visual narrative of the show and continues to intrigue viewers. The card carries three symbols. A circle, square, and triangle that equates to the hierarchies of workers who execute various tasks associated with the games, from food distribution to player termination and cremation operation. The real-world financial market commodifies the *Squid Game* card in the form of a Visa credit card. A recent advertisement from RHB, a Malaysian bank and financial services corporation, uses *Squid Game* as a medium to advertise a youth-targeted Visa card. The dark blue Visa card features three shapes, a circle, a square, and a rectangle in the middle. A hand holds the card to the right, and the phrase "Eyes on the Prize" is highlighted. This phrase connects to the prize money associated with the fictitious game and the financial game of life. Specifically, it serves as a clarion call to students to persevere in their journey to attain a college education, one that for many culminates with a maxed-out credit card or student loan debt.

To raise awareness about the impact of student loan debt, we designed an assignment called "the debt card." This project was carried out at a comprehensive four-year public university during the 2019–2020 academic year before the onset of the COVID-19 pandemic. Students used a 3 × 5 notecard to write down their student loan debt anonymously. Those cards were then put into a box and shuffled. Students took turns taking a card and looking at the number on the card. They carried the card with them for the next week and wrote down reflections on how the number made them feel. Two classes of students of 25 students participated in the exercise. In one class, the debt loads ranged from $0.00 to $101,000 with a class average of $38,000. In another section, the debt loads ranged from $0.00 to $60,000 with a class average of 17,500. In the second class, ten students reported zero debt loads contrasted with three students in the first cohort. Students wrote about living with their debt card and feelings associated with the number inscribed on their cards. Students talked about the essence of debt and how it makes them feel. One student noted, "To me, debt is an inescapable trap that terrifies me. I work about 50 hours a week to stay afloat as a college student." Another student discussed a sense of imprisonment, observing,

> Holding the debt card made me feel nervous about my future. There are many things I want to accomplish in my life but, with that amount of debt hanging over my head, it might not be impossible if I don't get a good-paying job.

Other students expressed an appreciation and empathy, noting they were not alone dealing with significant debt loads. One non-traditional student expressed compassion for other students, stating,

> It was humbling but also helped me feel like I'm not alone. I'm lucky enough to have little debt, but part of that is because I took such a long

> break from school and worked. Seeing some of the debt that my younger classmates had accrued made me feel for them because I know the kind of anxiety I would have had at that age if my debt was so high. It also made me worry for their health because I'm sure it has to weigh on their minds.

Other students assessed their situation and realized where their debt fell on the student debt continuum. One student remarked,

> I thought that I was in a lot of debt until this exercise. Seeing how much more money some people owed upset me because I don't believe anyone should pay such prices for college when a job isn't guaranteed. I feel like we are getting robbed.

Several students expressed concerns as to dealing with student loan debt and survival. One narrator writes,

> I envy people that have a limited amount of debt to pay off once they graduate. I, on the other hand, have the harsh reality of student loan debt. I was already struggling to pay for textbooks and living expenses to survive. I worry that because of my student loan debt, I may become homeless.

Other students expressed concerns about whether their chosen professions will pay them enough to cover their student loan debt and living expenses. Many feared having to work multiple jobs to make ends meet as one student recounts,

> When I end up leaving my parent's home and living on my own, I will have far more bills to pay. Having to pay off my student debt will make that hard to do and tough to save money. I'm concerned that I will have to work two or more jobs which is not something I want to do.

While several students recounted their fears and anxiety associated with debt, some expressed guilt in recognizing their financial situation was better than their peers, akin to survivor's guilt. One narrator wrote, "Holding the debt card with a higher number than my actual debt gave me overwhelming guilt. I felt my privilege first hand, and this made me want to fix the issue of student debt." Another student expressed a need to stay quiet about their student loan debt and talked about societal conditions of not talking about finances, observing,

> Since I am privileged enough to avoid student loan debt, I stay quiet about my situation. I know it is rare for someone to be in my position.

> I also never would want to hurt someone's feelings. I believe I have the responsibility, given my circumstances, to campaign to get others of debt for the good of society—so we can all thrive.

Another narrator reflects,

> I feel guilty that my parents put money aside for me so I could go to college. I now realize not everyone had people to do that for them. I am asking why are we as a society not making college free and accessible for everyone?

In the following section, we take up the notion of collective action and care, highlight ongoing efforts to resist internalized capitalism and student debt, and remind ourselves that money is not ineffable, and paying one's debts is not the essence of morality, but rather is a value to be interrogated and resisted.

Let the Games Begin: Internalized Capitalism, Collective Self-Care, and Debt Resistance

> Alone our debts are a burden. Together they make us powerful.
>
> The Debt Collective 2021

Each round of competition in *Squid Game* begins with a loudspeaker's announcement, hailing time to proceed to the great hall or arena. So too, the college application process is a competition with students putting on their best armaments, be it grades, test scores, co-curricular activities, and awards in the ring to battle not only for coveted slots at colleges and universities but also a chance at the prize of winning financial support in the form of scholarships, awards, or grants. The value placed on a politics of acceptance and a constructed mediated scarcity drives many students and their families to take out excessive student loans to pay for the price to play—or attain an undergraduate degree.

The value of a university education must be interrogated and go beyond discussions of business deals and transactions. As Gani (2021) asserts, "The value of education has moved away from a societal value to a 'value for money,' and the emphasis on students competing against each other is causing isolation, stress, and anxiety." Thus, education is commoditized. Knowledge is a possession with the "selling of education as a transaction, turning the sector into a conveyor belt" (Bassi 2020, 33).

The pressure for students to select market value degrees and get high marks becomes requisite for securing employment. Such classification marks "become fetishized with the journey of education displaced by an urgent desire to meet assessment criteria and make one's way through social and economic hierarchies" (Bassi 2020: 34). Much like the classification of workers in *Squid Game*, students become equated as circles, triangles, or squares in the market economy. Thus, capitalism creates expectations for students as they see themselves. The notion is reified in the idea that "the university will transform them into an instrument of use and exploitation depriving them of a sense of self" (Fromm 1956, 73). The drive to sell oneself prevents students from seeing the interests of their true selves and one another. Fromm (1956) contextualizes this commodity fetishism and relates it to human relations and mental health, or "where the relationships between things and money transcend social relationships between people" (Bassi 2020, 34). Capitalist alienation reifies estrangement from oneself and others.

To counter the exhaustion and alienation brought on by student debt, we turn to a discussion of care and the need for collective self-care as central to debt resistance. Foucault (1984 [1988]) situates the notion of self-care within a discourse of care for the soul. He emphasizes "the importance of knowing ontologically who one is, what one is capable of, and what is suitable to hope for in an ethical practice of personal freedom" (Lioro-Bidart and Semenko, 2017, 21). Care for the self and others is then equated with the capacity for collective self-care and freedom.

Collective self-care becomes a radical act to contest internalized capitalism and advanced debt mobilizing movements. In a recent speech, Angela Davis noted the most significant thing she had learned from today's youth was self-care. "Self-care has to be incorporated in all of our efforts. And this is something new. This holistic approach to organizing is, I think, what is going to eventually move us along the trajectory that may lead to some victories" (qtd. in Mirk 2018).

Therefore, self-care extends to an act of political warfare and solidarity. Sarah Ahmed (2018) puts forth this decree of self-care as warfare and suggests that we redirect care away from its proper objects in directing our care toward ourselves and each other. In his book *Debt*, David Graeber (2014) explores debt politics and offers insights about Occupy Wall Street, which included the occupation of Zuccotti Park, a space that brought together debt refugees. The clearing of Zuccotti brought new inspiration for debt activists. Graeber (2014) recalls, "After the suppression of the camps, we began assemblies that included Strike Debt and debt resistor collectives. We created projects such as the Rolling Jubilee, the Debt Resistors Operations Manual, and the Debt Collective" (397). Strike Debt is a decentralized network of debt resisters, activists, artists, academics, and organizers. The Debt Collective is a debtors' union fighting to cancel debts and defend millions of households (Debt Collective 2021). Education is a primary goal of the Debt Collective and remains paramount as one narrator who emphasized the need for more information about debt and debt cancellation states,

> In my senior year in high school, I took an economics class. The teacher briefly spoke about how people fall into debt and some consequences of being in debt; however, he did not touch on debt management or even debt resistance.

Another student underscored the need for agency and action among students grounded in critical empathy, care, and consolidation about debt,

> More extensive and empathetic education on debt management and the cycle of inequality seems to be an obvious starting point in combating the loan crisis. Students need knowledge of how these financial systems operate and what they're getting themselves into when taking out loans. And they should learn about debt resistance actions. We need to know about groups that care not just banks.

Collective self-care then is about creating a community assembled out of the experiences due to financialization and accelerated capitalism. We (re)assemble ourselves through the ordinary and often painstaking work of looking after each other (Kaltefleiter 2020). In this formulation, "self-care is no longer a litmus test for social equality; it is a way to insist to a violent and oppressive culture that the self- matters and that one is worthy of care" (Kishner 2016). The trajectory of collective self-care is intertwined within a framework of the self and one's fragility, constituting a fluid space of self-care, love, life, and social engagement (Kaltefleiter 2022).

The essence of collective self-care might contribute to, as Graeber (2014) put it, "a broader moral reassessment of the very idea of debt, work, money, growth, and the "economy itself" (398). We need only look to the COVID-19 pandemic to see this reassessment in motion as more people reevaluate their lives, and for some, opt out of work. To that end, Graeber (2014) foreshadows the next stages in the reimagining of debt and society, noting, "Many of our most cherished assumptions about the value of work, or the virtue of paying debts are likely to be stood on their heads" (ibid.). And, so it goes, the student loan crisis garners attention in the news as more young people combat not only the financial burdens of debt but also the anxiety and humiliation of being in debt. The student loan game is *Squid Game* in that we see the big and small humiliations of capitalism. Abdelmahmoud (2021) summarizes this sense of social survival, "The feeling of your worth tethered to your productivity; the magical thinking that once you're rich, you'll be a different person; the embarrassments we are willing to endure to afford what we think we deserve."

In the end, student debt subjects the borrower to a distinctly capitalist pedagogy, transforming higher education into an increasingly expensive commodity bought and sold on the open market. But as the legions of student loan debtors attest, investment in a college education is no longer a guarantee of remunerative employment or personal financial security (Maisano 2012). What emerges then is, as our narrators suggest, a need for greater collective self-care and action or as one student put it, "leaving no squid behind." Such collectivity enables us to counter the morality of debt, epitomized in the *Squid Game* quote, "Do you think money solves everything?" Further, collective action allows us to contest the financial imperatives that reduce us all, despite ourselves, to the equivalent of combatants in a game, eyeing the world simply for its economic value counted as money. To resist such domains requires a contestation of financialization of the neoliberal university and record-breaking college endowments in the wake of surging student debt. Student movements emulating the Rolling Jubilee could be enacted to redirect endowment funds directly to support all students.

Future research might address intersectional Post-COVID analyses of student loan debt, amplifying inequities of student debt loads among students of color and collection actions to mobilize black lives for monetary reform. Additionally, further study is needed to determine the prolonged effects of the pandemic on students' mental health and economic well-being.

In all, debt resistance accentuates mutual aid, direct action, and care for each other by embracing the authentic value of education and elevates possibilities to reimagine financial structures that allow all to reach their full potential without being weighed down by a number on a card. Collective action that incorporates care creates systems to dismantle constraints of student loan debt and offer pathways to authentic financial freedom and social survival for all.

References

Abdelmahmoud, Elamin. 2021. "Squid Game" Works Because the Despair of Capitalism Transcends Borders." *Buzzfeednews.Com*. https://www.buzzfeednews.com/article/elaminabdelmahmoud/squid-game-netflix-review-lupin-international.

Ahmed, Sarah. 2018. "Selfcare As Warfare." Blog. Feministkilljoys. https://feministkilljoys.com/2014/08/25/selfcare-as-warfare/.

American College Health Association. ACHA 2017. "National College Health Assessment." Part II. https://www.acha.org/documents/ncha/NCHA-II_Fall_2017_Reference_Group_Data_Report_Undergrads_ONLY.pdf.

American Psychological Association (2016). "Stress in America: The Impact of Discrimination." Retrieved from http://www.apa.org/news/press/releases/stress/2015/impact-of-discrimination.pdf .

Bassi, Camille. 2020. "On the Death Throes of Education: Erich Fromm's Marxism And A Rally Cry for a Healthy University." *In Neoliberalism and Academic Repression*. Leiden: Brill.

Bauman, Z. 2004. *Wasted Lives*. Cambridge, UK: Polity.

Bauman, Zygmunt. 2007. *Liquid Times: Living in an Age of Uncertainty*. Cambridge: Polity Press.

Bauman, Zygmunt. 2013. *Wasted Lives*. Cambridge, UK: Polity.

Camera, L., 2022. "Education Department Approves $8 Billion in Public Service Loan Forgiveness." [online] *US News and World Report*. https://www.usnews.com/news/education-news/articles/2022-06-27/education-department-approves-8-billion-in-public-service-loan-forgiveness.

Cassell, John A., and Thomas Nelson. 2013. "Exposing the Effects of the 'Invisible Hand' of the Neoliberal Agenda on Institutionalized Education and The Process of Sociocultural Reproduction." *Interchange* 43 (3): 245–264.

Clarke, Carrington. 2021. "Squid Game, The Most Popular Show on Netflix, Was Inspired by South Korea's Crippling Debt Crisis." Abc.Net.Au. https://www.abc.net.au/news/2021-10-16/squid-game-on-netflix-inspired-by-koreas-debt-crisis/100533282.

Debt Collective. 2021. Debtcollective.Org. https://debtcollective.org/.

Fromm, Erich. 1956. *The Sane Society*. London, UK: Routledge.

Foucault, M. 1988. History of sexuality. Vol. 3. The care of the self / Michel Foucault. translated from the French by Robert Hurley. New York: Vintage.

Foucault, Michel, Frédéric Gros, François Ewald, and Alessandro Fontana. 2006. *The Hermeneutics of The Subject*. New York: Picador.

Gani, Aisha. 2021. "Tuition Fees 'Have Led to Surge in Students Seeking Counselling.'" *The Guardian*. https://www.theguardian.com/education/2016/mar/13/tuition-fees-have-led-to-surge-in-students-seeking-counselling.

Graeber, David. 2014. *Debt: The First 5,000 Years*. London: Melville House Publishing.

Giroux, Henry A. 2004. *The Terror of Neoliberalism*. Aurora, ON, Canada: Garamond.

Giroux, Henry A. 2013. *America's Education Deficit and The War on Youth*. New York: Monthly Review Press.

Harvey, David. 2008. *A Brief History of Neoliberalism*. Oxford, UK: Oxford University Press.

Hess, Abigail. 2021. "The US Has A Record-Breaking $1.73 Trillion In Student Debt—Borrowers from These States Owe the Most on Average." CNBC.Com. https://www.cnbc.com/2021/09/09/america-has-1point73-trillion-in-student-debtborrowers-from-these-states-owe-the-most.html.

Heckman, Stuart, Hanna Lim, and Catherine Montalto. 2014. "Factors Related to Financial Stress Among College Students." *Journal of Financial Therapy* 5 (1): 19-39.

Kaltefleiter, Caroline, and Karmelisha Alexander. 2019. "Self-Care and Community: Black Girls Saving Themselves." In *The Black Girlhood Studies Collection*, 181–208. Toronto, ON, Canada: Canadian Scholars and Women's Press.

Kaltefleiter, Caroline. 2020. "Learning to Labor: (Anarcha)Feminism, The Myth of Meritocracy, Incivility, And Resistance for Women in The Neoliberal Academy." In *Neoliberalism and Academic* Repression. Leiden/Boston: Brill Press.

Kaltefleiter, Caroline. 2022. "'Tied to The Loom: Alienation.' In The Neoliberal Academy, Anarcha-Feminism, and A Politics of Resistance and Care." In *Neoliberal Schooling of Selfishness and Exploitation: Rubricization and Corporatization of Higher Education*. New York: Peter Lang Publisher. (Forthcoming).

Kelly, Alexandra. 2013. "David Graeber: 'There Has Been A War on The Human Imagination." Truthdig: Expert Reporting, Current News, Provocative Columnists. https://www.truthdig.com/articles/david-graeber-there-has-been-a-war-on-the-human-imagination/.

Kerr, Emma, and Sarah Wood. 2021. "See Ten Years of Average Student Loan Debt." US News and World Report, 2021. https://www.usnews.com/education/best-colleges/paying-for-college/articles/see-how-student-loan-borrowing-has-risen-in-10-years.

Kim, Victoria. 2021. "The Real World of Private Lending In 'Squid Game' Is A Real Temptation in South Korea." *Los Angeles Times*, 2021. https://www.latimes.com/world-nation/story/2021-10-16/the-seedy-world-of-private-lending-in-squid-game-is-a-realtemptation-in-todays-south-korea.

Kirstein, Peter. 2020. "Marx, Neoliberalism, and Academic Freedom: Toward a Dialectic of Resistance and Liberation." In *Neoliberalism and Academic* Repression. Leiden and Boston: Brill Press.

Kishner, Jordan. 2016. "The Politics of Conspicuous Displays of Self-Care." *The New Yorker*, 2016. https://www.newyorker.com/culture/culture-desk/the-politics-of-selfcare.

Levy, Cynthia. 2017. "African American Student Loan Debt." In *The Neoliberal Agenda and The Student Debt Crisis in US Higher Education*. New York and London: Routledge.

Lloro-Bidart, Teresa, and Keri Semenko. 2017. "Toward a Feminist Ethic of Self-Care for Environmental Educators." *The Journal of Environmental Education* 48 (1): 18–25.

Lustig, Meghan. 2021. "How Student Debt Affects Graduate School Options." *Usnews.Com*. https://www.usnews.com/education/blogs/student-loan-ranger/articles/how-your-existing-student-loan-debt-affects-graduate-school-options.

Maisano, Chris. 2012. "The Soul of Student Debt." *Jacobinmag.Com*. https://jacobinmag.com/2012/12/the-soul-of-student-debt.

Mirk, Sarah. 2018. "Audre Lorde Thought of Self-Care as an 'Act of Political Warfare'." *Bitch Media*. https://www.bitchmedia.org/article/audre-lorde-thought-self-care-act-political-warfare.

O'Connell, B. 2021. "Night of the Living Debt: Five Real Life Student Loan Horror Stories." [online] *Savingforcollege.com*. Available at https://www.savingforcollege.com/article/night-of-the-living-debt-five-real-life-student-loan-horror-stories.

Ramirez, Madison. 2021. "LMU To Replicate Squid Game, Giving Students A Chance to Cancel Their Student Debt." *The Los Angeles Loyolan*, 2021. https://www.laloyolan.com. LMU to replicate Squid Game, giving students a chance to cancel their student debt.

Reinicke, Carmen. 2021. "Biden Has Canceled $9.5 Billion In Student Loan Debt Yet Forgiveness for All Isn't Necessarily Coming." Cnbc.com. https://www.cnbc.com/2021/08/28/biden-has-canceled-9-point-5-billion-in-student-loan-debt-yet-forgiveness-for-all-isnt-necessarily-coming-.html.

Rottenberg, Catherine. 2018. *The Rise of Neoliberal Feminism*. New York: NY: Oxford University Press.

Son, Changwon, Sudeep Hedge, Alec Smith, Xiaomi Wang, and Farzan Sasangohar. 2020. "Effects Of COVID-19 On College Students' Mental Health in The United States: Interview Survey Study." *Journal of Medical*

Internet Research. 22 (9) https://www.ncbi.nlm.nih.gov/pmc/articles/PMC7473764/.

Seis, Mark. 2021. "Pondering the Neoliberal Public University with The Ghost of Foucault." In *Neoliberalism and Academic Repression*. Leiden: Brill.

Thompson, Derek. 2020. "How Capitalism Broke Young Adulthood." The Atlantic. https://www.theatlantic.com/ideas/archive/2020/01/boomers-have-socialism-why-not-millennials/605467/.

Tran, Alisia G. T. T., Christina K. Lam, and Eric Legg. 2018. "Financial Stress,Social Supports, Gender, And Anxiety During College: A Stress-Buffering Perspective." "*The Counseling Psychologist* 46 (7): 846–869.

Tran, A., Mintert, J., Llamas, J. and Lam, C., 2018. "At what costs? Student loan debt, debt stress, and racially/ethnically diverse college students' perceived health." *Cultural Diversity and Ethnic Minority Psychology* 24 (4): 459–469.

Turner, Cory. 2021. "Student Loan Forgiveness Is A Lot Closer for Some Borrowers, and They Are Pumped." NPR.Org. https://www.npr.org/2021/10/20/1046107687/student-loan-forgiveness-is-a-lot-closer-for-some-borrowers-and-they-are-pumped.

Wang, Victoria. 2019. "Killer Loans—College Debt Triggers Depression and Suicide." *Salon*. https://www.salon.com/2019/06/01/killer-loans-college-debt-triggers-depression-and-suicide_partner/.

Williams, Jordan. 2021. "What Squid Game's and Hunger Games Comparisons are Getting Wrong." *Screenrant*. https://screenrant.com/squid-game-hunger-games-survival-comparison-similar-differences/.

Wisconsin Hope Lab. 2018. "Still Hungry and Homeless in College." Madison: University of Wisconsin. https://midatlantic.compact.org/wp-content/uploads/large/sites/61/2021/04/Wisconsin-HOPE-Lab-Still-Hungry-and-Homeless.pdf.

Wong, W. 2022. "Netflix announced a 'Squid Game' competition series. Some fans say it 'goes against' the original show's message." [online] *NBC News*. https://www.nbcnews.com/pop-culture/pop-culture-news/netflix-announced-squid-game-competition-series-fans-say-goes-original-rcna33800.

How Are You Going to Pay for It? The Macroeconomic Benefits of Student Debt Cancellation

Stephanie Kelton

This chapter is a revision of the transcription of a talk Dr. Kelton gave at SUNY Cortland on February 20th, 2020. Benjamin Wilson drafted and edited Kelton's remarks for this volume. This talk was given before the release of Dr. Kelton's 2020 New York Times Bestselling book *The Deficit Myth: Modern Monetary Theory and the Birth of the People's Economy*, thus segments of the talk are supplemented by quotations from the book with footnotes identifying chapters in the book that go into greater detail about the topics discussed in this chapter.

To begin this talk, I shared a video featuring snippets of commentary from well-known politicians and high-profile media personalities. Each of them had something to say about the urgent need to deal with America's so-called debt problem. In the video, the sequence of speakers alternates between Democrats and Republicans in a way that makes it appear that they are intentionally completing one another's sentences. It's a striking way to show that when it comes to the federal government and

S. Kelton (✉)
Stony Brook University, Stony Brook, NY, USA

B. C. Wilson, *Care, Climate, and Debt*,
https://doi.org/10.1007/978-3-030-96355-2_9

its finances, the national discourse is dominated by a bipartisan chorus of voices who all appear to be singing from the same fiscal hymn book.

Until recently, there has been no serious disruption—politically or within economics—in the conventional way of thinking about the limits on government debt and deficits. Instead, the most widely recognizable politicians and the most highly visible economists from both ends of the political spectrum have complained about our nation's long-term fiscal outlook. Former Secretary of State Hillary Clinton is heard, in the videos, summarizing the need for fiscal responsibility: "You cannot cut taxes or increase spending unless you can pay for it." "Borrowing from China," a young Barack Obama tells a small crowd at a campaign stop on his way to becoming the nation's first African American president, is "unpatriotic." Others invoke the familiar "burdening of future generations," and we hear a leading FOX news host declare, "the national debt is America's biggest problem."

The message I am going to deliver in this chapter is that the dominant way of thinking about money, taxes, and government spending is rooted in a series of misunderstandings that have given rise to a powerful myth, the deficit myth.

I will deconstruct this myth in four stages. First, I will describe how the fear of adding to the national debt and deficit spending influences everyday politics. I will then point out that despite bipartisan agreement about the danger of increasing the national debt, the obstacles the deficit myth creates are treated by Republicans and Democrats in distinct ways. Next, I'll illustrate this difference by comparing republican tax cuts with the Democrats' proposal for student debt cancellation. This example illustrates some basic criteria for assessing and evaluating policy outcomes by using a macroeconomic model. Finally, I'll address the following questions: Where does the money come from and where does it go? We conclude by proposing a more appropriate constraint on government spending that dispels the deficit myth.

As the chief economist to the democrats on the US Senate Budget Committee (2015/16), I witnessed first-hand how the bipartisan angst over fiscal deficits hamstrings policymakers. For instance, it is widely understood that the US needs to invest in its crumbling infrastructure. But what would it take to get Congress to commit to spending $1 trillion to repair and modernize America's infrastructure? The process often involves Congressional staffers who work for the senator or representative who drafts the legislation. Staffers are frequently tasked with the job of drumming up support for their boss's legislation. To find supporters of the bill, the staffer must make the rounds and find other members of Congress who will co-sponsor, support, and ultimately vote for this legislation. The first question in the hallway, on the phone, via email comes in several forms but asks the same thing: What's your 'pay for'? Where is the money coming from? Are you asking me to vote to raise taxes? Before anyone will even consider pledging to support the bill, they want to know how the spending can be carried out without adding to the deficit. That's what it means to 'pay for' your spending in Congress. Given this question, we see the joining of spending and taxing in our legislative process and this, we will see, is not only unnecessary but one of the most corrosive aspects of the deficit myth.

The joining of taxing and spending, ratified under PAYGO, was reinstated by Democrats after they gained a majority in 2018. Republicans had waived PAYGO in order to pass their sweeping tax cuts in December 2017, but Democrats reinstated the self-imposed budgeting constraint immediately after coming to power. As a self-imposed procedural rule, PAYGO falls into the same category as other attempts to keep the federal government from overspending, such as the debt ceiling or the Senate's Byrd Rule. All of which Congress has shown can be waived off or suspended at their pleasure. The most recent iteration of self-imposed constraint is the PAYGO rule that says, in order to do X, I need to offset that spending somehow by either spending less in some other area of the budget or by raising revenues somewhere else. So why does Congress embrace these kinds of self-imposed constraints? Why do we join what are two distinct government policy operations together, spending and taxing? To answer this question we need a little history and to further describe the many moving parts that come together to move legislation through the House and the Senate.

The first of these moving parts is the Congressional Budget Office (CBO). The CBO was created in 1974 and is Washington's official budget scorekeeper. Whenever major legislation is being proposed the CBO (sometimes with input from the Joint Committee on Taxation) is enlisted to assess the bill. So for any significant legislation like major infrastructure investment, the Green New Deal, Medicare for All, tuition-free college, or cancelling student loan debt, the CBO must review and provide a "score" for the bill. A "good" score is one that shows that the spending can be carried out without adding much (if anything) to future deficits. With enough votes, Congress can still pass legislation even when the budgetary effects aren't completely neutralized. But a sufficiently "bad" score—one that includes dire warnings about future debt crises—can effectively stop a bill in its tracks.

The central problem with the bipartisan agreement about the dangers of the national debt, the series of self-imposed constraints and the linking of spending and taxing operations is that it unnecessarily prevents Congress from asking other more relevant questions about what the legislation is intended to do for the American people. The focus and number one question from lawmakers is, "Will this add to deficits over time?" Not, "Will it create millions of good-paying jobs?" Or, "Will it lift millions of kids out of poverty?" "Will it help families secure affordable childcare, ease the burden of paying for college, improve our public infrastructure, address our increasing vulnerability to the climate crises, and strengthen our democracy?"[1] In other words, our legislators are consumed and focused on zeroing out fiscal deficits, rather than working to tackle our most pressing social and environmental shortfalls.

This, however, was not always the case. The CBO is a relatively recent addition to the Washington institutional alphabet. Before the CBO's arrival in 1974 large and significant legislation was drafted and passed. For instance, President Lyndon B. Johnson passed Medicare and Medicaid in 1965 to address deficits in healthcare access. Other big legislative accomplishments in the twentieth century include: Social Security, the construction of major infrastructure projects, such as hydroelectric dams in the west, the interstate highway systems, and our national parks. None of these major legislative projects faced the scoring system of the CBO.[2] If FDR and LBJ had been forced to reckon with the CBO and to adhere to today's conventional scorekeeping exercises, it's entirely possible that programs like Social Security, federal unemployment insurance, Medicare, and Medicaid would not exist today.

The popular fear of this thing we call "the national debt" and fear of voting for spending that increases the fiscal deficit isn't just a political issue. It has become a cultural phenomenon as well. Many have seen the debt clock in Times Square, and that image is plastered on the front

[1] Each of these "deficits" is covered at length in Chapter 7 "The Deficits that Matter" in *The Deficit Myth* (2020).

[2] Social Security provides a point of reference throughout *The Deficit Myth*, as it is a direct target of contemporary attacks grounded by pernicious PAYGO logic, with specific budgetary history and discussion found in Chapter 6 "You're Entitled!".

covers and magazines and newspapers to terrorize members of Congress, the public, and the punditry. Everybody looks at this. Why? Because my God, the debt relative to the size of the US economy, I mean, it's just projected to grow and grow and grow. We are looking into a future where the debt just continues to climb higher and higher. This is obviously a crisis. This is unsustainable. Think about the next generation. Think about what it means for our national security. Think of China. I mean, think about all the standard talking points. Behind this image of the debt's rapidly increasing numbers lies all of those anxieties. So we have this scary picture of our government and its inability to be responsible, and it's a huge obstacle.

This obstacle, however, is treated by Republicans and Democrats in distinct ways. While both parties agree that the debt and deficit spending are to be feared, they differ in their approaches to expanding the economy using the government's powers to tax and spend. Republicans generally support tax cuts. Tax cuts increase the deficit but are claimed to grow the economy and thus pay for themselves through increased future tax revenues. This is supply-side economics—sometimes called "trickle-down" theory—and its supporters frequently defend the approach by referencing the Laffer Curve. Recent studies have found a complete lack of empirical support for these policies (Hope and Limberg 2020). Basically, they have not delivered after some five decades of trying. This argument, however, allows Republicans to fight their policy battle on one front, cutting taxes. In contrast, Democrats frequently want to spend money to build infrastructure or expand access to things like health care and education. So what happens is Democrats, under PAYGO and other self-imposed budgetary constraints, get locked into these epic battles where the tax piece and the spending piece are linked together.[3] In order to spend another dollar into the economy you need to come up with a dollar of new revenue (or a way to offset some other kind of spending). This is a much more challenging political battle, even though both policy actions, spending and tax cuts, increase the deficit.

To illustrate, why spending and taxing can be viewed as distinct policy proposals and do not need to be debated or linked together by PAYGO or any other arbitrarily constructed budget rule in Congress, I'm going to examine student debt cancellation and use the Trump tax cuts as a

[3] At the time of the writing of this chapter, an example of this very kind of battle was playing out over the Biden Administration's Build Back Better agenda.

comparative point of reference. One is a spending operation that requires PAYGO, the second is justified by Republicans as paying for itself. This exercise also helps illuminate why the government's deficit is always good for someone, and where and how the deficit is distributed matters much more than its size. This is a big piece for understanding the deficit myth.

The comparison of the Trump tax cuts and the cancellation of student debt is a strong exercise because both policies are roughly the same size, roughly $1.4 to 1.7 trillion, according to estimates. The second similarity between these two policies is that they both stimulate the economy through two processes that economists call income and wealth effects. Given these parallels, we can compare the real-world impact of the Trump tax cuts to modeled simulations of student debt cancellation. To build and execute the student debt cancellation simulations, our team was fortunate to have input from Mark Zandi and some of his research staff at Moody's Analytics. In addition to studying the effects of cancellation using the "Zandi Model," we also made use of the FAIR model, a large-scale macro model developed by Ray C. Fair, an economist at Yale. So, our formal analysis of student debt cancellation was undertaken using two different models, which gave us a way to compare the results and see if everything made sense. So what do you think happened? What were the macroeconomic effects of student debt cancellation?

Our report, which was published in February, 2018, showed what might happen to a wide range of economic indicators—employment, inflation, interest rates, and real output—if the entire stock of outstanding student loan debt was eliminated (Fullwiler et al. 2018). From a macroeconomic perspective, we saw just what one might expect. The freed-up income and jump in household wealth led to more consumer spending, a faster-growing economy, and lower levels of unemployment, with only a very small (and temporary) rise in inflation. These results compared favorably to the stimulus and macroeconomic impact early data were showing from the tax cuts. To understand why, it's helpful to break down, at a more micro level, why and how people were spending the additional money they gain from the policies.

The first way we can break down spending is to analyze what is called the income effect. Eliminating a bill that comes due every month for a student loan repayment means that there's just more money left in their bank account. Cancelling student loan debt boosts disposable income. So you have more money available to spend on other things, what are you going to do? You're going to spend a lot of it. People will save a portion of it, but taking away this monthly obligation allows them to go out and spend on a variety of other things. In short, relieving people of a monthly obligation increases the amount of money they have to spend. It feels similar to when you just get a pay raise, which is why economists refer to it as an income effect.

To know just how much of an economic boost cancellation might bring through the income effect, it's important to get a sense of how much of this freed-up income might be used for consumption and how much might be added to savings or used to pay down other debts. That makes a big difference when it comes to estimating the macroeconomic benefits and is one of the big differences between tax cuts for the wealthy and corporations and cancelling student debt. Because many student debt holders are in the early stages of their professional lives, the boost to spending is likely to be large, as people can use that addition $150, $500 or in extreme cases $2000 to move into their own apartment, buy a home, afford a car payment, maybe start a new business, or simply eat out more often because they can afford to do so. Whereas the spending changes created by tax cuts often do not create the same effects, because, among other reasons, their asset and income structures are so very different (Hope and Limberg 2020).

But remember, the income effect is just one of the two benefits that economists look at when assessing such a policy. In addition to the income effect, student debt cancellation also delivers a wealth effect. The wealth effect operates by changing your net worth. Your net worth is the difference between your assets, what you own, and your liabilities, what you owe. So if your assets stay the same, but your liabilities go down because the government eliminated all of your student loan debt, then your net worth rises proportionately. This wealth effect is particularly beneficial for young people looking to build wealth for the future. Relieved of a significant debt burden, they will not only find more disposable income in their bank accounts but discover that their credit scores have also likely improved. Strong credit scores expand access to and make mortgages, car loans, and small business loans more affordable. Given the opportunity to start from a stronger financial footing, young people can start investing in themselves and their families much earlier.

The income and wealth effects give us a view of what student debt cancellation might look like for the household, but let's return to the macroeconomic impacts that our models estimated? While the magnitude of the improvements to the variables across our models varies, in each case the stimulus generates positive outcomes in the variables studied. For instance, the model finds that with student debt cancellation the economy adds somewhere between 1.2 and 1.5 million jobs per year at the peak of the cancellation. The creation of jobs, in particular, is an important indicator of economic stability for individual households, but this stability also filters up and supports our communities more broadly. Economists often refer to this kind of indirect benefit as a spillover effect, and one such spillover effect from student debt cancellation is the improvement of state-level balance sheets.

The State of New York, the State of California, the State of Kansas, all the states in our union have their own budgets. These budgets are used to support schools, infrastructure, and often folks who are struggling with benefits payments like unemployment insurance. Thus, when the federal government acts to stimulate the macroeconomy in ways that grow the economy and add jobs it helps out states as well. States find direct benefits from these spillover effects. Increasing employment reduces their spending on unemployment insurance and other benefits. Additionally, when people use their new or extra income to help them purchase homes the state's income and property tax receipts both increase, as well. Therefore, both the spending and income sides of the state's balance sheet improve and enhance stability across our communities.

Additionally, while our model was not constructed to examine the impact student debt cancellation would have on other important social measures like crime rates, educational attainment, household formation, small business startups, or public health outcomes, there are large bodies of research (some of which you can find in this volume) that support claims that these indirect benefits or spillover effects are likely outcomes from this macroeconomic stimulus (Fulwiler et al. 2018). There is significant evidence that student debt cancellation is an economic policy that improves the balance sheets of individuals directly, but is also able to generate positive spillover effects in neighborhoods, communities, and even at the level of state budgets. In sum, when people and communities are more financially stable they are able to take on risks and experience the rewards of being less vulnerable to business cycle downturns.

There is one balance sheet, however, that does not improve, at least immediately, with the cancellation of student debt, and that is the balance sheet of the federal government. Like the Republicans' tax cuts, this policy adds to the deficit and therefore increases our national debt. So the next question we want to address is where does the money come from that makes all of these economic benefits possible. How is Congress able to cut taxes leaving money in the accounts of the wealthy and corporations, cancel student debt, or spend money on new projects or programs without a so-called pay for or other offsets in the budget?

The answer to this question is a little technical but begins when Congress passes legislation that requires additional spending. The spending that Congress outlines in any bill is called an appropriation. To appropriate the funds for student debt cancellation or new infrastructure does not mean Congress has the money in its possession and is going to transfer it to someone else's account. Rather, the appropriation means that Congress has made the decision, through democratic debate and voting, that this money needs to be spent, after that it is really a matter of accounting. Congress authorizes the creation of new dollars. This is Modern Monetary Theory's starting point: "our national currency, the U.S. Dollar, comes from the U.S. government, and it can't come from anywhere else" (Kelton 2020, p. 17).[4] One way I like to describe this is—Congress has the power of the purse. The appropriation means Congress is spending money it did not previously possess. By law, this appropriation commits the US to spending this money. When Congress appropriates funds the execution of this spending must be carried out.[5] This is where the real 'pay for' comes from. Congress authorizes the spending through the act of passing legislation. Step one: Congress takes care of it. So there it is. Spending by our federal government does not require the collection of revenue. It requires the collection of the votes necessary to pass the law. So, when you hear these politicians say, we have to find the money they are telling a deficit myth story. They do not need to find the money, they need to find the votes.

Votes fund our federal spending. Here is a very clear example: In late 2019, Democrats and Republicans together, very enthusiastically voted for the $738 billion Defense Reauthorization Act. $738 billion, that's for an annual appropriation. That's one year, $738 billion. This

[4] Details describing the process of US government spending can be found in Chapter 1 "Don't Think of a Household" in *The Deficit Myth*.

[5] For a detailed legal description of how this works, the reader is encouraged to listen to the "This is How They Could Literally Mint a Trillion Dollar Coin" episode of Odd Lots. In this interview with legal scholar Rohan Grey, they provide the listener with extensive details about federal funding operations and how the debt ceiling disrupts this process.

was more than the White House had requested. It is more than the Pentagon requested. Why did they give them extra? Did Congress just feel generous? Did they have a couple extra billion dollars in a closet? No, it is because they could, because they have the power of the purse. 87 members of the US Senate voted for the $738 billion defense authorization, overwhelmingly bipartisan, take the money and go. Another aspect of this spending worth noting is that there was also no discussion about how we are going to pay for billions of dollars of new spending on the military. We did not see a series of press conferences or media personalities asking what was going to be sacrificed or whose taxes are we were going to raise to get the money for this legislation. It was simply authorized and spent. Now that this money is authorized; it will be spent into existence. That's how it works. That's where the money comes from.

What these examples, tax cuts, student debt cancellation, and military spending, demonstrate is that the linking of taxing and spending is a political choice. If our elected members find military spending, or tax cuts, or student debt cancellation to be important for the well-being of their constituents, then those laws can be passed without the offsets that arbitrary rules like PAYGO demand. So why do we spend so much time and energy obsessing over the debt and deficit spending? Should we fear deficit spending? Can we trust our elected officials with the power of the purse? We know, for example, that the government is going to continue to make trillion-dollar deposits to the non-government sector next year, the year after that, the following year, and so forth. Should this cause us to panic? Are the talking points about the debt going to come true? Deficit spending and the national debt do not cause me to panic, because there is another way to look at this. It is all a matter of perspective.

The most useful perspective for understanding deficit spending is to look at it through the lens of basic accounting. What is happening on the balance sheets of all those who are involved. At the macroeconomic level, there are three parties, the US government,

all the households and all the businesses in the US economy, and the rest of the world. Those three groups are all there is. Those three groups include everyone and their balance sheets. In short, there's the government, the private sector, and the rest of the world. When we break things down into these three basic categories, we can investigate how money moves between them. This simple perspective and its consequences are what the late economist Wynne Godley helped us to see. Godley's point is very simple. If you think of the world as a system of interlocking balance

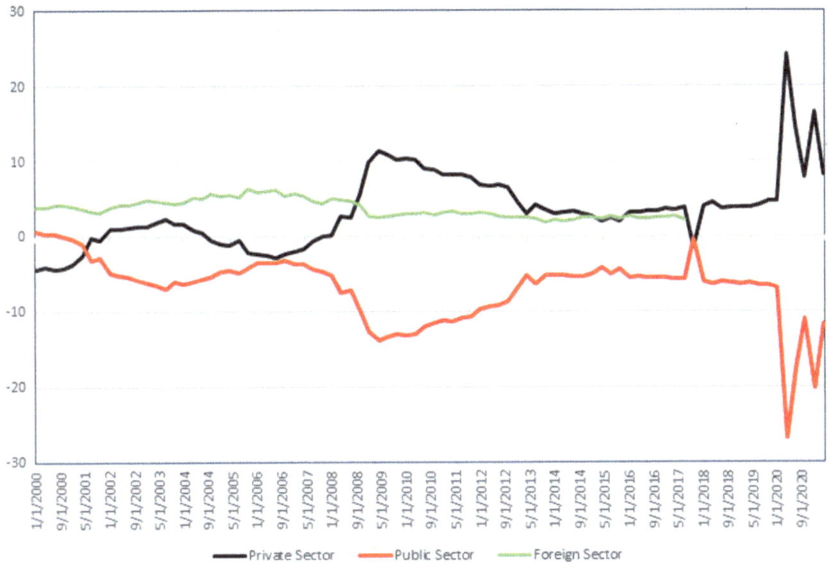

Fig. 1 Quarterly sectoral balances (% of GDP) 2000—September 2020 (*Source* U.S. Bureau of Economic Analysis, Net lending or net borrowing [-], NIPAs: Private [W994RC1Q027SBEA], retrieved from FRED, Federal Reserve Bank of St. Louis; https://fred.stlouisfed.org/series/W994RC1Q027SBEA, November 8, 2021 and authors calculations. Note Foreign Sector data reporting ends in the fourth quarter of 2017)

sheets, then a payment that flows out of any one sector has to arrive in some other sector. Wynne would describe it to me this way, every payment that comes from somewhere must go somewhere. Okay, that makes sense. If a $10 payment leaves the government sector, a $10 payment has to be received in some other part of the economy. This relationship is called sectoral balances and it has a very simple equation and their relationships can be observed graphically in Fig. 1:

Government financial balance + Nongovernmental financial balance + foreign sector financial balance = 0.

The critical observation here is that all deficits are good for someone. The government's red ink is your black ink.[6] The government's spending is always credited on another balance sheet somewhere in the economy. We observed this process above with our student loan cancellation. By cancelling student debt and increasing its deficit, the federal government would grow the balance sheets of millions of Americans. The same is true of defense spending. Those dollars increase the deficit, but also increase the balance sheets of defense contractors and others for whom the bill appropriates those dollars.

A very important difference to recognize, and what brings the significance of this relationship into view, is that when households or businesses spend money and credit another person's balance sheet, they must have already obtained access to that money, either by earning it or being awarded the credit they need to spend it. They are revenue constrained and must find the money. As we have seen, however, this is not the way the federal government works. The government's power of the purse comes from the US Constitution. It has the power to pass legislation and appropriate money, because it is written in the law of our land. Specifically, it was given unto Congress by our founding fathers who wrote in Article I, section eight, that: "The Congress shall have Power… To coin Money, regulate the Value thereof… and fix the Standard of Weights and Measures." Constitutional authorization to coin money definitively establishes that Congress is not like a household. In fact, our founding fathers go on to write that if others attempt to create dollars, then Congress has the power to punish those for "counterfeiting the Securities and Coin of the United States." Private businesses and households do not create new US dollars. State and local governments cannot authorize dollars into existence. They do not have the power of the purse. The federal government is different. It is not a household.

Just like creating a series of tweets, or adding points to scoreboards, Congress can authorize the spending of money that they do not have in their possession because they have the power of the purse. A power that is afforded to them through our Constitution. So the question is, if they do not need to find the money, then how much can they safely spend before offsets become necessary? In other words, how much can they grow the bank accounts of non-governmental actors before inflation

[6] Chapter 4 is called "Their Red Ink Is Our Black Ink".

(a general increase in prices) begins to damage the value of the currency and threaten macroeconomic stability? When does taxation or other forms of inflation management become necessary? Was it safe to cut $2 trillion dollars in taxes, can we spend $3.5 trillion on infrastructure, what about a $16 trillion Green New Deal? If Congress has the power of the purse, and it does not need to collect revenue before it spends, then what is its true constraint?

To find its constraint, Congress must examine the economy. The economy has its own internal constraints. The economy can only handle so much new demand before reaching its capacity constraint. These constraints can be examined by looking at what economists call real resources. These include things like lumber, hotel rooms, batteries, food, and all of the stuff we use to make our lives possible, but the best indicator of whether or not we have reached our capacity is to look at workers. Are there enough people to cut the lumber, fill reservations and service the hotel rooms, grow and distribute our foods? If we have people who are unemployed or sitting on the sidelines, then our economy can do more and is able to absorb additional spending to ensure we are using all of our labor power. When restaurants can't find another busboy or there is not another worker to be hired in a hospital or an accounting firm, at that point, the economy has reached full employment, its true capacity constraint. Once this is achieved, any additional new spending will only drive prices higher because it can't drive output higher. It can't increase supply to match higher demand.

This is why MMT, "recommends a federal job guarantee, which creates a nondiscretionary automatic stabilizer that promotes both full employment and price stability" (Kelton 2020, p. 63).[7] Given this framework, the first question policymakers should consider is whether or not the spending moves the economy beyond our employment constraint? If it does not, then we can execute the spending program without any revenue offsets and our fight for the bill can be grounded by questioning its economic, social, and environmental impacts, not how it affects the government's balance sheet. Like the Republican tax cuts, it only needs to be debated on the spending front. The revenue or tax piece is a separate policy question.

[7] The topic of inflation is the subject matter of Chapter 2 "Think Inflation".

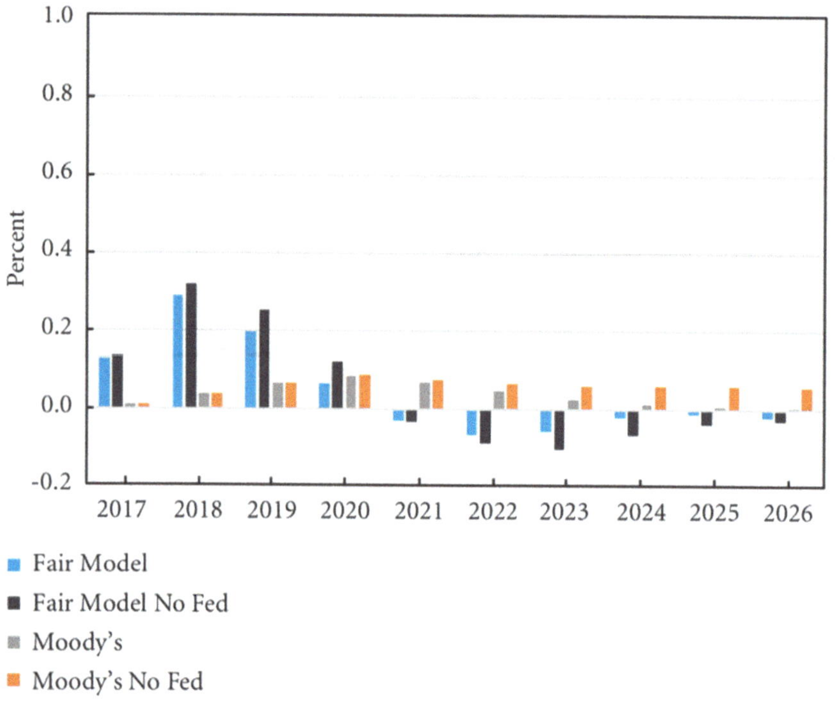

Fig. 2 Estimated inflation impacts of student loan debt cancellation (*Source* Fulwiler, Scott, Kelton, Stephanie, Ruetschlin, Catherine and Marshall Steinbaum. The Macroeconomic Effects of Student Debt Cancellation. The Levy Economics Institute of Bard College. February [2018])

To illustrate how this works, let's return to our student loan cancellation simulation, remember, just like Republicans, this cancellation came with no offsets. So, to know if we surpass the economy's internal constraints, if this policy spends more money into the economy then it can handle, then we will see increases in inflation. In our model simulations, we observe employment and output going up, but inflation hardly budges. The inflation effects are shown in Fig. 2. The results are consistent across each of the models we estimated. In each model, we observe a mild uptick in prices at the peak of the cancellation, about three-tenths of a percentage point. To put this into context, inflation before the COVID-19 pandemic consistently ran in the neighborhood of 1.8%. This means that student debt cancellation would have increased inflation to roughly two percent, or the Federal Reserve's generally stated inflation target. A target, in fact, that they struggled to hit with any regularity during the post financial crisis era.

So the point is that instead of picking the PAYGO fight and saying, if we want to cancel student loan debt, we also need to line up the offsets and address the CBO's deficit concerns, we can just pay for it, that's it. No need to tie this publicly beneficial policy to a tax on Wall Street speculation or add a wealth tax to our legislation. The economy is more than capable of absorbing this appropriation and improving the balance sheets and lives of millions of Americans. Just as the economy routinely absorbs large military appropriations.

From this perspective, we can imagine a much healthier and civil public discourse about public spending and taxing. If we separate these two distinct policy operations and debate them on their own terms, then we relieve ourselves of one of the most toxic elements of the deficit myth. Public spending does not need to be constrained by redistribution. We do not need to take money from one group of people in order to help and invest in others. The deficit myth traps us in the world of Robin Hood. What an understanding of Congress's power to appropriate, sectoral balances, and the economy's real resource constraints allow us to see is that taxes play a very different role in our economy.[8]

Rather than paying for the federal government's spending, taxes ensure that our money has value by creating demand for the currency. Thus, tax increases or offsets are one lever the government can use to stabilize prices and inflation. Another important role that taxes play in our economy is that they can be used to discourage behavior. Sin taxes, like on cigarettes or gambling are prime examples. We can also use taxes to improve economic distribution and reduce inequality by implementing progressive income taxes or taxes on inheritance. The point is, while taxes do not directly pay for our federal spending, they do serve very important roles and can be levied to help make room for new money in other parts of the economy, if we are approaching our real resources constraints. This is a much different debate, then saying that federal tax dollars pay for public goods and services. They simply do not.

[8] Summaries of the taxing and borrowing functions are discussed in Chapter 1 "Don't Think Like a Household".

The deficit myth and the associated Congressional rules like PAYGO represent broken thinking that is poisoning our politics. We must, I think, fix the idea proffered by former British Prime Minister Margaret Thatcher when she argued, "the government has no money of its own. It has got to find the money from somewhere. There is no public money. There's only taxpayer money."[9] To fix this idea, we can draw from a different Margaret, Margaret Atwood, when she argues that in order to change how something works, we must change how we think about it.

To change how we think about the deficit and our national debt, I would like to conclude by offering a simple mnemonic device. I call this the TaB(S) model, But simply put, TaB stands for Taxing and Borrowing and the S stands for spending. The deficit myth narrative and Margaret Thatcher argue that Taxing and Borrowing TaB proceed spending, because the government does not have its own money. To change how we think about public finance and thus change how it works, we simply need to reverse the mnemonic. Spending proceeds and does not require taxing and borrowing for the US government, as the Constitution and empirical evidence clearly tell us. If we embrace this new perspective, a perspective grounded in history and law, we can reject all of the parsimonious stories the deficit myth perpetuates. The US Congress is most decidedly not a household. Instead, the US Congress, empowered by votes, can appropriate the financial resources we need to help all of our households contribute to the building of an economy that is strong, fair, and sustainable, if we simply let go of the deficit myth.

References

Fulwiler, Scott, Kelton, Stephanie, Ruetschlin, Catherine and Marshall Steinbaum. The Macroeconomic Effects of Student Debt Cancellation. The Levy Economics Institute of Bard College. February (2018). http://www.levyinstitute.org/pubs/rpr_2_6.pdf.

Hope, David and Limberg, Julian. The Economic Consequences of Major Tax Cuts for the Rich. International Inequalities Institute Working Papers (55). London School of Economics and Political Science, London, UK (2020).

Kelton, Stephanie. The Deficit Myth: Modern Monetary Theory and the Birth of the People's Economy. New York, NY: Public Affairs Hachette Book Group (2020).

[9] Margaret Thatcher, Speech to the Conservative Party Conference, Winter Gardens, Blackpool, UK, October 14, 1983, Margaret Thatcher Foundation, www.margaretthatcher.org/document/105454.

Weisenthal, Joe and Tracy Alloway. Odd Lots. This is how to Literally Mint a trillion Dollar Coin. Bloomberg. November 1, 2021. https://www.bloomberg.com/news/articles/2021-11-01/this-is-how-they-could-literally-mint-a-trillion-dollar-coin?srnd=oddlots-podcast.

The Aesthetics and Potential of Alternative Monetary Design

“Solidarity Is a Force Stronger Than Gravity”: Money, Aesthetics, and the Abstractness of Care

Scott Ferguson

In this essay, I re-imagine Western modernity’s fraught and, by most accounts, exhausted dialectical opposition between money and aesthetics. To do so, I rethink the social character and value of abstraction in general—a matter that, I believe, critical theory has largely misconstrued. I challenge previous critical theorists from Theodor Adorno to Fredric Jameson, who focus on abstraction’s central role in ordering modern life but judge abstraction and, with it, money to essentially alienate ecosocial relations from their allegedly primary material bases. On my analysis, such presumptions have long impaired critical theory’s forays into aesthetics as well as its capacities to envision radical social and ecological transformation. Instead, I take my cue from the galvanizing adage oft-repeated by labor organizer and current International President of the Association of Flight Attendants, Sara Nelson: “Solidarity is a force stronger than

S. Ferguson (✉)
University of South Florida, Tampa, FL, USA
e-mail: sferguson@usf.edu

B. C. Wilson, *Care, Climate, and Debt*,
https://doi.org/10.1007/978-3-030-96355-2_10

gravity."[1] Playing on the fact that the commercial air travel flight attendants regularly facilitate must directly negotiate material forces, Nelson's apothegm suggests that collective action is irreducible to the physics of flight. Political organization, that is, partakes of remote and hence abstract orchestrations in ways that at once subtend and exceed the physics of gravity. Abstractness, therefore, conditions not only the distribution of power across political economy and aesthetics, I contend, but also the difficulties and possibilities of care.

To reorient money and aesthetics toward this more capacious understanding of abstraction, I turn to the conception of money articulated by the contemporary heterodox school of political economy known as Modern Monetary Theory, or "MMT" for short. MMT has become increasingly important in political and economic debates since the Great Financial Crisis and now sits at the heart of most discussion about the Global Green New Deal. For MMT, monetary abstraction is not a private, finite, and hence alienable technology that is co-extensive with the market, as both mainstream and Marxist economics hold. At bottom, MMT argues, money is an *inalienable public utility*. Unlike the variable finitude that defines material resources, however, money operates through abstract inscriptions and is therefore genuinely inexhaustible. According to MMT, then, it is *because* not in spite of abstraction that money contains still-unrealized possibilities for inclusive transformation and, as I argue, care.

Mobilizing MMT, I move beyond tired dialectical oppositions that pit aesthetic abundance and communality against monetary privation and greed. Rather, I affirm the emphatically abstract bases of embodied social production across monetary and aesthetic domains. I set the modern relationship between political economy and aesthetics on more expansive and interdependent premises. And I inaugurate a new practice of critical theory, which seeks to actualize money's curative potentials in a sensuous here-and-now. To do so, I critique Western modernity's ongoing repression of abstraction's *aesthetic* possibilities by way of a fresh critical examination of its physics-obsessed visual culture from Renaissance perspectival painting to what I call "hyper-Newtonian" blockbusters and video games.

[1] Sara Nelson, "Solidarity Is a Force Stronger Than Gravity," LGBTQ Nation, June 5, 2019, date accessed September 20, 2021, https://www.lgbtqnation.com/2019/06/solidarity-force-stronger-gravity/.

Such are the principal arguments and stakes of my first published book, *Declarations of Dependence: Money, Aesthetics & the Politics of Care* (University of Nebraska Press, 2018). In what follows, I share some of my book's primary provocations in an effort to transcend the deadlocks that haunt aesthetic praxis from the Renaissance to the neoliberal present, while making critical theory freshly answerable to future politics. Before doing so, however, I return to MMT to more thoroughly flesh out my reading of its counterintuitive intervention in economics.

As I have already begun to suggest, whereas modernity's dominant Liberal political economy construes money as a private, finite, and decentered exchange instrument that is always in short supply and can never seem to be everywhere it is needed, MMT conceives money as an unlimited public utility, which harbors untold capacities for ensuring political inclusion and sustainable prosperity. According to MMT's state-based or "chartalist" theory, money does not bubble up from spontaneous barter-like exchanges at the fringes of society, as orthodox yarns about money's origins presuppose. Money is, rather, a centralized fiscal project, promulgated by governments from ancient Sumer to medieval China to the contemporary United States. As a primarily fiscal infrastructure, money organizes finite material production through an abstract government writing instrument that no currency-issuing polity can be said to lose or lack.

On MMT's argument, money arises whenever a governing institution or stakeholder at the center of a community imposes obligations on the wider collective in the form of taxation, including fees, fines, or tithes. Denominated in a unit the stakeholder sets, governs, and enforces, such obligations form the backbone of all economic activity, public and private alike. In this way, the tax obligation renders money a thoroughly political institution. It is subject to no special or cordoned off "laws of motion" beyond the supreme challenges of political contestation, social valuation, and technical knowhow.[2] In this way, money hinges on what MMT describes as a vertical rapport between stakeholder and community, defined by interdependence in all directions and a numerically unconstrained fiscal center. Only secondarily does money's

[2] Burkett, John P, "Marx's Concept of an Economic Law of Motion." *History of Political Economy* 32, no. 2 (2000): 381–394, https://muse.jhu.edu/article/13208.

macro-economic constitution make possible localized horizontal transactions, which Liberal modernity mistakenly reduces to finite barter-like exchanges and frequently metaphorizes as so many unhinged flows.

As a consequence, MMT surmises, a currency-issuing polity can forever afford to guarantee persons employment and involvement, access, and care, regardless of the going quantity of federal tax receipts or bond sales. So long as fiscal expenditures activate meaningful and productive activities, public spending can usher forth a robust, ecologically sensitive, and socially inclusive system of production and distribution without causing deleterious inflation.

MMT economist Stephanie Kelton encapsulates her school's singular approach to political economy with an elegant maxim: "Money is no object."[3] At first glance, Kelton's maxim seems to echo Karl Marx's oft-cited language in his book, *The Poverty of Philosophy:* "Money is not a thing, it is a social relation."[4] For Marx, this means that money is not simply an exchanged object; it is an abstract social system that, rather paradoxically, engenders estranging phantom-like relations at a remove through the immediate exchange of material things. Kelton's maxim similarly de-naturalizes of money. However, Kelton goes much further and in a quite different direction. A deliberate pun, her quip "money is no object" puts a critical twist on Marx's characterization of money's social form by re-conceiving its fundamental locus, shape, and capacity.

Namely, Kelton anchors the money relation, not in the spectral objectivity Marx discerns in far-flung individuated exchanges but, rather, in the government's broad and inalienable fiscal-tax system. And when it comes to the public purse, Kelton declares, *politics,* not affordability or private profit, is the only serious constraint. With this, Kelton and her MMT colleagues not only liberate the treasury for common use and disputation, but also crucially sever money's spatial locus—or *topology*—from what Marxists often describe as the "real abstraction" or "mediated immediacy" of the cash nexus. Whereas the Marxist critique of Liberal political economy lambasts money for organizing ghastly relations between remote things, MMT's argument for money's irreducibly wide and inexhaustible

[3] Stephanie Kelton, *The Deficit Myth: Modern Monetary Theory and the Birth of the People's Economy* (New York Public Affairs, 2020), 182.

[4] Karl Marx, *The Poverty of Philosophy,* trans. Harry Queltch (New York: Cosimo Inc., 2008), 87.

fiscal architecture reveals Marxism's preoccupation with ghostly objectification to be topologically misplaced and politically misleading. In contrast, MMT discloses radical and imminently realizable possibilities for social and ecological transformation by transmuting money from the perceived root of all evil into the most capacious revolutionary weapon within reach.

In *Declarations of Dependence*, I take MMT's chartalist view of money as provocation to re-conceive abstraction and reground critical theory's traditionally Marxist approach to modern culture and aesthetics. The book's key theses unfold across four main body chapters, which I will briefly summarize. Chapter 1 is titled "Transcending the Aesthetic." In it, I sketch a genealogy of MMT in critical dialog with Marxism, as I have here. Next, I read modernity's dialectical opposition between money and aesthetics as a debilitating symptom of the hegemonic Liberal conception of money that Marxism shares. In place of this seemingly interminable dialectic, I draw the aesthetic's historical dedication to sensory and social enrichment entirely within money's commodious fiscal structure, aiming to redeem money and aesthetics alike.

Chapter 2, titled "Declarations of Dependence," risks the surprising thesis that money constitutes the center of collective caretaking in modernity. Developing what I term a "politics of care," I turn to the Roman "myth of Cura" to tease out an alternative definition of care. Reading the Cura myth alongside works by Martin Heidegger and Judith Butler, I claim that care is irreducible to the embodied, altruistic, and often feminized activity to which Liberal modernity often reduces it. Rather, care, as I characterize it, is an inescapable and enigmatic charge that derives from collective dependence but frequently goes unheeded. On this expanded reading, then, care is not a willing altruism but rather the constitutive problematics that condition collective and individuated responses from macro to micro registers. Approaching money through this alternative conception of care, I shift critical theory's principal concern from overwrought problems of freedom and power in modernity to repressed riddles of social dependence and ecological maintenance. Finally, I outline a fresh symptomology of care by drawing on the object-relations school of psychoanalysis. Whereas psychoanalysis's traditional Oedipal logics root symptoms in contradictions between desirous subjects and paternal laws, the object-relations school permits me to read cultural artifacts as cryptic signs of care's historical contradictions and failures, while leveraging the resulting insights toward broad political demands.

My third chapter develops a new historical and theoretical framework for imagining the money relation in modernity. It does so by contesting conventional accounts of modern history that foreground the allegedly spontaneous emergence of merchant and banking activity in the Italian peninsula during the High Middle Ages. Titled "*Medium Congruent-tisimum,*" or "communal medium," Chapter 3 traces money's modern European ascent back to the late medieval papacy's broad-scale fiscal-tax system and the aesthetics and theology that supported this system. Specifically, I track a well-known shift in Western metaphysics that, on my analysis, first reveals, then conceals the topology and capacities of money that MMT makes perceptible. During the High Middle Ages, for example, the scholastic theology of Thomas Aquinas and the Gothic aesthetics represented by cathedrals envisioned social and material provisioning as a far-reaching and centralized cascade of dependence mediated by multiple levels of abstraction. In the tumultuous fourteenth and fifteenth centuries, however, Franciscan theologians and humanist writers and artists rejected this vision of the real for an immediate metaphysics of "thisnness" or, in Latin, "haecceity." Deeming broad-scale mediation an artificial, arbitrary, and ultimately unnecessary assertion of sovereign will, Franciscans and humanists reduced being in general and money in particular to a contingent and ever-alienable haecceity, setting the groundwork for the rise of Liberal modernity. In Chapter 3, I recuperate something to the spirit of high medieval mediation as way of attuning critical theory anew to the crises and possibilities of modern money.

Chapter 4, "Allegories of the Aesthetic," uncovers what I see as the repressed historical secret of the modern aesthetic project within what I call Western modernity's "gravitropic visuality." Born with perspectival painting during the Florentine Renaissance, the modern era's gravitropic visuality simulates spectatorial immersion, contiguous movement, and a universally enjoyed material gravity. In doing so, I claim, it represses inscription's abstract and paratactic or non-contiguous qualities that shaped medieval iconography, while expressing a wish to redeem the proximate haecceity that later British Sentimentalists and German idealists make the basis of the modern aesthetic project. In time, various modernisms and avant-gardes challenged this gravitropic visuality. Yet it returned with a vengeance in the neoliberal epoch with the rise of New Hollywood blockbusters and triple-A video games. Following a symptomatic analysis of such hyper-Newtonian media, I conclude *Declarations of Dependence* with an exhortation to divest modern sensory existence of visual culture's gravitropic assurances and to embrace abstraction across monetary and aesthetic realms.

In the remainder of this essay, I want to highlight and expand some of my book's interlocking claims over the course of three sections. First, I explicate the constrictive modern metaphysics of haecceity that so constrain care in Western modernity. Second, I turn a critical eye toward modernity's gravitropic visuality in order to rethink the historically vexed problem of aesthetic abstraction. Third, I consider abstraction's present political and aesthetic stakes by looking closely at the hyper-Newtonian Disney blockbuster *Big Hero 6*.

Part I. Modern Metaphysics: The Big Squeeze

My contention in *Declarations of Dependence* is that while the center of care ontologically precedes the money relation, money becomes the dominant means for politically organizing the mystery of social dependence during the modern period. Yet as I argue in my third chapter, the calamity of Western modernity is that the hegemonic conception of money is predicated upon a contracted metaphysics of haecceity, or *thisness*. Arising in Franciscan theology and humanist methods during the fourteenth and fifteenth centuries, haecceity forecloses care's central locus and wide mediating breadth.

To understand this historical break in Western metaphysics one must comprehend the Thomas Aquinas's synthesis of the scholastic tradition from which haecceity departs. Writing during the great political and economic expansion of the High Middle Ages, Thomas argued that being takes the shape of a centralizing, inalienable, and inescapably interdependent cascade of being. While no doubt reliant upon the contiguous comings and goings of individual creatures and things, this boundless cascade realizes the broad labor of Creation all at once via its entire interconnected infrastructure. Thomas's metaphysics sought to make sense of the late medieval period's ballooning political economy and converging cultures. Such metaphysics are perhaps best emblematized by the inexhaustible transubstantiation of the Eucharist on disparate altars. But they also undergird Thomas's writings on angels, whose non-locomotive movement permits instant passage from one location to another without coursing through intervening space. Still more miraculous from a modern perspective is the fact that Thomas's metaphysics served as the basis for late medieval chartalist conceptions of a boundless fiscal apparatus, what jurists from Bracton to Accursius referred to as the "fiscus sanctissimuss," or the "most holy fisc."[5]

In the centuries following Thomas's time, late medieval Europe entered a long and painful twilight beset by countless political, economic, and environmental crises. Responding to these crises, Franciscan theologians such as Duns Scotus and William of Ockham and humanists from Petrarch to Erasmus challenged the Thomistic synthesis with a new metaphysics and a recognizably modern social topology. This metaphysical *topos* decentered Thomism's boundless cascade, reconstituting the Christian God as an absolute and immediate willing power in the world. In so doing, the Franciscans and humanists variously contracted dependency's wide causal breadth into a contiguous and ultimately alienable "thisness" which, as I've noted, Scotus famously dubbed "haecceitas" or "haecceity." Increasingly, this new modern topology of being reduced causality to efficient relations, while deeming anything like concurrent mediation at a distance either unnecessary, artificial, or downright impossible.

Over time, the *topos* of haecceity became the unquestioned metaphysical backdrop for an ascendant modernity, lending direction, rhythm, and significance to everything from political economy to aesthetics. It enabled influential Franciscans and humanists to reject Thomist visions of an incorruptible holy fisc and to re-envision money as an alienable medium of exchange. It spurred Renaissance visual and literary culture to supplant Gothic and Byzantine abstraction for figurations of immediate sensuous embodiment and a passionate material *gravitas*. At the same time, metaphysical commitments to an immediate willing potency saw political philosophers from Machiavelli to Hobbes think the polis primarily in terms of power, subordinating care's vast scaffolding to the status of a weak, naïve, and often feminized supplement.

The key historical contribution to this process was the rise of Reformed Christianity. Staging what was essentially a tax revolt against the Papacy, Reformed Christianity variously jettisoned the Church's feminized mediations symbolized by the Virgin Mary, while promising a more intimate relationship with the divine Father through an intensified personal faith and direct access to biblical interpretation. Justifying a period of destructive religious wars, Reformed Christianity and corresponding Counter-Reformation precipitated the exclusionary political consolidations now

[5] Ernst Kantorowicz, *The King's Two Bodies: A Study in Medieval Political Theology* (Princeton: Princeton University Press, 1997), 184.

erroneously associated with the so-called Westphalian settlement, which in turn birthed the modern system of fiscally strapped and financially unstable nation-states. Finally, modernity's haecceity metaphysics cast the mold for an emergent philosophy and practice of the aesthetic. Set against monetary exchange while mirroring its dreams of expansive proximity, the aesthetic aimed to cure the inadequacies of Liberalism's alienating and destructive money form. Only, it sought to save the modern bourgeoisie by redeeming the same poisonous haecceity metaphysics that conditioned Liberal money's myriad deficiencies.

Part II. The Aesthetic: There, There

Rethinking the rise and nature of the modern aesthetic project, my book reposes what is arguably critical theory's central historical problem: abstraction. For critical theorists, the problem of modernity lies in the inscrutable relationship between monetary abstraction and the production of sensuous life as a whole. Generally speaking, critical theory's contribution to this problem rests upon two inter-related insights. The first Fredric Jameson puts well: money is what he calls "the fundamental source of all abstraction" in modern life.[6] The second concerns monetary abstraction's central influence on representation writ large. In T. J. Clark's words, "money is the root form of representation" in modern society.[7] I concur with both of these insights. However, I part company with critical theory's commitment to an ordinary thisness because this attachment to haecceity presumes monetary abstraction inevitably subtracts something from embodied sociality. What is worse, it tacitly accepts that social production governed by abstraction must be stamped by carelessness.

To rebuff this reduction of abstraction to carelessness is to recuperate aesthetics for politics and transfigure critical theory's interpretation of aesthetic artifacts. Refusing vulgar reductions and determinations, the best critical theory reads sensuous artifacts as genuine sociohistorical riddles in the face of the aesthetic project's historical failures to redeem the modern world. Such work gives voice to historical suffering, while grasping toward a more just tomorrow. For my part, I not only place

[6] Fredric Jameson, *The Cultural Turn* (New York: W. W. Norton & Company, 2000), 162.

[7] T. J. Clark, *Farewell to an Idea: Episodes from a History of Modernism* (New Haven, CT: Yale University Press, 1999), 10.

money's boundless center at the heart of such inquiries. I also diagnose the modern aesthetic project itself a symptom of Liberal modernity's relentless attachment to haecceity and I disclose the unconscious wish that drives the aesthetic project through a fresh reading of modernity's dominant gravitropic visuality.

Born with the perspectival painting of Renaissance Florence, modernity's gravitropic visuality has been long recognized for its pursuit of mimetic likeness, or the so-called *imatatio naturae* principle (Fig. 1). On the standard interpretation, Quattrocento perspective is said to break with the abstract, iconic, and unapologetically paratactic pictorial strategies of Gothic and Byzantine visual culture and, instead, derive its forms from the structure of nature and natural perception. With parallel lines that converge at one or more vanishing points, Renaissance perspective promises to open a transparent window onto embodied relations in the real world. Suspicious of the viewpoint perspectivalism produces, Marxist aestheticians have underscored its links to the possessive individualism of modern life. Such arguments follow Marxist critiques of money in that they accuse an abstract form of naturalizing social domination and economic alienation. The abstractions of Renaissance perspective carve out a disembodied and idealized position of mastery for the viewing subject to whom they extend an illusion of transparency. The result allows the bourgeois subject to imagine holding dominion over the world and possessing myriad objects. As in Marxist critiques of money, however, the dubious mathematics of Renaissance perspective in fact dominate the subject they establish and alienate its illusory viewpoint from connections to the material and social world.

On my interpretation, Renaissance perspective is neither "natural" nor properly "abstract," and the historical significance of Quattrocento pictorialism has little to do with oppositions between transparency and opacity. Instead, I argue, Renaissance perspective constructs a gravitropic phenomenology that aims to materially embrace viewer and viewed in a relationship of material propinquity—no matter how stable or unstable, transparent or opaque, that relation may appear. This phenomenology places the spectatorial body in the here-and-now of a geometrically projected scene. More important, it physically anchors the embodied viewpoint in a distributed array of light and heavy figures suggesting a world held together by invisible forces of gravitational attraction that include the viewing position itself. Meanwhile, this overlooked

Fig. 1 The Holy Trinity

phenomenology harbors an unconscious collective wish: a wish to physically secure social mediation at a distance through gravity's invisible contiguous force. In the face of money's alienable thisness, gravitropic visuality cradles the sensorium in its all-encompassing material grasp. It mediates social relations between near and far, seen and unseen, and does so in a manner that abjures what humanist Lorenzo Valla dismissed as the "weightless ravings" of Thomistic scholasticism and the dizzying ethereality of Gothic visuality.[8]

With this, Renaissance perspective's gravitropic phenomenology seeks to make good on the anemic haecceity that organizes the money relation conceived in the Florentine Republic. By rendering haecceity a totalizing and all-inclusive relation of material propinquity, Quattrocento perspective at once reduces relationality to contiguity and imagines that this contiguity is capable of holding the social totality together. "There, there," it whispers, there's still a "there, there," just as "all that is solid melts into air."[9]

In the centuries that followed the rise of Renaissance painting, its passionate gravitropism became the underlying *topos* of modern consciousness and, I suggest, the very archetype of the modern aesthetic project. Indeed, as scholar Michael Friedman has demonstrated, Immanuel Kant's *Critique of Judgment* is not only responsible for giving this project its fundamental expression, but also did so by refashioning Isaac Newton's theory of universal gravitation to imagine the aesthetic as a distinctly modern site of sensuous and communal salvation. It is true, Friedman explains, that Kant's transcendental thinking eschewed the substantive forces proffered by Newton. He made no explicit mention the Englishman's theological characterization of gravity as "an emanative effect of God and an affection of every kind of being."[10] Yet throughout his later writings, Friedman shows, Kant fashioned the aesthetic project in the image of gravity's universal materiality and affectivity. "Kant saw a deep analogy," Friedman writes, "between the community of all rational beings in a moral realm of ends and the thoroughgoing community effected by among all material bodies in the universe by universal gravitation."[11]

[8] Lorenzo Valla, ed., and trans. Brendan Cook, Correspondence (Cambridge, MA: Harvard University Press, 2013), 111. I am indebted to Brendan Cook for this alternative translation.

[9] Karl Marx and Friedrich Engels, *The Communist Manifesto* (Chicago: Pluto Press, 1996), 54.

[10] Isaac Newton, *Isaac Newton: Philosophical Writings*, ed. A. Janiak (Cambridge: Cambridge University Press, 2004), 21.

[11] Michael Friedman, "Newton and Kant on Absolute Space: From Theology to Transcendental Philosophy," in *Constituting Objectivity: Transcendental Perspectives on Modern Physics*, ed. Michel Bitbol, Pierre Kerszberg, and Jean Petito (New York: Springer, 2009), 49.

This brings me to my book's culminating thesis: that is, modernity's gravitropic visuality reveals both the hidden secret of the aesthetic project and its catastrophic limitations. Like perspectival painting, the aesthetic constitutes a gravitropic form of care. Rejecting abstract mediation at a distance, the aesthetic's gravitropic embrace stretches haecceity to its maximal capacity in hopes of saving the social totality. Tragically, however, the aesthetic has proven incapable of fulfilling its historical charge of securing the social and material order. On my argument, then, the aesthetic signals the failure of haecceity, the constraining limits of modern care, and the punishing austerity of modern political economy.

A vital and by now inextricable feature of modern life, the aesthetic project has in many ways replaced the Church as the primary contributor of sensuous artifacts and experiences to political and economic domains. In making the aesthetic's bounded gravity the site of collective salvation, however, Liberal modernity turned us away from money's limitless center, obliging aesthetic praxis to contribute far more than it can afford. Contemporary aestheticians know the hopelessness of this charge; but they do not perceive its conditions. Melancholically renouncing the dialectic between money and aesthetics, they fail to detect the problematic history of this relation or to imagine a genuinely curative way forward.

To transcend this impasse, critical theorists after MMT must discern and treat its entrenched symptomology. Such symptoms include Marxism's own preoccupation's with gravity as well as the immersive Baroque physics of New Hollywood blockbusters and triple-A video games. As I demonstrate in my book, these "hyper-Newtonian" media announce both the collapse and exhaustion of the historical dialectic between money and aesthetics in the neoliberal era by compulsively making gravitropic salvation into a global commercial spectacle. Their immersive "thrill rides" collapse the difference between abstraction and physics, pronouncing the death of the aesthetic's moneyless utopia by serving as corporate cash cows, while rendering the phenomenological structure of money's boundless center illegible.

Still, far all of their problems, such media forms represent deeply meaningful symptoms that call out for attention and care. While riddled by self-destructive contradictions, hyper-Newtonian media unconsciously express their own "declarations of dependence," impassioned demands for a more expansive, diverse, and secure collectivity in the face of neoliberalism's debilitating reduction of monetary and aesthetic abstraction to an unanswerable global flux.

Part III: Wither Abstraction: Are You Satisfied with Your Care?

To model a form of treating today's hyper-Newtonian symptoms, I conclude with Disney's computer-animated feature *Big Hero 6,* which raises a question that cuts to the core of neoliberal media and the fate of the aesthetic project. Each time the film's inflatable healthcare robot, Baymax, performs treatment, he asks: "Are you satisfied with your care?" According to his programming, only a "yes" will suffice. For a media form that doles out lessons to its consumers, this affirmation seems cunningly reflexive and ideologically pernicious. Throughout *Big Hero 6*, Baymax's programming is played for humor. At the film's climax, his query becomes the source of a fatal and seemingly impossible decision. Free-floating in an alternative dimension of ponderous volumetric space, Baymax is damaged and can no longer use the majority of his powers. Thus stranded, he and protagonist Hiro reach out to stabilize each other's movements (Fig. 2).

With this, Hiro and Baymax return us to the origins of early modernity's gravitropic visuality. Recalling the figure of Francis reaching toward God's hand in Giotto's *Saint Francis Renounces His Father* (Fig. 3), the pair evoke above all Michelangelo's *Creation of Adam* (Fig. 4), wherein God's outstretched finger expresses the narrow and contingent foundations of human existence. Conjuring countless similar arrangements in hyper-Newtonian media, their interlocked grip also points to the original computer-generated hand created by Pixar founder and president of Walt Disney Studios, Ed Catmull in 1972 (Fig. 5). A wire-form construc-

Fig. 2 Big Hero 6 Reaching

Fig. 3 Giotto Francis

Fig. 4 Creation of Adam

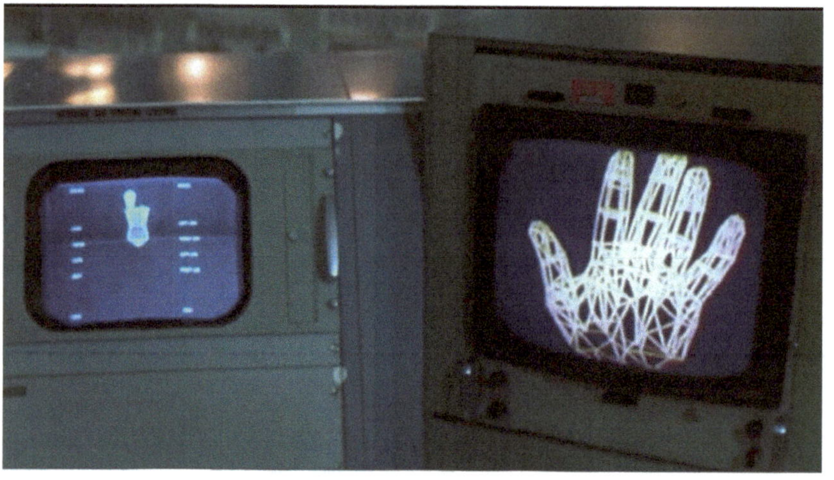

Fig. 5 Future World Catmull Hand

tion featured in the 1976 film *Futureworld,* Catmull's hand pioneered the Renaissance-style polygon projection techniques that have grounded more than four decades of abstract practical and computer graphics in fantasies of immediate material touching.

As they drift together and without recourse, Baymax offers to use his fist, an operational rocket, to propel Hiro back to safety. Because every hyper-Newtonian action has its reaction, however, this means Baymax will be pushed deeper into the ether, where he will perish alone. Committed to this strategy, Baymax must nonetheless ask his routine question and receive an affirmative answer. When he asks Hiro, "Are you satisfied with your care?," the boy struggles to discover a way to save them both. "There is no time," Baymax retorts before reiterating his question. Rebuffed again, Baymax summons the origins of the blockbuster by way of Obi-Wan Kenobi. "Hiro," he pledges, "I will always be with you," to which the boy weepingly replies after another embrace: "I'm satisfied with my care." Riding Baymax's fist to safety, Hiro's caretaker drifts toward the image's vanishing point and will eventually be swallowed by Quattrocento perspective's crushingly limited schema of the infinite.

Are we satisfied with our care: yes or no? Such is the choice we face when it comes to the modern dialectic between money and aesthetics. The conclusion to *Big Hiro 6* offers the neoliberal path forward. At the end of the film, Baymax returns to Hiro in the form of a memory chip, clenched securely in the detachable fist he rode to safety. A token of haecceity, the chip is a compact vehicle for storing abstract information that attains its place and significance against a gravitropic background. Delimited in space and contingent with respect to time, the memory chip permits Hiro to give back to Baymax and thereby help him keep his caregiver's promise. As with the aesthetic project as a whole, *Big Hero 6* answers neoliberalism's zero-sum logic with a caring and mutually reciprocating haecceity. From MMT's vantage, of course, takes the very form of neoliberalism and, as such, represents a historical road to nowhere.

That is why, to truly retain the force of the aesthetic project for a just and sustainable future, we must refuse neoliberalism's false and austere choices and enfold both money and aesthetics into abstraction's boundless and inalienable embrace. Care, in other words, is a distinctly abstract business, which should never be reduced to immediate material forces or the delimited to possibilities ascribed therein. Indeed, if, as Sara Nelson tirelessly reminds us, "solidarity is a force stronger than gravity," then it will be necessary to collectively seize the means of abstraction before we can even hope to take flight.

References

Theodor W. Adorno, *Aesthetic Theory*, trans. Robert Hullot-Kentor (London: Bloomsbury, 2013).

Thomas Aquinas, *The Summa Theologica of St. Thomas Aquinas* (London: Burns Oates & Washbourne, 1912).

Michael Baxandall, *Giotto and the Orators: Humanist Observers of Painting in Italy and the Discovery of Pictorial Composition, 1350–1450* (Oxford: Clarendon Press, 1971).

John P. Burkett, "Marx's Concept of an Economic Law of Motion." *History of Political Economy* 32, no. 2 (2000): 381–394. muse.jhu.edu/article/13208.

Judith Butler, *Notes Toward a Performative Theory of Assembly* (Cambridge: Harvard University Press, 2015).

T. J. Clark, *Farewell to an Idea: Episodes from a History of Modernism* (New Haven CT: Yale University Press, 1999).

Eamon Duffy, *The Stripping of the Altars, c. 1450–c. 1580* (New Haven CT: Yale University Press, 1992).

Terry Eagleton, *The Ideology of the Aesthetic* (Oxford: Blackwell Publishers, 1991).

Scott Ferguson, *Declarations of Dependence: Money, Aesthetics & the Politics of Care* (Omaha: University of Nebraska Press, 2018).

Michael Friedman, "Newton and Kant on Absolute Space: From Theology to Transcendental Philosophy," in *Constituting Objectivity: Transcendental Perspectives on Modern Physics*, ed. Michel Bitbol, Pierre Kerszberg, and Jean Petito (New York: Springer, 2009).

Martin Heidegger, *Being and Time*, trans. John Macquarrie and Edward Robinson (New York: Harper Perennial Modern Classics, 2008).

Fredric Jameson, *The Cultural Turn* (New York: W. W. Norton & Company, 2000).

Fredric Jameson, *Postmodernism, or, The Cultural Logic of Late Capitalism* (Durham, NC: Duke University Press, 1997).

Immanuel Kant, *Critique of Judgment*, trans. Werner S. Pluhar (Indianapolis, IND: Hackett Pub. Co, 1987).

Ernst Kantorowicz, *The King's Two Bodies: A Study in Medieval Political Theology* (Princeton: Princeton University Press, 1997).

Stephanie Kelton, *The Deficit Myth: Modern Monetary Theory and the Birth of the People's Economy* (New York Public Affairs, 2020).

Karl Marx, *The Poverty of Philosophy*, trans. Harry Queltch (New York: Cosimo Inc., 2008).

Karl Marx and Friedrich Engels, *The Communist Manifesto* (Chicago: Pluto Press, 1996).

Sara Nelson, "Solidarity Is a Force Stronger Than Gravity," *LGBTQ Nation*, June 5, 2019, date accessed September 20, 2021. https://www.lgbtqnation.com/2019/06/solidarity-force-stronger-gravity/.

Isaac Newton, *Isaac Newton: Philosophical Writings*, ed. A. Janiak (Cambridge: Cambridge University Press, 2004).

Thomas H. Ogden, *The Primitive Edge of Experience* (London: Aronson, 1989).

Paul Vincent Spade, *Five Texts on the Mediaeval Problem of Universals* (Indianapolis: Hackett Publishing Company, 1994).

Steven Ozment, *The Age of Reform, 1250—1550: An Intellectual and Religious History of Late Medieval and Reformation Europe* (New Haven CT: Yale University Press, 1980).

Warrant T. Reich, *Encyclopedia of Bioethics*, revised edition, ed. Warren Thomas Reich, 5 vols. (New York: Simon & Schuster Macmillan, 1995).

Lorenzo Valla, *Correspondence*, trans. Brendan Cook (Cambridge: Harvard University Press).

L. Randall Wray. *Understanding Modern Money: The Key to Full Employment and Price Stability* (Northampton, MA: Edward Elgar Publishing, 2006).

D. W. Winnicott, "The Theory of the Parent-Infant Relation," *International Journal of Psychoanalysis* 41 (1960): 585–95, 590.

Water, Money, and the Job Guarantee

Jakob Feinig

> Foolish parents attempt to hold their children back from willful destruction by asserting that the things they wish to destroy cost money! Instead of explaining to their children the value of the object itself, their economic response begins with an emphasis on the money spent. (Simmel 2004: 270, translation adapted)

When he wrote the comment in the epigraph, the sociologist Georg Simmel expressed his frustration with a way of looking at things that reduces everything to its cash value. He thought that instead of emphasizing their monetary cost, sensible parents should teach children to appreciate objects because of the work it takes to produce them, their usefulness, or their beauty. If only adults instructed children about the true worth of things, children would cease to destroy them. But if we remember many parents' pain when they cannot buy shoes or school supplies for their children, calling them foolish sounds unreasonable: In

J. Feinig (✉)
Department of Human Development, Binghamton University, Binghamton, NY, USA
e-mail: jfeinig@binghamton.edu

B. C. Wilson, *Care, Climate, and Debt*,
https://doi.org/10.1007/978-3-030-96355-2_11

practical terms, the monetary perspective is often the most important one for impoverished households.

At the level of society at large, however, Simmel's remark rings true. Often, policymakers, pundits, and other actors who operate at the level of monetary governance act like Simmel's "foolish parents." Under certain conditions, the availability of cash does not constrain governance institutions because they are not powerless relative to money creation.[1] Actors and institutions of monetary governance do not face monetary constraints comparable to households. Instead, for monetary governance institutions, cash is a means for mobilizing resources, coordinating the activities of people, and organizing society. Unlike parents, they can afford to value things, resources, and human labor according to criteria they choose. Yet instead of debating the inherent value of ecosystems, public infrastructure, or human health, public commentators think only in terms of "the money spent." Even though money is a means toward socially defined ends, saving money seems to become an end in itself.

Simmel argued that large-scale institutions such as money or the military end up obfuscating the ends for which they have been established. They leave their imprint on society because they become ends in and of themselves:

> Aside from money, militarism is perhaps the most striking example [...]. The regular army is a mere preparation, a latent energy, a contingency, whose ultimate goal and purpose not only very rarely materializes but is also avoided at all costs. [...] we have reached the very pinnacle of the contradiction that lies in the *drowning out of the end by the means: the growing significance of the means goes hand in hand with a corresponding increase in the rejection and negation of the end*. And this factor increasingly permeates the social life of the people; it directly interferes with personal, political, and economic relationships. (Simmel 2004: 486, emphasis added)

For Simmel, the means-ends confusion takes place whenever a realm of practice with its own logic is established. Its practitioners tend to overlook its character as means, and come to see it as an end to which other spheres are subordinate (Simmel 2004: 371). Informed only by their internal logic, and shielded from influences such as meaningful democratic

[1] See, e.g., Kelton (2020).

participation, large institutional formations become ends in themselves, and subordinate the social world to their own logic.

While for Simmel, the confusion of means and ends is a necessary effect of large institutions, I offer a more optimistic perspective on the institutions that create money. I show that, in the realm of money, the means-ends confusion depends on a set of historically changing conditions, including how we think about money and public debt. Margaret Atwood (2008: 203) commented that "notions about debt form part of the elaborate imaginative construct that is human society. [...] because it is a mental construct, how we think about it changes how it works." If possibilities change according to how we think institutions work, it is worthwhile looking at the conditions of our knowledge about monetary systems and public debt. Could it be that the means (money) doesn't always drown out the public purpose?[2] Can we institutionalize money—the "means of means" (Simmel 2004: 490)—in a way that enables more democratic forms of living together?

Eighteenth-century New York City is an instructive entry point for addressing these questions. This city was marked by rigid exclusions and hierarchies and far from a democratic society. But the methods through which the municipal government attempted to reorganize water provisioning are instructive because at first, the end (water provisioning) did not overwhelm the means (money).

Money and Water in New York City

The lack of clean drinking water was a constant problem in eighteenth-century Gotham, where horse carriages distributed water from a suburban well to urban households. In 1774, an engineer proposed to build underground pipes connected to a steam pump, a pioneering effort in the British North American colonies. He estimated that the high-tech system would cost £18,000 when the city's yearly revenues were £3,000 and its outstanding debt £13,000 (Koeppel 2001: 42). This estimate, however, did not intimidate city officials: To pay for the infrastructure, they ordered that notes in different denominations be printed. The municipal treasury promised to accept them in payment of taxes (Minutes of the Common

[2] On money and the public purpose, see Ehnts and Höfgen (2020).

Council 1905: 41, 55, 59), and they became "current as money" (Bangs 1890: 25).

When it made them legal tender for debts owed the municipality, policymakers ensured the currency's acceptance within New York City and surrounding areas: Because households routinely had to pay taxes, fees, or fines to the city, these pay tokens became desirable, and people were willing to work for them, knowing that others would also accept them. When it issued this currency, the city government used the certainty that people would incur obligations to it to finance an urgent investment without having to acquire types of money over which it had no control.

This is an example of how water works currency entered and exited circulation: When the city paid the business that delivered trees for the wooden water pipes, its owner paid the workers. These workers used the money to pay off debts or to purchase goods and services, passing it on to others. The money would remain in circulation until someone used it to pay taxes, fees, or fines to the monetary system's central actor: The City of New York. Even though the city's debt increased, the municipal treasury would not have to pay back its obligations in a currency it did not control. The circulating water works debt was nothing but the money it had spent but not withdrawn through taxes.

Water provisioning was tenuous, but the municipal government also acted in a context in which colonists struggled with imperial authorities over the right to issue currency. While colonial legislatures had long claimed the right to create money for public infrastructure and credit to small farmers, Britain limited this practice in the middle decades of the eighteenth century. As a result, debtors struggled to pay back loans, prices for agricultural staples decreased, and colonists had to rely on ledger entries with merchants to get credit and make purchases. Imperial currency policies were unpopular and caused massive tensions with Britain (Greene and Jellison 1961; Bouton 2007; Edwards 2017). New York City's water works currency was suspicious from the standpoint of imperial authorities, but it was in line with a long-standing and popular practice of colonial money creation. Even as colonists inched toward war with Britain, even as inhabitants fled and a fire ravaged the city, work continued on what had become an entire sector of the economy, fueled by water works money. When British soldiers entered the city, they destroyed the already-functioning steam pump and the rest of the water infrastructure (Koeppel 2001: 49).

After the war, lack of clean water continued to plague the city, a concern that became more pressing when yellow fever reappeared. But this time, policymakers took a different financial route. When the New York state legislature passed an act "for supplying the city of New-York with pure and wholesome water" (1799), they established a corporation that promised to create water infrastructure. Unbeknownst to lawmakers and the population at large, the assembly granted privileges far beyond water provisioning, including the right to issue currency. The company prioritized currency creation over water provisioning, and its bank became known as Chase Manhattan (Hammond 1962: 152; Koeppel 2001: 71–101; Wright 1998). Water provisioning had become a pretext for authorizing corporate money creation. The means—money—began to drown out the end: Reliable access to clean water.

Contrasting the water works currency and the Manhattan company's bank notes is instructive. The municipal currency carried an elaborate engraving of the steam pump at the heart of the water provisioning system and instructed money users about the public purpose for which the city had issued the currency. Conversely, corporate money informed its beholder only about the issuing bank. Both types of currency were debt: Water works money was municipal debt, and the city promised to accept it in payment of debts owed to it. Conversely, the bank's currency was the bank's debt, and it also promised to accept it in payment of debts to itself. Both were creatures of government. The municipal currency was a governmental practice in a direct and visible way. The corporate currency, in contrast, was part of an institution the state assembly had authorized to issue currency. These two currencies, these two forms of circulating debt, shaped notions of a community's fiscal elbow space, and a community's capacities to coordinate activities and mobilize resources for public infrastructure.

When they chartered the Manhattan Company, New York State lawmakers acted in a context in which the United States Constitution had categorically prohibited money creation by state assemblies. Congress was now the only actor allowed to create money. Faced with complaints about money scarcity, state lawmakers argued that while the Constitution had outlawed legislative money creation, they could charter currency-creating banks. The Manhattan Company was one of the first examples, and legislatures later chartered hundreds of banks, each with its own distinctive currency.

The new mode of corporate money creation reshaped how the population understood cash and credit: In the colonial era—when state legislatures had issued currencies similar to water works money—settlers had understood cash as a public good. It had been a means to mobilize collective resources, coordinate production, and make exchanges. After the Constitution, money seemed to become a creature of corporate banks, creatures animated by the profit motive. The economist Farley Grubb (2003: 1778) argues that this shift was "a usurpation of state sovereignty by rent-seeking bankers." The intertwined history of New York City money and water is an extreme example, but the tension between seeing and practicing money as a public good, or the product of a for-profit entity, remains in place today.[3] The character of debates about money, currency, and public debt changed when people focused on corporate banks' abuses and unearned profit but forgot to think about money as a potentially democratic means. The very loathing of corporate banks, a popular practice in the antebellum United States, helped drown out the end.

This brief visit to colonial and antebellum New York City allows us to rethink Simmel's claim about how money's character as a means disappears from view. If we look at the Manhattan Company's corporate bank notes in isolation, Simmel's claim rings true: The means (money creation) eclipsed the end (water provisioning). But water works money—the bank notes' predecessor currency—allows us to think about money in a more open-ended way. There is no reason to think that money has to sideline the public purpose. How a society understands and practices money depends, at least in part, on how it institutionalizes money creation. Money's character as a means for organizing society becomes visible or invisible depending on the institutional conditions of its creation.[4]

What People Know About the Monetary Coordination of Society

A strand of sociological inquiry its creators call Institutional Ethnography argues that in capitalist modernity, texts mediate the relation between governing institutions and publics: laws, regulations, memos, and instructions coordinate actors, and organize their lives-in-society. From the

[3] On money as a public infrastructure, see Kelton (2020). On money creation by corporate banks, see, e.g., Hockett and Omarova (2017).

[4] On this point, see Desan (2014) and Feinig (2022).

perspective of Institutional Ethnography, "the social as the focus for study is to be located in how people's activities or practices are *coordinated*. Individuals are there, they are in their bodies, they are active, and what they're doing is coordinated with the doings of others" (Smith 2005: 59, emphasis in the original). For instance, issuing bus tickets is a textual practice that connects potential bus riders to municipal policymakers.[5] By deciding about pricing and subsidies, and whether to distribute free passes to certain community members, policymakers coordinate access to and exclusion from public transportation, and organize individuals into two groups: Those who can ride the bus, and those who are excluded from it.

Through the processes we call "money," governance bodies also coordinate people's activities. First, when a government spends money to purchase goods and services, it mobilizes collective resources for what it has defined as a public good—from public housing to warfare. In the past, monetary-coordination-for-public-purpose was often more visible than today. Water works money is one example. Issuing money meant claiming the right to mobilize resources and to coordinate people's activities: Through water works currency, policymakers brought together raw materials, workers, and planners: the city government used them to pay for labor power, the trees out of which workers made the wooden pipes, and the engineer who developed the steam pump. The United States government created a similar currency to mobilize the resources it needed to fight the states that wanted to continue enslaving people of African descent. During the Civil War, the federal treasury paid soldiers and suppliers with a currency that became known as Greenbacks. In sum, monetary coordination occurs when a government deploys money for public purposes, when money animates the relation between governance bodies and a population (Desan 2016; Ingham 2004; Wray 1998). But governmental monetary practices also enable private actors to coordinate their activities once they have received the currency—they can now buy and sell things from each other but also settle debts.

Institutional Ethnographers claim that coordination mechanisms such as money separate those who do the coordinating from those whose lives are being coordinated, and place some actors in positions of knowledge denied to others, creating conditions for public silence and ignorance.

[5] I borrow this example from Campbell and Gregor (2004: 29–32).

Textual relations are "being put together systematically, but more or less mysteriously and outside a person's knowledge, and for purposes that may not be theirs" (Campbell and Gregor 2004: 18, see also Smith 1990, 2005). In a context of illegible relations, the texts that reach individuals' lives often appear as things—a bus ticket, for example, becomes a thing used to ride a bus. Similarly, from the perspective of everyday life, money—pay tokens—become things used to pay, to save, and to gauge the value of goods and services. Dorothy Smith (1987) calls this disconnect—which she considers a typical feature of ruling relations—"ideological rupture:" The break between "the world known in experience and the textual realities representing it in relations and apparatuses of power (Smith 1990: 103). For groups that are immersed in everyday struggles and concerns, the larger relations of money seem out of reach.

But this ideological rupture is not a necessary part of textual coordination, as water works and Civil War money show. Money users understood how these currencies worked, and they served a publicly defined purpose. They remained an intelligible means for a public purpose.

How can we recover the promise of intelligible currency, of public debt that serves a public purpose?

Money as a Means to an End: The Job Guarantee

New York City's water works money shows that, in the case of money and public debt, ideas about money shape possibilities for public action: Had policymakers attempted to borrow or tax *before* starting construction, work on the steam pump might never have begun. And had the New York State Assembly been able to create money to address the water issue after the war, they might have repeated the engineering feat. Instead, they chartered a corporate bank that had other priorities. Because of the way New York City and later the State Assembly institutionalized money creation, people's knowledge of money and debt changed. While public water works currency did not drown out the end, corporate cash functioned according to the logic of a for-profit institution. Money, then, is an example of "the elaborate imaginative construct that is human society. [...] because it is a mental construct, how we think about it changes how it works" (Atwood 2008: 203). Money has no inherent logic it imposes on societies, and there is no reason this large-scale mechanism for coordinating activities has to be opaque from the perspective of the population at large.

What would be today's equivalent of water works money—the practice of using money for a public purpose, and intelligibly so? An increasingly popular policy proposal, the federal Job Guarantee (e.g., Tcherneva 2018, 2020; Ehnts and Höfgen 2019), at first glance appears as just another social policy, but it could lead to a profound rethinking of money and society. The Job Guarantee would guarantee a publicly funded job to anyone willing and able to work. It would end involuntary unemployment, and provide jobs tailored to people's already-existing skills, allowing them to serve their communities. But the Job Guarantee is more than a promising social policy: it has the potential to transform our current understanding of money. If we begin to understand that governmental bodies can create money to coordinate the activities of people in communities, we can reconnect with money's character as a means. Collectively, we no longer think like Simmel's "foolish parents" who only ask what something costs. We can, instead, value the contributions and skills of real, living individuals on our own terms, and organize their contributions for tasks small and large, from municipal water provisioning to addressing the myriad emergencies of climate change.

References

Atwood, Margaret. 2008. *Payback: Debt and the Shadow Side of Wealth.* Toronto, Canada: Anansi.

Bangs, Isaac. 1890. *Journal of Lieutenant Isaac Bangs.* Cambridge, MA: John Wilson & Son.

Bouton, Terry. 2007. *Taming Democracy: "The People," the Founders, and the Troubled Ending of the American Revolution.* Oxford, UK: Oxford University Press.

Campbell, Marie L., and Frances Mary Gregor. 2004. *Mapping Social Relations: A Primer in Doing Institutional Ethnography.* Walnut Creek, CA: AltaMira Press.

Common Council of the City of New York. 1905. *Minutes of the Common Council of the City of New York, 1675-1776.* Vol. 8. New York: Dodd, Mead & Company.

Desan, Christine. 2014. *Making Money: Coin, Currency, and the Coming of Capitalism.* Oxford, UK: Oxford University Press.

———. 2016. "Money as a Legal Institution." In *Money in the Western Legal Tradition: Middle Ages to Bretton Woods*, ed. D. Fox and W. Ernst. Oxford: Oxford University Press.

Edwards, Andrew David. 2017. "Grenville's Silver Hammer: The Problem of Money in the Stamp Act Crisis." *Journal of American History* 104 (2):337–62.

Ehnts, Dirk, and Maurice Höfgen. 2019. "The Job Guarantee: Full Employment, Price Stability and Social Progress." *Society Register* 3 (2):49–65.

———. 2020. "Modern Monetary Theory and the Public Purpose." *Berlin School of Economics and Law Working Paper No. 133.*

Feinig, Jakob. 2022. *Moral Economies of Money: Politics and the Monetary Constitution of Society*. Redwood City, CA: Stanford University Press.

Greene, Jack P., and Richard M. Jellison. 1961. "The Currency Act of 1764 in Imperial-Colonial Relations, 1764-1776." *The William and Mary Quarterly* 18 (4):485–518.

Grubb, Farley. 2003. "Creating the U.S. Dollar Currency Union, 1748-1811: A Quest for Monetary Stability or a Usurpation of State Sovereignty for Personal Gain?" *American Economic Review* 93 (5):1778–98.

Hammond, Bray. 1962. *Banks and Politics in America: From the Revolution to the Civil War*. Princeton, NJ: Princeton University Press.

Hockett, Robert, and Saule Omarova. 2017. "The Finance Franchise." *Cornell Law Review* 102:1143–218.

Ingham, Geoffrey. 2004. *The Nature of Money*. Cambridge, UK: Polity.

Kelton, Stephanie. 2020. *The Deficit Myth: Modern Monetary Theory and the Birth of the People's Economy*. New York: PublicAffairs

Koeppel, Gerard. 2001. *Water for Gotham: A History*. Princeton, NJ: Princeton University Press.

Simmel, Georg. 2004. *The Philosophy of Money*. London: Routledge.

Smith, Dorothy. 1990. *The Conceptual Practices of Power. A Feminist Sociology of Knowledge*. Boston: Northeastern University Press.

———. 2005. *Institutional Ethnography: A Sociology for People*. Walnut Creek, CA: AltaMira Press.

Tcherneva, Pavlina. 2018. "The Job Guarantee: Design, Jobs, and Implementation." *Levy Economics Institute of Bard College Working Paper No. 902*, http://www.levyinstitute.org/pubs/wp_902.pdf.

———. 2020. *The Case for a Job Guarantee*. Cambridge, UK: Polity.

Wray, L. Randall. 1998. *Understanding Modern Money: The Key to Full Employment and Price Stability*. Cheltenham, UK; Northampton, MA: Edward Elgar.

Wright, Robert E. 1998. "Artisans, Banks, Credit, and the Election of 1800." *Pennsylvania Magazine of History and Biography* CXXII (3):211–40.

The Uni Currency Project: Democratic Finance for Public Higher Education After COVID-19

William O. Saas, Benjamin C. Wilson, Scott Ferguson, and Maxximilian Seijo

The COVID-19 pandemic exposed critical structural vulnerabilities in the funding models of US public colleges and universities. Rather than engage with radical proposals that might finally remediate those vulnerabilities and so furnish durable protections against future such crises, public higher

W. O. Saas (✉) · B. C. Wilson · S. Ferguson · M. Seijo
Global Institute for Sustainable Prosperity, Granville, OH, USA
e-mail: wsaas@tulane.edu

W. O. Saas
Tulane University, New Orleans, LA, USA

B. C. Wilson
State University of New York College at Cortland, Cortland, NY, USA

S. Ferguson
University of South Florida, Tampa, FL, USA

M. Seijo
University of California, Santa Barbara, CA, USA

B. C. Wilson, *Care, Climate, and Debt*,
https://doi.org/10.1007/978-3-030-96355-2_12

education's managers defaulted early in the pandemic to what resembles a new *crisis routine*: first, solicit emergency funding from state and federal legislators and, second, while awaiting Congressional action that will almost certainly be insufficient to the problem, pass the costs of the crisis onto workers and students through firings, freezes, flexibilization, and coerced-cum- "essential" work.

While the public higher education system today resides at center of numerous crises, its continued financial dependencies on flexible labor, over-indebted students, and hostile legislatures go largely unremarked upon. This is likely the case because—with some notable exceptions and confounding the estimates of even the most sanguine prognosticators—much of the US public higher education system remains in serviceable financial shape at the time of this writing. That this feat was accomplished at great physical, mental, and emotional toll to those that represent public higher ed's greatest democratic and redemptive promises—students, staff, researchers, and teachers—is already being forgotten. It remains likely that the next great crisis to affect higher ed will beget the same policies of financial reaction that predominated the administrative playbook leading up to and throughout the COVID pandemic.

There are of course many ways to account for ongoing administrative recalcitrance to responding to the COVID crisis proactively, with an eye toward improving the resilience of their institutions to recurrent and future crises. We believe that one plausible (if charitable) explanation is that, like most people, administrators of public higher education simply do not understand money. That is, they lack comprehension of the substantial fiscal agency of their institutions as those institutions exist and operate within the modern US monetary economy. Unreflexively in thrall to a neoliberal money politics that valorizes revenue while vaporizing money, these administrators and their supporters perhaps cannot help but acquiesce to calls by self-serving industry consultants and milquetoast politicians to slash budgets, raise tuition, and email their Congressperson. These policies, and the money politics that authorize and structure them, are all that such administrators know.

We contend, however, that acquiescence to the neoliberal vision of a fiscally nimble and financially reactionary public higher education system must be halted at all costs.[1] Indeed, from the vantage of Modern Monetary Theory (MMT), many of the actions taken by administrators and boards of regents in the wake of COVID-19 were heedless and totally unnecessary. If money is, as MMT so clearly demonstrates, a capacious public utility, then what is required of college and university administrators in times of financial crises is not accession to the austere directives of reactionary neoliberalism (Fraser 2018). What is required instead is to recognize and engage creatively with the tremendous fiscal and financial powers that constitute and emanate from our unheard-of but eminently public center—that space and system for collective provisioning which is constrained only by nature and political imagination (Ferguson 2018).

Large private corporations have long had imagination and influence enough to harness the near-limitless capacity of this unheard-of center to their own benefit in times of great crisis. The largest of these continue to tap easily accessible lines of credit that help them grow richer and more secure in a period of mass unemployment, ecological devastation, and collapsing public infrastructures. In this chapter, we build on previous work to provide advocates of public higher education—even and especially administrators—with a means by which to demand that public colleges and universities receive the same consideration given to large private corporations throughout and beyond the COVID-19 crisis. The policy mechanism is simple: Colleges and universities will issue local currencies, or "Unis," which will function as short-term notes. These notes will be used by colleges and universities to make payments for any and all services that they render. Simultaneously, and similar to the bottom-up pressure placed on the Fed by private actors, Unis will demand the same privileges and guarantees afforded to both public and private debt issuers through the Federal Reserve's extensive collection of lending facilities. When implemented, the two-stage Uni program will fend off threats to the health and welfare of public college and university students and workers. It will do so by activating a funding source that guarantees the salaries, wages, and benefits of all campus workers for the duration of this crisis and future crises, while also providing funds for the development

[1] Included in this view is the assumption that higher education budget cuts—resulting in campus layoffs and furloughs—would be a natural and even uncontestable outcome of the COVID-19 crisis. This misguided position is evident in an online petition signed by over 3,000 academics, many of them very prominent in their respective fields ("COVID-19" 2020).

and implementation of safe alternative approaches to post-secondary and graduate pedagogy. Especially when grounded in principles of workplace democracy, the salutary consequences of the Uni program will be myriad and durable, enabling meaningful systemic change in both the near- and the long-term. In what follows, we provide a more thorough accounting for the political, economic, legal, and pedagogical frameworks for the Uni program.

Public Finance in Crisis

Crises like those precipitated by the global spread of COVID-19 too rarely encourage critical reflection, careful planning, or creative thinking by economists and policymakers. Instead, as Naomi Klein (2007), Philip Mirowski (2013), and others have amply documented, crises throughout the neoliberal period have tended primarily to function as logically thin but politically hardy conceits for doubling down on the worst impulses of an entrenched neoliberal elite. Privatization of public resources; financialization of private life; the precaritization and globalization of work—each of these defining trends of the neoliberal era has been substantially advanced in response to one or other modern moments of global upheaval.

Unfortunately, the contemporary tendency toward disaster capitalism proceeded apace through the early days of COVID-19. As Milton Friedman and other charter school advocates levered the human and ecological catastrophe of Hurricane Katrina to finally unmake the public-school system in New Orleans, so did Donald Trump and his appointees weaponize COVID-19 to terminally weaken the United States Postal Service (Daly 2020). As the worst offenders in the scandal-ridden housing and financial collapse of 2008 registered record profits in the wake of that crisis, so did some of the most successful global corporations in 2020 using the Federal Reserve's largesse to stage stock buybacks, consolidate monopoly power, and pad shareholder and executive pockets (Dayen 2020b, July 22; Linnane 2020; Knox and Sussman 2020; Sorvino 2020; Spector and DiNapoli 2020). For the wealthiest and most powerful among us, crises like COVID *never* go to waste. Meanwhile, workers across all sectors were forced back into their workplaces, consumers were urged into brick and mortar storefronts, and teachers and students were pushed back into classrooms—long before it was believed to be close to reasonable or safe for any of them to do so.[2]

All of which makes the Federal Reserve's experimentation with the Municipal Liquidity Facility (MLF) especially remarkable. Historically, the Fed's monetary experiments in times of crisis have served primarily to bolster the balance sheets of those who least needed or deserved financial assistance, leaving it to other bodies of government to offer only meager forms of relief for those worst affected (Taibbi 2019). The MLF marks a clear departure for the Fed, then, by offering to purchase up to 20% of 2017 revenues in municipal bonds, or "Munis," from qualifying state and city governments—bodies that are often best positioned to directly provision (and employ) their local populations (Federal Reserve Board 2020). Moreover, given the past outcomes of similar experiments in direct monetary financing by the Fed, MLF loans may be more accurately regarded as *grants* than as debts that must be repaid. The MLF thus stands as a meaningful corrective for the Fed's worst decisions in the aftermath of 2008. Critically, the MLF experiment also clarifies and underscores the Fed's position as a world historical *choreographer of credit*, responsible for animating and directing the boundless financial capacities of the United States—where and as needed and, in this instance, in direct service of a greater public purpose.

State and municipal governments proved sheepish in response to the Fed's inducements to movement. Reluctant governments no doubt monitored the very few that received MLF funds to track how the program played out.[3] We found such caution, which is likely rooted in deep misunderstanding of public monetary systems, to be ill-advised. In fact, during the early days of the crisis, we exhorted *all* public institutions to seize immediately upon the MLF, even and especially if their state and local governments would not. Institutions of public higher education, we argued, ought especially to leverage their positions as essential local hubs of employment, real estate, and economic development to apply for and maximize the benefits of the MLF (Seijo et al. 2020; Ferguson et al. 2020). In order to satisfy its dual mandate to achieve full employment and

[2] There is good reason to conclude that the lackluster and haphazard fiscal policy responses by Congress and the White House have extended the duration of the coronavirus pandemic (Dayen 2020a, July 6).

[3] Only the state of Illinois has so far formally participated in the MLF program, according to the Fed's July 10 transaction report.

stabilize prices and, further, to avoid repeating previous critical mistakes, we further argued that the Fed must accommodate all notices of interest by colleges and universities for funding that would have kept them operating—safely—for the duration of the COVID-19 crisis (Federal Reserve Bank of New York 2020).

That this proposal may strike some as alien or outrageous is only an indictment of the constricted political economic imagination that has been actively cultivated by policymakers and economists since at least the 1970s. Crises of the early-twentieth century famously generated programs of collective care and wellbeing that, for reasons documented thoroughly elsewhere, faded from collective memory after midcentury.

The MLF may eventually help to restore such visions to prominence in US public life. It is incumbent upon advocates of public higher education, however, to take even more direct ownership over the task of changing the formula for university finance in the wake of COVID-19. It simply will not do to outsource the work of imagination to boards of regents and politically appointed Federal Reserve officers. To that end, we propose to even more vividly reanimate our collective memory through implementation of complementary currencies, called "Unis," as an additional and more direct means for colleges and universities to build new foundations for a just and sustainable future.

Unis in Practice

"Unis" is our broad designation for complementary currencies issued by colleges and universities in response to the COVID-19 crisis. Much like their US dollar counterpart, Unis will be spent into existence and disbursed to remunerate or encourage only those activities determined to be most essential to the wellbeing and prosperity of the issuing institution and its stakeholders. Also like the dollar, the purchasing power of the Uni will be constrained only by the relative availability of desired resources and the continued willingness of Uni issuers to receive them as means to pacify non-reciprocal obligations. Most critically, Unis will obtain value as they circulate within and beyond their local communities because they will be accepted by their issuers—public colleges and universities—in payment for any services rendered, including tuition, fees, meal plans, and rents.

Ideally, and in recognition of its statutory obligations, the Fed will extend accommodation to these complementary currencies and, thereby, greatly enhance the Uni's effective money-ness. Even if the Fed chooses not to accommodate them, however, Unis ought still to be immediately developed, issued, and circulated among local and regional campus communities. This is because Unis can and will make immediate positive impacts for their issuing institutions and broader communities, even without help from the Fed, and in spite of a dearth of any real fiscal support from federal and state legislatures. We provide an example—which, though it focuses on an institution in Central New York, describes a process that is applicable across many different geographic and institutional variations—of the latter scenario below.

SUNY Cortland & BLOCK Unis

In the heart of Central New York is one of 64 State University of New York campuses, SUNY Cortland. In order to staunch its financial bleeding and support its faculty, staff, students, and the regional community in which it resides, SUNY Cortland announces it will begin issuing the Cortland Uni through its student ID credit system. Unis will be paid to all those working to address increasing food insecurity due to the pandemic. In addition, they will help to fund contact tracers, marketing of public health best practices, and host open town halls with the public to identify additional urgent needs.

Initial demand for the Cortland Uni will be created by the university's promise to accept the currency back in payments for tuition or any other school-related cost.[4] While this payments circuit will generate a significant demand for the Uni, local circumstances in Cortland suggest an additional institutional relationship to simultaneously enhance Cortland Uni acceptability *and* resolve a tension between SUNY Cortland and its host community. Despite the fact that colleges and universities frequently boast significant positive local economic impacts, they also often create local economic strain due to their tax-exempt status. Toward a remedy, Cortland offers to alleviate local budgetary strain by paying the City of Cortland a percentage of its property taxes in Cortland Unis. Through doing so SUNY Cortland immediately provides new liquidity for their local municipality and encourages the city to accept Unis from all of its residents. If local property taxes can be paid in Unis, then all property

[4] Nathan Tankus (2020) has called these promises "University Payments Anticipation Notes," or UPANs.

owners and even most renters will become willing to accept and exchange Unis.

Observing the extraordinary and rapid success of their member institution in Cortland, the SUNY system—building upon their newly signed Memorandum of Understanding with the Department of Financial Services to launch the virtual currency program SUNY BLOCK—initiates statewide implementation of the Uni program (State University of New York 2020). Under the new BLOCK Uni, CUNY, Cornell, and other institutions across New York state are invited to join the currency consortium. Immediately higher education is providing not only liquidity flows, but innovative social production across the state. Students are moved from online isolation into local spaces where they are afforded opportunities to contribute directly to community health and wellbeing. And they will do this *where they are,* rather than being made to traverse the state in order to generate residential dormitory income—income that has now been rendered unnecessary by the Uni. Through meaningful financial innovation, and by tossing out the austerity handbook, the SUNY system finds success in achieving its stated core mission to "support and participate through facility planning and projects, personnel policies and programs with local governments, school districts, businesses and civic sectors of host communities regarding the health of local economies and quality of life" (State University of New York).

A Uni designed to leverage both the fiscal tax circuit and university payment systems will generate a positive feedback loop that encourages increased collaboration between municipalities and their anchor institutions.[5] This structure will not only utilize the traditional tax circuit emphasized by MMT, but also diversify the hierarchy of money across democratically structured institutions. Freed from the constraints of the tuition-as-revenue model, and no longer beholden to the wills of wealthy donors, the university system may restore priority to strong faculty governance and intellectual freedom on their campuses. Meanwhile, Unis will further empower colleges in smaller rustbelt and rural communities to reinvent themselves and restore prosperity to their communities after decades of disinvestment and giveaways to agribusiness (Berry 1977).

[5] On anchor institutions and their role in monetary architecture, see Benjamin C. Wilson (2019).

Unis as Experiential Learning

In addition to its immediate beneficial economic effects, the Uni program also presents tremendous opportunities for deep experiential learning across multiple layers of the US higher education system. Most straightforwardly, Uni stakeholders will become closely acquainted with neochartalist ideas as they design and mobilize their local currencies. First-hand observation of the Uni's fiscal tax circuit will trouble previously held notions regarding the uses and abuses of "taxpayer money" and the desirability of balanced budgets.[6] Indeed, real-time empirical study of the public bases and democratic possibilities of their local Uni system will make Uni stakeholders more capable critics of *all* of neoliberalism's entrenched economic falsehoods.[7] Guided by a pragmatic pedagogy of embedded demystification, Uni users may even come to embrace and refine what Jakob Feinig (2020) has described as a "moral economy of money," or a framework for political economy that celebrates rather than eschews the radically democratic potentials of the modern money form.

The field-tested lessons of the Uni will also ramify throughout the leadership structures of individual campus communities. As with any public currency, questions of who Unis are for and to what ends they ought to be mobilized will quickly and inevitably become matters for serious debate among all concerned parties—i.e., the staff, students, faculty, administrators, unions, and community members that keep colleges and universities running. Critical and open engagement between each of these stakeholder communities will be crucial to the success of the Uni experiment. Such engagement will, in its unfolding, help to more clearly disclose the various gaps, calcifications, and blockages that constitute current structures of campus governance. Those structures may then be refashioned, as needed, in order to more effectively advance the democratic aims of the local Uni project.

Lessons learned locally will, in turn, shape how Uni users understand and engage with leadership in the upper echelons of the higher education system, from members of state boards of regents to the chair of the

[6] For more on the myth of taxpayer money, see Raúl Carrillo (2020). On the place and function of balanced budgets in US political discourse, see William O. Saas (2018).

[7] In this way, the Unis project builds on previous work on classroom and campus currencies, like the Denison Volunteer Dollar (DVD) and the "Buckaroo" program at University of Missouri, Kansas City (Kaboub 2012).

Department of Education. Confronted by popular demands greatly sharpened by close comprehension of how public money really works, those higher education leaders will have little choice but to concede that the regimes of austerity and financial indenture they had previously overseen have no place in a post-Uni world.

These are, no doubt, ambitious projections for the future of public higher education. Yet they are perfectly proportionate to the tremendous task that now confronts students, faculty, and staff in public higher education institutions across the country. They also align nicely with the contemporary preference for learning by doing, whether through community service or intensive fieldwork. Moreover, the strategy currently taken by most leaders in public higher education—roughly, hoping for the best while idly waiting for the fate of their industry to be decided by a largely anti-social and anti-democratic Congress—is not a viable option. To that end, we are heartened that an organization like the Resident Assistant Peer/Mentor Union (2020) at the University of Massachusetts-Amherst took the fight for the Uni to their management. For the Uni to succeed, many more such worker-led bodies will need to follow their example.

Conclusion

Much as happened in 2008, the COVID-19 crisis dispelled multiple dangerous myths regarding the economic constraints and political possibilities that obtain within a public monetary economy. Now, as then, critics in the school of political economy known colloquially as MMT have provided some of the most incisive commentaries and most promising proposals for surviving and even thriving through a catastrophic political and economic period.[8] It is likely for this reason that MMT continued to be the target of ire for some conservative members of Congress (Hern 2020). Fortunately, such opposition has repeatedly proven a poor match for a burgeoning modern money movement that only grows broader,

[8] For an example of a contemporary MMT-driven policy that would make meaningful long-term economic impacts, see Congresswoman Rashida Tlaib's BOOST Act proposal (2020), which was co-authored by Modern Money Network president Rohan Grey. For a more speculative proposal for policy intervention in US media, see Maxximilian Seijo et al. (2020).

more diverse, and more effective in response to every new legislative feint toward needless austerity (Money on the Left 2019).

Still, MMTers must not rest on their laurels. Neoliberalism's advocates have proven time and again their resilience against movements for a more democratic and just political economic order—and against movements of far greater in size and scope than ours.[9] At the same time as the ongoing COVID crisis provides meaningful opportunities to re-forge our most critical public institutions upon more democratic, equitable, and just foundations, then, it also marks a critical opportunity for inviting more and diverse audiences into the fold by expanding the public imaginary regarding what is possible in a modern monetary economy. The Uni proposal goes some way toward accomplishing both of these important goals, revitalizing public college and university budgets at the same time as it discloses the tremendous fiscal authority that previously lay (mostly) dormant within the multiple local nodes and regional federations that comprise our national public higher education system.

The time for the Uni is now. As the novel coronavirus threatens lives and reactionary governments across the globe lash out in violent insecurity, a national movement for #BlackLivesMatter marches in our collective streets demanding new investment in our public and social infrastructures. We need an economy that advances BLM's vision. We need an economy that provides health care to all and allows people of all classes, genders, races, and ethnicities to contribute to not only ending the pandemic, but also building our recovery. Through the Uni and related proposals, this recovery can be an inclusive recovery that grants ownership of its direction and magnitude to all. As strong public anchor institutions with substantial resources already in place for robust public provisioning, colleges and universities must be unleashed in support of the construction of a just society that cultivates the human spirit through knowledge and collaboration.

While the Uni program does not require any immediate action by the Fed, it would be a dereliction of duty for the central bank to pass up the opportunity. Fed leadership clearly recognizes the shortcomings of the central bank's most recent facility experiments, as Minnesota Fed chair Neel Kashkari nicely summarizes:

[9] For one such humbling account, see Money on the Left (2018).

> There are two big mistakes when I look back at 2008 that we made that I think are relevant today. Number one, we were always too slow and too timid in responding to the crisis. The reason is we didn't know how bad it was gonna get. And we didn't wanna overreact. And it turned out it got really, really bad. And the right answer should've been overreacting to try to avoid the devastating recession that we ended up happening. So today, whether it's healthcare policy makers, fiscal policy makers, which means Congress or the Federal Reserve, we should all be erring on the side of overreacting to try to avoid the worst economic outcomes. And number two, in 2008, we tried to be very targeted in helping homeowners. Only helping homeowners who needed a little bit of help because a lot of Americans were angry at the thought of their neighbor getting a bailout for being irresponsible or so they thought. So we tried to target our program. It ended up we didn't help very many people. We would've been much better off if we had been much more generous in our support for homeowners, deserving and not deserving. We would've had a less crisis. So my advice to Congress as they're designing their programs to help workers and to help small businesses, err on being generous. (Pelley 2020)

Unfortunately, not helping very many people has been a consistent outcome of the Fed's monetary experiments. Not being generous enough has reliably resulted in massive transfers of wealth to the top 1%, and to the disproportionate impoverishment of communities of color and vulnerable populations across our urban and rural municipalities.[10]

The Uni system clearly and elegantly addresses the shortcomings described by Mr. Kashkari. Our present crises mark as good a time as any to reject not only austerity, but also the narrow neoliberal notions of self that foreclose our capacities for collective care and mutuality. By embarking on the Uni experiment, we will make critical forward progress toward unifying our communities and allowing the power of the people to be truly recognized.

References

Berry, Wendell. *The Unsettling of America: Culture and Agriculture* (San Francisco: Sierra Club Books, 1977).

Carrillo, Raúl. "Challenging Monetary Sanctions in the Era of Racial Taxation," *UCLA Criminal Law Justice Review* 4, no. 1 (2020), 143–155.

[10] As thoroughly documented by organizations like Fed Up: The National Campaign for a Strong Economy.

"COVID-19: A Statement of Academic Solidarity," *Academicsolidaritystatement.com,* https://www.academicsolidaritystatement.com/?fbclid=IwAR1bkD7-LB30lIUfvGN4RYpZs0qlsshnbgAddL6CiFiO8PFxTfQ2_Cahkac

Daly, Matthew. "Mail Delays Likely as New Postal Service Boss Pushes Cost-Cutting," *WHYY,* July 16, 2020a, https://whyy.org/articles/mail-delays-likely-as-new-postal-service-boss-pushes-cost-cutting/

Dayen, David. "Unsanitized: How the CARES Act Contributed to the Pandemic Surge," *American Prospect,* July 6, 2020a, https://prospect.org/coronavirus/unsanitized-cares-act-led-to-pandemic-surge-state-fiscal-aid

Dayen, David. "Unsanitized: How the Pandemic Expands Corporate Power," *American Prospect,* July 22, 2020b, https://prospect.org/coronavirus/unsanitized-how-the-pandemic-expands-corporate-power-monopolized/

Federal Reserve Board. "Municipal Liquidity Facility," *Federalreserve.gov*, 2020, https://www.federalreserve.gov/monetarypolicy/muni.htm

Federal Reserve Bank of New York. "Municipal Liquidity Facility Notice of Interest," *NewYorkFed.org*, https://www.newyorkfed.org/medialibrary/media/markets/mlf-notice-of-interest

Fed Up and The Center for Popular Democracy. "A People's Fed: To Serve the Public Interest, the Federal Reserve Must Become Fully Public: Here's How," *WhatRecovery.org,* https://drive.google.com/file/d/0Bx9EptRDW4_NUlFZNUpVUzhqaGs4cE9qT202TW1VR2xiSnVN/view

Feinig, Jakob. "Toward a Moral Economy of Money? Money as a Creature of Democracy," *Journal of Cultural Economy* (2020).

Ferguson, Scott. *Declarations of Dependence: Money, Aesthetics, and the Politics of Care* (Lincoln, NE: University of Nebraska Press, 2018), 4.

Ferguson, Scott, Benjamin Wilson, William Saas, and Maxximilian Seijo. "Overcoming COVID-19 Requires Rethinking University Finance," *b2o,* July 8, 2020, http://www.boundary2.org/2020/07/scott-ferguson-benjamin-wilson-william-saas-maxximilian-seijo-overcoming-covid-19-requires-rethinking-university-finance/

Fraser, Nancy. "The Crisis of Progressive Neoliberalism," *Law and Political Economy,* January 25, 2018, https://lpeblog.org/2018/01/25/the-crisis-of-progressive-neoliberalism/

Hern, Kevin. "Hern Introduces Resolution Condemning Modern Monetary Theory," *Hern.House.Gov,* July 17, 2020, https://hern.house.gov/news/documentsingle.aspx?DocumentID=219&fbclid=IwAR2Pe7kR1x-_6gOGSWroUSJiScH3HTM0Mrt6MbHsaCNu-UChpNf-8yM3zVM

Kaboub, Fadhel. "Denison Volunteer Dollars: The Currency of Civic Engagement," *YouTube,* July 2, 2012, https://www.youtube.com/watch?v=vSQ6POEV86U

Klein, Naomi. *The Shock Doctrine: The Rise of Disaster Capitalism* (New York: Picador, 2007).

Knox, Ron and Shaoul Sussman. "How Amazon Used the Pandemic to Amass More Monopoly Power," *The Nation*, June 26, 2020, https://www.thenation.com/article/politics/amazon-bezos-pandemic-monopoly/

Linnane, Ciara. "Apple Plans Four-Part Bond Deal for Later Monday," *Marketwatch.com*, May 4, 2020, https://www.marketwatch.com/story/apple-plans-four-part-bond-deal-for-later-monday-2020-05-04

Mirowski, Philip. *Never Let a Serious Crisis go to Waste: How Neoliberalism Survived the Financial Meltdown* (New York: Verso, 2013).

Money on the Left, "The Job Guarantee as Historical Struggle with David Stein," *Monthly Review Online*, May 27, 2018, https://mronline.org/2018/05/27/job-guarantee-as-historical-struggle-with-david-stein/

Money on the Left, "The Modern Money Movement with Andrés Bernal," *Monthly Review Online*, August 15, 2019, https://mronline.org/2019/08/15/the-modern-money-movement-with-andres-bernal/

Pelley, Scott. "Coronavirus and the Economy: Best- and Worst-Case Scenarios from Minneapolis Fed President," *60 Minutes*, March 22, 2020, https://www.cbsnews.com/news/coronavirus-and-economy-best-and-worst-case-scenarios-60-minutes-2020-03-22/

Resident Assistant Peer/Mentor Union, "RAPMU Reopening Proposals," 2020, https://docs.google.com/document/d/1psWUI4PGVVYOJ9flQiwsWKWHK9qhdLPFjonToNo4R7M/mobilebasic?fbclid=IwAR2pKwOHzggugNSJsrrQGFtm1Bl7D-1eYJDfQNgzD4s5yIfnu2VgmkJCTkc

Seijo, Maxximilian. "Governing Media Information through a Green New Deal: History, Theory, Practice," *Journal of Environmental Media* 1, no. 2 (forthcoming 2020).

Seijo, Maxximilian, William Saas, Scott Ferguson, and Benjamin Wilson, "#Unis4all: An Open Letter to the U.S. Higher Education Community," *MROnline*, May 15, 2020, https://mronline.org/2020/05/15/unis4all-an-open-letter-to-the-u-s-higher-education-community/

Saas, William O. "The Econo-Rhetorical Presidency and the U.S. Fiscal Situation," *Advances in the History of Rhetoric* 21, no. 2 (2018, Summer), 131–146.

Sorvino, Chloe. "Uber's Grubhub Play: A Desperate Bid to Save a Business Everyone Hates," *Forbes*, May 13, 2020, https://www.forbes.com/sites/chloesorvino/2020/05/13/ubers-grubhub-play-a-desperate-bid-to-save-a-business-everyone-hates/#df7f71f43894

Spector, Mike and Jessica DiNapoli, "On Eve of Bankruptcy, U.S. Firms Shower Execs with Bonuses," *Reuters*, July 17, 2020, https://www.reuters.com/article/us-health-coronavirus-bankruptcy-bonuses-idUSKCN24I1EE

State University of New York, "Mission Statement," https://www.suny.edu/about/mission/.

State University of New York, "State University of New York and Department of Financial Services Sign Landmark MOU to Launch a Virtual Currency Program," June 24, 2020, https://www.suny.edu/suny-news/press-releases/06-20/6-24-20/virtual-currency-program.html

Taibbi, Matt. "Turns Out the Trillion-Dollar Bailout Was, in Fact, Real," *Rolling Stone,* March 18, 2019, https://www.rollingstone.com/politics/politics-features/2008-financial-bailout-809731/

Tankus, Nathan. "Responding to the University Budget Crisis with University Currencies," *Notes on the Crises,* May 14, 2020, https://nathantankus.substack.com/p/responding-to-the-university-budget

Tlaib, Rashida. "BOOST Act," *Tlaib.House.gov*, 2020 https://tlaib.house.gov/issues/boost-act

Wilson, Benjamin C. "A Dirigisme Approach to a Monetary Policy Jobs Guarantee and the Green New Deal," June 27, 2019, https://doi.org/10.2139/ssrn.3411111

Index

B. C. Wilson, *Care, Climate, and Debt*,
https://doi.org/10.1007/978-3-030-96355-2

FSC
www.fsc.org
MIX
Papier | Fördert gute Waldnutzung
FSC® C083411

Kolibri 360 GmbH
Ferdinand-Jühlke-Straße 7
99095 Erfurt, Deutschland
produktsicherheit@kolibri360.de